If You've Raised Kids, You Can Manage Anything

Also by Ann Crittenden

THE PRICE OF MOTHERHOOD:
WHY THE MOST IMPORTANT JOB
IN THE WORLD IS STILL THE LEAST
VALUED

SANCTUARY:
A STORY OF AMERICAN CONSCIENCE
AND LAW IN COLLISION

KILLING THE SACRED COWS:
BOLD IDEAS FOR A NEW ECONOMY

If You've Raised Kids, You Can Manage Anything

LEADERSHIP BEGINS AT HOME

Ann Crittenden

GOTHAM BOOKS

GOTHAM BOOKS
Published by Penguin Group (USA) Inc.
375 Hudson Street, New York, New York 10014, U.S.A.
Penguin Books Ltd, Registered Offices: 80 Strand, London WC2R 0RL, England
Penguin Books Australia Ltd, 250 Camberwell Road,
Camberwell, Victoria 3124, Australia
Penguin Books Canada Ltd, 10 Alcorn Avenue, Toronto, Ontario, Canada M4V 3B2
Penguin Books (NZ), cnr Airborne and Rosedale Roads,
Albany, Auckland 1310, New Zealand

Published by Gotham Books, a division of Penguin Group (USA) Inc.

First printing, September 2004
10 9 8 7 6 5 4 3 2 1

Gotham Books and the skyscraper logo are trademarks of Penguin Group (USA) Inc.

LIBRARY OF CONGRESS CATALOGING-IN-PUBLICATION DATA
Crittenden, Ann.
   If you've raised kids, you can manage anything : leadership begins at home /
   by Ann Crittenden.
      p.   cm.
   ISBN 1-592-40073-6 (hardcover : alk. paper)
   1. Working mothers.   2. Women in the professions.   3. Women executives.
   4.   Personnel management.   5. Success in business.   I. Title.
   HQ759.48.C75 2004
   306.874'3—dc22   2004007023

Printed in the United States of America
Set in Goudy
Designed by Lovedog Studio

This book is printed on acid-free paper. ♾

To my son,
James Crittenden Henry

Contents

If You've Raised Kids, You Can Manage Anything

Introduction

When a two-year-old throws a tantrum in the grocery store, or a teen-ager yells "I hate you!" parents often think, "If I can get through this, I can handle anything."

Most mothers and fathers know in their bones that raising a child is the hardest job they've ever had. And, even if child-rearing is not that difficult for some, it is certainly comparable to dealing with adults, whether they are superiors, clients, coworkers, employees, or thin-skinned friends. Anyone who has learned how to comfort a trouble-some toddler, soothe the feelings of a sullen teenager, or managed the complex challenges of a fractious household can just as readily smooth the boss's ruffled feathers, handle crises, juggle several urgent matters at once, motivate the team, and survive the most byzantine office intrigues.

Leadership begins at home.

Women have always known this on some level. For eons, they have understood that the skills, the organization, and the sheer character it takes to manage a family are relevant to coping with other chal-lenges in life. "It's obvious that the skills of parenting cross over into business," says Jeanne Liedtka of the Darden School of Business at the University of Virginia. "People are people, and the same basic principles apply."

As long as mothers remained confined to a domestic ghetto this insight could be ignored, dismissed, or chuckled over. The subversive maternal insight that childish behavior often suspiciously resembles the behavior of grown men in groups could be treated as a joke. Now that women have risen in the professions, business, and politics, however, they can see for themselves that conscientious parenting is one of life's great credentials. They recognize that the considerable skills they practice at home are transferable to the workplace. At long last, that truth is coming out of the closet.

Two recent surveys of successful female managers have confirmed, almost by accident, that parenting teaches transferable skills. A survey of sixty-one white, well-educated female managers by the Center for Creative Leadership in Greensboro, North Carolina, looked at whether multiple life roles enhanced or detracted from effectiveness at work. The women reported that *all* private roles enhanced their professional performance, but mothering was by far the most frequently cited. Some of the women had even been told by coworkers that they were much better managers after they had children. "Get a life!" in other words, may be sound career advice.[1]

Another study by the Wellesley College Center for Research on Women of sixty prominent female leaders, including CEOs, college presidents, lawyers, doctors, and writers, also found that virtually all those who had children thought that being a mother had made them better executives. The authors were surprised by this unexpected finding. Having children, the women reported, had been an excellent training ground for leadership. "If you can manage a group of small children, you can manage a group of bureaucrats. It's almost the same process," said one of the women.[2]

Interestingly, the younger leaders were more apt to see child-rearing as a relevant credential than the older generation of female executives, who had often had to behave like a man in order to get ahead in a man's world. Nearly half those age forty-five or younger viewed the maternal role as a preparation for leadership, compared with only 10 percent of older women. "It's a sign of their comfort with motherhood," said Sumru Erkut, author of the study. "In the past, women checked their womanhood at the door."[3]

Surveys like this don't prove a causal link between being a parent and being a better manager. They may simply reflect the supermom phenomenon: Highly energetic and talented women who become successful also tend to take on multiple life roles, including motherhood. The fact remains that many competent mothers are convinced that the practice of parenting contributes to a higher performance at work. Nancy Drozdow, a management consultant with the Center for Applied Research in Philadelphia, and a mother and stepmother, sums it up neatly: "People become better managers when they take their parenting seriously."[4]

Intriguingly, new brain research suggests that there may actually be a genetic basis for a relationship between nurturing and certain competencies. A recent study done on mice by two Virginia neuroscientists found that hormones released during pregnancy and nursing enrich parts of the brain involved in learning and memory. Moreover, these positive changes appear to be permanent. The news prompted headlines that PREGNANCY MAY MAKE YOU SMARTER.[5]

These findings challenge the conventional wisdom that pregnancy turns women inward and dulls their analytical skills. Clearly, that antiquated assumption makes no evolutionary sense. We know that human infants require more intensive care, for a much longer period of time, than the offspring of other mammals. We also know that the preponderance of this care has always been provided by females. It would be logical to assume that millions of years of evolutionary selection pressures may have given the human female brain certain cognitive advantages that facilitate the survival of offspring—such as the ability to remember and keep multiple tasks in focus simultaneously, the ability to read nonverbal danger signals, and a certain fearlessness when danger threatens. Research on how reproductive roles have shaped our brains, particularly the female brain, is still in its infancy. As this research is extended from mice to social primates, we may discover fascinating confirmation that responsibility for a child stimulates capabilities in parents that were never before imagined.

This book is based primarily on my own extensive interviews with more than 100 prominent mothers and fathers who have been the primary caregivers in their family. I talked with people who have been active, involved parents as well as successful in business, law, politics, diplomacy, academia, the entertainment industry, and the nonprofit world. (I tried to avoid interviewing the kind of parents described in the *New Yorker* cartoon showing two toddlers being wheeled in their strollers by nannies, as one tot says to the other: "My parents are the same way. Lots of ostentatious child-rearing, very little direct nurturing.")

I interviewed far more women than men, simply because the daily work of child-rearing still remains an overwhelmingly female occupation. In 2002, for example, 11 million children had stay-at-home mothers and 189,000 had stay-at-home dads.[6] Single mothers greatly outnumber single fathers (16.5 million vs. 3.3 million), and among married parents, mothers spend at least three times as much time on child care as fathers, and even more than that in the early years.[7]

What's more, the multifaceted individuals who have been conscientious, hands-on parents *and* successful professionally also tend to be women. Of 1,200 executives interviewed by the Families and Work Institute in 2002, an almost equal percentage of men and women had children (79 percent of the women, 77 percent of the men). But 75 percent of the men had stay-at-home wives, compared with only a handful of the women.[8] So, the great majority of the people who are in a position to compare the work of child-rearing with professional work are women.

I asked these people directly whether they thought they had learned valuable management skills from motherhood. Only a handful failed to see a connection. Here are a few typical comments.

✳ "Both parenting and managing adults require that you accept people for who they are, find out what they are good at, coach them on how to do their best, support them when they need help, and get out of their way when they don't." Pamela Thomas-Graham, CEO, CNBC.

✳ "Running a large organization is pretty darn close to running a kindergarten." Louise Francesconi, who manages 11,000 people as head of Raytheon's Missile Systems Division, which supplied the laser-guided bombs used against al Qaeda in Afghanistan.

✳ "I'm concerned about all this commentary that you cannot have children if you're a successful executive. Nonsense! You're a *better* executive if you have kids!" Shelly Lazarus, chairman and CEO of Ogilvy & Mather Worldwide.

✳ "I'm a better manager *because* I'm a parent, not *in spite of* being a parent." Deb Henretta, president, Global Baby Products, Proctor & Gamble, and, with Lazarus and Francesconi, one of *Fortune* magazine's top fifty women in business.

✳ "I learned more about managing my subordinates and my superiors from raising my children than from any management course. . . . Two-year-olds taught me a lot about customer service, managing by objectives, and utilizing a system of rewards to improve performance. Women who have managed toddlers can manage just about any crisis situation." Geraldine Laybourne, chairman and chief executive of Oxygen Media.

✳ "There is no better career preparation than parenthood." Shirley Strum Kenny, president of the State University of New York at Stony Brook and mother of five.

✳ "When you need to lead people, when you need to organize people, there's probably not a skill set better than what the average mother knows at home. The same lessons you yell at your ten-year-old in a twenty-four-hour period are probably the same lessons you ought to apply in the business world." Ann Moore, chairman of Time Inc. (Moore's four basic rules: no whining;

listen to the teacher; do your homework; and always remember
to say thank you.)

Harold Saunders, the American diplomat who negotiated the peace
settlement between Israel and Egypt in 1979, told me he could never
have persuaded the two sides to accept a settlement if he hadn't been
widowed and left the sole parent of two youngsters, who for years sent
him Mother's Day cards. In particular, Saunders said, he never would
have understood the Israelis' profound sense of insecurity had he not
had the experience of comforting his own children for their loss.

Management gurus, authors of business books, and executive trainers have connected the dots between managing a home and managing
an organization. Joshua Ehrlich, an executive trainer with Beam, Pines
in New York City, gives all his clients copies of *Leadership Effectiveness
Training*, a sequel to *Parent Effectiveness Training*, based on the assumption that the same management techniques work at home and in the
office. Martha Brest, an executive recruiter in Boston, says her clients
see a clear connection between the way they are with their kids and
the way they operate in the workplace.

"I have one client, a very senior person in an investment management firm—one of the brightest guys I know—who has had children
since I was last in touch with him. He volunteered that he had learned
a lot about how to manage his staff from managing his kids. He
thought that managing children actually took more raw managerial
skill, because there's no protocol, no structure, no real training. I think
people are acknowledging these connections."[9]

Stephen R. Covey, bestselling author of *The 7 Habits of Highly Effective People*, has written a sequel called *The 7 Habits of Highly Effective Families*, in which he admits he learned it all at home. "Applying
the 7 habits material to the family is an absolute natural," writes the
father of nine. "It fits. In fact, *it's where it was really learned.*" (emphasis
added).[10]

In still another sign of the growing willingness to credit the leadership capabilities of the person in charge of the home, a majority of em-

ployed adults polled recently said their mothers could do just as well or better than their current chief executives. Ajilon Office, a New Jersey recruiting services firm, surveyed 632 people and found that nearly three-fourths thought their mothers would be better or at least as capable at communicating with employees as their CEOs. Two-thirds thought Mom would be just as good or better at resolving employee disputes, and almost two-thirds thought she could handle company finances just as well or better. Not surprisingly, fully 80 percent thought their mothers could teach their CEOs a thing or two about ethics.[11]

When Judy Blades, an executive vice president of The Hartford, was honored in 2002 as Insurance Woman of the Year at a luncheon at the Russian Tea Room in Manhattan, she told the assembled insurance executives, speaking off the cuff and from the heart, that she had learned everything she knew from her family, including her children. She later told me that she had never had such positive feedback from any talk she had ever given.

My own "ah-ha!" moment came soon after my son was born in 1982. I was busily devouring baby books, and noticed an uncanny resemblance between the advice found in many books on parenting and the material in books on management that I had read as a business reporter. I wondered if the how-to books aimed at new mothers and the how-to books aimed at aspiring executives could in fact be the same material, packaged differently for different audiences.

I pursued this hunch a few years later by signing up to attend a three-day seminar at Harvard called "Dealing with Difficult People and Difficult Situations." The course was taught by William Ury, co-author of *Getting to Yes*, the bestselling business book of all time. And, sure enough, the management tips that the assembled business executives and military officers were paying almost two thousand dollars per head to hear were largely the same lessons anyone could read by picking up a ten-dollar paperback on parenting.

Ury attributed his advice to such impeccably masculine sources as Sun Tzu, the legendary Chinese general and author of *The Art of War*, and Carl von Clausewitz, the Prussian military strategist and author of

On War. But, over lunch, he good-naturedly confirmed that much of what he taught came straight from Haim Ginott, the humanistic psychologist whose 1956 classic, *Between Parent and Child*, became a parenting bible. His largely male audience at Harvard, thinking they were learning how to apply the lessons of the battlefield to the modern organization, were in fact learning the lessons of child psychology that mothers had been applying at home for decades.

What are these lessons? What skills do conscientious mothers and fathers learn that cross over and enrich their professional lives? In my conversations with parents, four categories of transferable skills were mentioned over and over again.

The first and most oft-cited is *multitasking*, the ability to keep a dozen balls in the air at once. Among the elements of multitasking are the ability to establish priorities, to maintain focus in the midst of constant distraction, to manage complexity with efficiency, and to handle crises with a steady hand. As a friend of mine once summed it up, "Life is not a final; it's daily pop quizzes."

Working with children also develops the *interpersonal skills* that enable people to understand and successfully work with adults. *People* skills are increasingly understood to be part and parcel of every competent leader's repertoire. They include the ability to handle irrational and immature individuals of every age; understanding the importance of *win–win negotiation*; the ability to *listen* to others' concerns; to practice *patience*; express *empathy*; and *respect individual differences*, by learning to appreciate and use the talents of every individual.

A third category of parental skills comes under the heading *growing human capabilities*. These are the empowering, mentoring techniques that enable a manager or leader to develop others' strengths, and bring out the best in others. They include positive reinforcement; the ability to articulate a vision and to inspire others to join in creating and executing that vision; and the wisdom to *let people go*, by giving them the freedom to grow and make their own mistakes while still providing enough structure and feedback to keep them from stumbling too badly.

The fourth category of parental strengths comes under the heading of character, or what political scientist Valerie Hudson calls *habits of integrity*. Good parenting requires the habitual practice of certain, admittedly old-fashioned, virtues. To be done at all well, it demands steadfastness, courage, humility, hope, selflessness, creativity, and a degree of self-mastery that is often at odds with our indulgent culture. No wonder one cultural psychologist has described child-rearing as "routine, unexamined heroism."

Joseph Campbell, the great chronicler of mankind's myths, once defined a hero as someone who has given his life to something bigger than himself. "Losing yourself, giving yourself to another, is part of it," Campbell told Bill Moyers in a television interview. "Heroism involves trials . . . tests, and ultimately revelations . . . it is the soul's high adventure." I can't think of a better description of the child-rearing experience.

The first habit of integrity is simply *being there*. Most mothers say that the most important thing they can do for their children is to be there for them. By this they mean being that solid someone their child can always count on in all the ways that count. It also means establishing a stable environment, a home base, that predictably meets the needs and expectations of those around you.

Virtually every parent I interviewed also told me that raising kids gave them greater *perspective*: an ability to distinguish between what's truly important in life and what isn't. Children, like nothing else, set your priorities straight.

Every parent who's ever divided up a birthday cake also knows that children are hard-wired to detect unfairness. The good parent, like the good manager, strives to be fair and impartial.

There is one more lesson children can teach. I believe that all those who have dreams for their children have to have a certain faith in the future. For parents, the future matters. It is hard for us as parents not to think of the time that will come after us, and the legacy we will leave behind. In the end, conscientious child-rearing includes working for a world we would want our children to inherit.

Those are the big lessons learned; the major insights the parents I interviewed said they had gained. Obviously not all parents learn all these lessons, and some parents may not learn any. This isn't about people who simply *have babies*; it's about the people who conscientiously *raise children*. And even conscientious parents are not necessarily equipped to take on serious managerial responsibilities—although many are.

Nor do I want to claim that the *only* way to acquire these life skills is by having children. These lessons can be learned from any number of profound personal experiences, including serious illnesses and other crises that put one in touch with one's deepest self. As a rabbi I interviewed eloquently put it, "I don't want anything I say to be construed to imply that those who are not parents don't have access to the same lessons I've learned from my children. You can learn this wisdom as an older sibling caring for a younger, or as an aunt or godmother or stepfather, or by caring for a sick parent, or simply by growing older. Parents don't have a monopoly on the lessons learned from caring for others."[12] I couldn't agree more.

So, let's just stipulate at the outset that this book is not about glorifying motherhood per se, or reconceptualizing leadership as maternal or parental behavior. It is really a book about people who believe that children did make a positive difference in the way they conduct their work lives, recognizing that this is not everyone's experience.

Above all, this book is simply about giving credit where credit is due. As the Wellesley study put it, "Crediting good mothering with leadership qualities has been overdue."[13]

A final section examines how far we've come in recognizing parenting as relevant work experience. The answer is important to the millions of women whose primary job is raising their kids, but who will be reentering the work force in the future. A recent article in the *New York Times Magazine* warned that ". . . [i]t is unclear what women like these will be able to go back to. This is the hot button of the work-life debate at the moment. . . . For all the change happening in the office, the challenge of returning workers—those who opted out completely, and those who ratcheted back—is barely even starting to be addressed."14 This book addresses that question of re-entry.

On the one hand, there is a growing recognition that a so-called female or benevolent management style is highly effective, and the beginnings of an inkling that the skills associated with that style are very similar to parenting skills. "There is an awakening," says Martha Brest, "but it's been long in coming. It should have happened years ago."

On the other hand, most employers still don't take child-rearing experience seriously. When I was working on this book and told people what it was about, their first reaction was to laugh. Their second take was often, "Oh! It's so true! " So why the laugh? What's so funny?

Why does the notion persist that the job of raising children is easy, unskilled, and not even real work? Why do we have management books gleaning lessons of leadership from whale trainers, Winnie the Pooh, even Jesus Christ, and not one book on the teachings of Mom, our original leader, guide, and mentor? Why do employers assume your brain goes on holiday when you take time out for children? (I spotted this headline in the *Daily Telegraph* in London: BOSS SAYS MOTHERHOOD TURNS WOMEN'S BRAINS INTO JELLY.)

And why, when you mention you've been a stay-at-home mom or dad to a job interviewer, do you run the risk of ridicule?

A few years ago, I was on a search committee charged with selecting a new executive director of an environmental organization. One highly qualified man had a so-called mother's resume. He had been out of the job market for seven years as a stay-at-home father of three children. In that period he had also served on a school's board of directors, and worked on at least four grassroots environmental campaigns. I thought he sounded like a credible candidate, but a male member of our committee, looking over his resume, snickered, "A househusband." We didn't even interview the guy.

In the end, we gave the job to a woman who had more than fifteen years of uninterrupted experience as an officer at a major environmental organization. She had two school-aged children who were never mentioned during the interview process. We pretended that she had a surrogate wife to take care of that side of life, and we took it for granted that her experience as a parent was utterly unrelated to her ability to run an organization.

Several months after she was hired, she told me that she had learned many of her management skills in a Parent Effectiveness Training course. She had wisely left that out of her resume.

Research has revealed a significant cognitive bias against housewives that apparently extends to men who spend any time raising children. This bias—that those who care for children are close to incompetent—is so strong that it can rear its ugly head in the most unlikely situations. Nancy Segal, a former Senate staffer and an expert on discrimination against parents in the workplace, in 2003 applied for a job at the Labor Department. The man conducting the interview asked her if she was good at juggling different projects, handling interruptions, and the like.

"Are you kidding?" she blurted out. "I'm the mother of two kids!" Oops. She immediately realized that was the wrong answer.

"Now that you bring it up," the clueless bureaucrat continued, "and I hesitate to say this considering the kind of work you do, but do you really think you can handle this job?"

Segal was momentarily speechless. She recovered enough to assure him that she was up to the task, and she was eventually offered the job. She didn't take it.[15]

The persistence of these negative stereotypes poses a real dilemma for women and men who want to be active parents. We look at some of the ways mothers have handled this dilemma, particularly the tricky question of whether to put child-rearing on a resume.

Finally, the book summarizes two of the more interesting and unexpected findings that came out of my research. As someone who has written about the obstacles confronting mothers in the workplace, I was pleasantly surprised to discover just how many mothers have managed to combine engaged parenting with a highly successful career. I found mothers at the top of every kind of institution, from defense contractors to the National Science Foundation, and in every profession, from movie production to the ministry. Moreover, I learned that high-achieving women are no less likely to be married and have children than the average full-time working woman.

Secondly, the presence of all these mothers in high places is already changing the workplace. The language of power is definitely changing, to include metaphors based on childbirth and children's books. Talking about one's children in the office is no longer a liability, but can even be an asset, according to several female executives.

I also heard numerous stories describing how mothers at the top of organizations have made them more congenial places for parents to work. I predict that we will see more of this as women come to run institutions, as opposed to being merely high-ranking females in male-dominated environments.

This is not to say that mothers are or will be any nicer or more caring or better managers than anyone else as they come into their own. As Marjorie Scardino, CEO of Pearson PLC, observed, at a conference for women in business several years ago, "We've all seen difficult, authoritarian women running organizations and feeling, participatory, collegial inclusive men. We musn't fall into stereotypical thinking." I whole-heartedly agree.

But one thing, it seems to me, is very clear. When mothers and others with different life experiences attain leadership positions, they introduce new ideas, find new ways of doing things, and discover innovative solutions to problems that no one even realized were problems before. In the stories I heard, mothers and involved fathers were introducing change, from a better-designed diaper to a more creative way of managing engineers to a fresh way of thinking about international "relationships." They were expanding our human repertoire. For that reason, acknowledging their skills, listening to their voices, and heeding their wisdom will enrich us all.

CHAPTER 1

Multitasking and the Rise of the Life Manager

"In politics, if you want anything said, ask a man. If you want anything done, ask a woman."

—Margaret Thatcher,
former prime minister of Great Britain

Madeleine Albright, whose career trajectory went from stay-at-home mother to Secretary of State of the United States, has described multitasking as *the* essential parenting skill, the "ability that comes from having one eye on the child while you try to talk to the plumber and worry about something else (like your doctoral dissertation) at the same time."[1] Multitasking is the only skill mothers are universally credited with possessing. Almost everyone acknowledges that the person who can run a household and raise kids, not to mention hold down a paying job at the same time, is an expert manager of *life*.

A rundown of all the things most life managers have to do could never be fit into a seven-second sound bite in response to the question, "And what do *you* do?" Ric Edelman, a financial services executive in Fairfax, Virginia, has calculated that mothers' responsibilities include components of at least seventeen different professions, making mothers, along with chief executives, the last nonspecialized generalists in the skilled work force.

Here's my own list of the dozen or so most important tasks of a life manager (bound to be incomplete).

1. Supervise child development: emotional, intellectual, and physical. This includes daily psychological support; listening to and resolving family problems; assuring and maintaining proper school environment; assisting with homework; nightly reading; interceding with teachers and school officials; responsibility for routine medical care; attending meetings at schools, sporting events, and neighborhood functions; and constant reassuring, supervisory presence.

2. Maintaining a home environment for family, including housecleaning, upkeep, and repairs; shopping for household items, from furniture to light bulbs to toothpaste to gifts to toilet paper. This effort to make sure the family is never out of X, Y, or Z involves a constant mental inventory of all the countless things it takes to keep a household stocked and in order.

3. Assuring family nutrition, including food shopping, preparation of meals, school lunches, cleanup, kitchen maintenance and repairs, and research to keep abreast of latest food trends and alarms.

4. Laundry and ironing, purchase and repair of clothing, from gloves and mittens to sporting equipment, new shoes, and back-to-school outfits to wardrobe monitoring to keep spouse as well as children presentable.

5. Crisis management, including handling accidents, fires, floods, auto accidents/repair, thefts, insect infestation, and calls from school principal.

6. Financial management, including managing the household budget; getting quotes and contracting for home improvement projects; investing the family's savings; budgeting for major expenditures, such as Christmas.

7. Project planning and organizing, including birthday parties, bar and bat mitzvahs, weddings, graduations, funerals, school events.

8. Provide transportation to school, afterschool sports, and other appointments, weekend sporting events, and so on.

9. Care for pets, from daily feeding, vet appointments, and delousing treatments, to repair of damage to household by puppies, cats' claws, and incontinent animals.

10. Maintain the family's social ties with friends, relatives, other supportive adults, and children's friends, through gifts, cards, thank-you notes, regular calls, and emails, and weekly planning of get-togethers with friends.

11. Nursing care for sick and injured family members, from doctor's appointments to emergency hospital visits to staying home from work to make chicken soup for laid-up children.

12. If married or in partnership, provide emotional support, business advice, psychological counseling, entertainment/toleration of business associates, and so on.

One of the funniest tributes to this Herculean performance was written a few years ago by Shirley Kenny, a mother of five, former English professor, now president of the State University of New York at Stony Brook. Kenny described a typical day during her teaching years at Catholic University in Washington, D.C.:

"Drag out of bed, get kids up, make breakfast and school lunches, pick up baby sitter, drive car pool ('My mom puts on her lipstick at the same stoplight you do'), hurry to campus for first class, teach, hold office hours. . . . sit on committee *du jour*, hurry home, return babysitter to home base, locate Hamburger Helper and fix dinner, supervise homework and lesson practice, give orders for cleanup and K.P. Duty, write notes to teachers, kiss kids, send big ones to bed, tuck little ones in, kiss them again, and again, drag out briefcase, grade papers or get back to research, stumble to bed in the wee hours, comfort Danny when he wakes up from a nightmare, sleep a little. Start over."[2]

Can anyone be surprised that this woman ended up as the head of a major university? Or that once there, she would notice, as she later told me, "Administration really *is* like housekeeping, although men hate to hear you say it. Once I did make the comparison in an academic group and I got curious stares, followed later by a present of a can of Endust. But look at the similarities: hundreds of little chores that are never really finished; if you don't keep up every day it gets ahead of you; none of it is very important in the abstract; all of it is important in the concrete."[3]

One of the first women to make this comparison between home and organizational management was Catherine Beecher, in her 1841 best seller, *A Treatise on Domestic Economy*. Beecher argued that running a household required the "wisdom, firmness, tact, discrimination, prudence, and versatility" of a politician and the "system and order" of a business. Domestic money management, she added, often surpassed the "desultory" practices of many businesses.[4]

One hundred years later, Eleanor Roosevelt made the same argument, in almost the same language: "A home requires all the tact and all the executive ability required in any business."[5]

The first serious conceptualization of business management as "multitasking," however, didn't appear until 1973, when Professor Henry Mintzberg published a now-classic book called *The Nature of Managerial Work*. At the time it was assumed that a manager sat in his splendid, isolated office thinking about the company's future direction and issuing commands to cadres of underlings. Mintzberg's data, based on time diaries of male executives, revealed that this picture was highly inaccurate. The executives actually spent very little time on planning or long-range strategy. What they really did closely resembled the day of a harried housewife: They answered calls, put out fires, reacted to crises, responded to people, and dealt with constant interruptions, all in a fairly incoherent pattern.

As Mintzberg put it, managerial work was characterized by "brevity, variety, and fragmentation."[6] Any attempt by managers to stick to a task usually failed because of constant interruptions. Sound familiar?

In the three decades since Minzberg's observations, managerial work has, if anything, become even more hurried and harried and more like a life manager's neverending day. The pace of action, around-the-clock economy, the constant juggling of projects, demands from different masters, rapid changes in technology, and frequent career reinventions all challenge managers and mothers alike.

Mothers today sew Halloween costumes, bake Christmas cookies, help with homework, *and* make major investment decisions, handle clients, teach courses, write reports. Mothers today include the executive at TIAA-CREF with triplets, an hour's daily commute into Manhattan, and a schedule that would put the Swiss railways to shame. They include her boss, who raised three kids, hosted a scout troop for eight years, threw regular Friday movie nights for preteens, did grocery shopping and meal planning and weekend chauffering while holding down a demanding job that required travel. (She left notes around the house when she was out of town, with messages like "I'm looking at you—don't forget to brush your teeth!")

Mothers today include the divorced World Bank official with a young son. She arrives in the office at 8:00 A.M. with the sense that she's already worked a full day: up at 5:00 A.M., fix breakfast, pack a school lunch, plan dinner, clean up someone's mess, wrap two birthday presents, clean up dog poop, and answer emails. On her way to work one day, she spied a man coming out of his house in his robe to pick up his morning paper. Her thought: "That guy has *no concept* of what my life is like!"

Mothers today include the former top Justice Department official whose typical weekend calender included:

* Dan's soccer game
* Sophia's birthday party with Dana
* National Security Council meeting
* Groceries

Most people still assume that the birthday parties, the Halloween costumes, the soccer games, and the grocery store somehow *detract* from the performance at an NSC meeting. There is absolutely no evidence of that. On the contrary, female managers report that planning and prioritizing multiple tasks promotes *efficiency*, *focus*, and *organization*. As one female manager put it in a recent study, "Taking on all those roles . . . being a mother, tending a household, working with an *au pair*, being a spouse, friend . . . adds organization into your life so that you're much more efficient and organized at work."[7]

Intriguingly, evidence is emerging that there may be a biological reason for this.

The Maternal Advantage

It is frequently assumed that the ability to handle multiple tasks at the same time is a female characteristic. In his wildly successful one-man show "Defending the Caveman," comedian Rob Becker demonstrates that focusing like a laser beam on a single goal is a guy thing, while taking it all in, doing a dozen things at once—gathering fruits and berries while chewing hides, nursing the baby and keeping an eye out for predators—is the female *modus operandi*. As one woman summed it up. "I try to take one day at a time, but sometimes several days attack me at once!"

Psychologists have known for some time that the female brain is different from the male. Women tend to gather in more details of the world around them, and integrate that data into a more holistic picture of the world. Anthropologist Helen Fisher calls this "web thinking," and contrasts it with men's greater propensity for linear thinking and mental compartmentalization.[8]

Now new research is linking the adaptability of the female brain to changes in hormone levels associated with maternity. It is beginning to appear that motherhood, and caring for the young, may actually promote enhanced brain functioning. A study done on mice at two universities in Virginia has found that *dendrites*, special cell structures which are necessary for communication between neurons, doubled in pregnant and nursing lab mice. The number of the brain's *glial* cells, which act as communication conductors, also doubled. The mother mice learned mazes more quickly, and were bolder and more curious than control animals. A subsequent study found that the new neural structures and pathways—and the associated gains in learning and spatial memory—were long-lasting, until the equivalent of eighty years in a human being.[9]

In one experiment on pregnant and nursing rats, the test animals were placed in the middle of a well-lit, five-foot-square open space, a nerve-wracking place for a prey animal like a rat, whose primary defense is to hide in the dark. The exposed mother rats were bolder, less fearful, more likely than the others to explore for food, according to University of Richmond neuropsychologist Craig Kinsley, who conducted the study with Randolph Macon psychologist Kelly Lambert. In another study at Monkey Jungle in Miami, Lambert and graduate student Anne Garrett found that marmosets who had experience caring for young were also more efficient than childless animals in foraging for hidden Fruit Loops. In preliminary pilot studies, male marmosets who were fathers were also better at remembering where Fruit Loops were hidden than childless animals.[10]

Lambert, thirty-nine, is planning new experiments with primates, and she admits that her research is partially motivated by her own experience. The mother of two daughters, ages five and nine, she is writing a book, teaching, conducting research, and serving as chairman of the psychology department at Randolph Macon. To get it all done, she often works until well past midnight, long after everyone else has gone to bed. She says she feels smarter, more daring, more productive, and in less need of sleep than at any time in her life. "One of the most enriching things for our brains is novelty," she told a reporter. "New connections are made with novelty, and every day there's something new with the kids."[11]

The measured gains in mammalian maternal brain functioning should hardly be surprising. By all logic, our relatively defenseless female ancestors would have had to have been extremely clever and brave to keep their infants alive during all the years of helpless dependence. If human mothers hadn't been more enterprising and creative than your average Flintstone, *homo sapiens* would have never have made it out of the Stone Age. Scientists are learning more every day about neuro-plasticity, the adult human brain's capacity to keep on developing well past puberty. Imagine—we may eventually discover that busy, con-cerned mothers are to brain-building what Arnold Schwarzenegger was to bodybuilding!

Interestingly, several of the women I interviewed described their multitasking in almost physical terms, as if it were brain exercise. Film producer Sarah Pillsbury said, "There are times in film production when you have to think about so many things, in so many parts of your brain—the sheer range of thinking—that I don't even know if men are biologically equipped to do it. At the very least you get better at it by *exercising* all parts of your brain simultaneously—the creative side, the efficient, practical side, and the relationship side. . . . For example, when you're producing a film, you have to be simultaneously thinking of the story; the physical needs in terms of telling the story—how much crew, what about the sets, et cetera; how much time you have in the day to shoot; the moods of the different actors; how do you add something to the schedule; or how can you shorten the schedule to get out of an expensive location; and on and on."[12]

I was also struck by the comments of mothers who said that engag-ing in a variety of quite different activities actually enabled them to be fresher and more creative in their work. As organizational psychologist Marian Ruderman, whose children are thirteen and ten, described it, "My children took my mind off work stress and made me more objec-tive about my work, because they took me into another domain in which I was deeply embedded. It is such a different domain of life that it refreshes you. It gives you a completely different frame of reference, and enables you to be freer to think more creatively about the issues you confront in your professional life. A lot of good ideas came to me while I was diapering the baby."[13]

Sue Shellenbarger, the Work & Family columnist for the *Wall Street*

Journal, has also been told by many high-achieving women that their best ideas come while playing with their kids, jogging, or just relaxing. The brain doesn't always work in lockstep, linear fashion, and a change of scene or focus can stimulate ideas and connections that might not emerge otherwise. Many people find that some of their most creative insights and breakthroughs come when they "get away from it all" while on vacation, hiking, gardening, or whatever. We now know that children and even housework can do the same trick. The late Felice Schwartz, an authority on women in the corporate world, once told me that in her early years as a stay-at-home mother she came up with some of her better ideas while doing the laundry.

Finally, mothers' capacity to take in more information helps them detect the early warning signs of change. One of the managers participating in the study by the Center for Creative Leadership reported that her ability to anticipate problems had improved "tenfold" since she became a parent. She worked in an organization that had undergone a lot of change, taking many people by surprise. She saw people in meetings scratching their heads because they didn't know what had happened to them. But she hadn't been surprised at all because, as she put it, "When you have kids, you have all of your antennae out . . . As a parent I have to be able to know by a cough if my kid is going to be sick. If so, I'd better be thinking about childcare tomorrow morning. That's my life. . . . It's like you're like that all the time. There is no time your guard is down. . . . You read signs much better because of parenting."[14]

She sounds like a prehistoric mother in the wild, constantly alert for signs of danger.

Efficiency

Judith Rapoport of the National Institute of Mental Health believes that efficiency is *the* lesson learned by people who raise children and manage households. Rapoport has found this to be an enormous asset

The Difference between Mom and Dad Brains

This story was emailed to countless mothers around the time of Mother's Day 2003.

Mom and Dad were watching TV when Mom said, "I'm tired, and it's getting late. I think I'll go to bed." She went to the kitchen to make sandwiches for the next day's lunches. Rinsed out the popcorn bowls, took meat out of the freezer for supper the following evening, checked the cereal box levels, filled the sugar container, put spoons and bowls on the table, and started the coffee pot for brewing the next morning. She then put some wet clothes in the dryer, put a load of clothes into the wash, ironed a shirt, and secured a loose button. She picked up the game pieces left on the table and put the telephone book back into the drawer. She watered the plants, emptied a wastebasket, and hung up a towel to dry. She yawned and stretched and headed for the bedroom. She stopped by the desk and wrote a note to the teacher, counted out some cash for the field trip, and pulled a textbook out from hiding under the chair. She signed a birthday card for a friend, addressed and stamped the envelope, and wrote a quick note for the grocery store. She put both near her purse. Mom then washed her face with 3-in-1 cleanser, put on her Night Solution and age-fighting moisturizer, brushed and flossed her teeth, and filed her nails. Dad called out, "I thought you were going to bed."

"I'm on my way," she said. She put some water into the dog's dish and put the cat outside, then made sure the doors were locked. She looked in on each of the kids and turned out their bedside lamp, hung up a shirt, threw some dirty socks in the hamper, and had a brief conversation with the one still up doing homework. In her own room, she set the alarm, laid out clothing for the next day, straightened up the shoe rack. She added three things to her six most im-

(continued)

portant things to do list. She said her prayers, and visualized the accomplishment of her goals. About that time, Dad turned off the TV and announced to no one in particular. "I'm going to bed." And he did ... without another thought. Anything extraordinary here? Wonder why women live longer ...? 'CAUSE WOMEN ARE MADE FOR THE LONG HAUL.

in directing collaborative research. As she explains, "as you progress in research medicine, you attract postdoctoral students who want to work with you. You have to organize all these different people—how they use their time, their flow of information, how they meet to discuss their findings, teaching them how to work on one data set, and at the same time be generating the next one and the one after that. Everyone should always have another paper ripening, in addition to the one they're working on, because that output is how they will be judged."[15]

At Kentucky Fried Chicken, so many women with children are good at structuring this kind of workflow that there is a name for them: *arrangers.*

"We tend to be list-makers and schedulers and arrangers," says Cheryl Bachelder, KFC's former CEO. "This always comes out on strength-finder tests." She cites the example of one woman executive who loves to draw up the flow charts showing what steps have to happen next, in which order, on a project.[16]

An acquaintance of mine calls this the *dinner-party* skill. Think of all the details that went into Mrs. Dalloway's important dinner: the guest list, the menu, the invitations, the decor, the seating arrangement. Then, on the day of the big party, the details and the precise timing multiply: trips to the grocer, the butcher, the baker, the florist, the wine merchant, and supervision of the final performance—making sure the house is clean, the silver polished, the table set, the wine chilled, the food prepared properly, the flowers arranged ... finally, bathe and dress and greet the guests as if entertaining them were the easiest and most pleasant thing in the world!

Even in the computer field, the tendency of women to be the arrangers has become apparent. Some 20 percent of computer professionals are women, and a pattern has emerged, with female programmers often becoming program managers. No one is sure why women tend to drift from the technical, engineering side of the industry to the business and management side. It is possible that the women have a relatively greater facility for organizational efficiency, and are going into areas in which they have this competitive advantage.

The most savvy employers are aware of mothers' efficiency. Lewis Mander, an internationally known chemist from the National University in Australia told me that "Some people think women with children will be distracted and diverted from their work, but I find they are the most efficient people around. I love to hire them. It's like that old saying, 'Always give the important new assignment to the busiest person in the office.' "[17]

Ann Moore of Time Inc. has said that some of her best managers are mothers because "They have no time for politics—they have no time to waste! They get the job done because they have to be out of there. Some of my most productive people are the ones who have come back after having a baby."

In this 2002 interview on *www.satellitesisters.org*, Moore, then executive vice president of Time Inc., had this to say:

> **Moore:** "Maybe one of the reasons I think working mothers make really good managers—and I particularly love working mothers who have very young children at home, because they don't waste any time. They're the most kind of sleep-deprived, time-pressed people, and I find them to be really efficient when they come back from maternity leave."
>
> **Host:** "That's interesting because I think a lot of bosses are reluctant to hire working mothers with young children because they think they're so distracted."

Moore: "No, I think just the opposite—I am always in awe of how much they can accomplish."

In most offices, people spend a certain amount of time just warming up—getting a cup of coffee, schmoozing with colleagues, making a few personal calls. Then, after a few hours, comes lunch. Working mothers rarely do lunch. Once when I turned in a manuscript with a reference to a business lunch of soft-shelled crabs, a young editor, the mother of a toddler, scribbled in the margin, "What's a soft-shelled crab?" She worked in midtown Manhattan, an area full of good restaurants, and she never went out to lunch. She had to get the job done and get out of there.

Another working mother, a writer for television, told me that one of the biggest changes in her life since having a baby was how much more efficient she had become. "When I used to have a script due, I would say, 'I'm writing,' and I couldn't do anything else," said Becky Hartman Edwards, one of the writers on the series *American Dreams*. "I would procrastinate, mull over it, wait until 2:00 A.M. to start working . . . Now I'm much more organized and much more productive during work hours, because I have to get out of here. I've got two kids at home."[18]

Fathers with child-rearing responsibilities can suddenly become just as efficient. Ruth Harkin of United Technologies has male attorneys in her office in Washington, D.C. who share parenting, including the chief trade counsel, a father of two. He recently asked her permission to work at home on Wednesdays. I asked her if she had granted it.

"Sure! And now I see *he's* getting more organized."

Marian Ruderman told me that she had been concerned that motherhood might affect the quality and quantity of her work, but she felt she did *better* work after her first child was born than before. She found that, among other things, she had more focus and was more efficient with her time; she was better able to deal with difficult people; and she gained more distance from the stresses of work by having a different dimension to her life. Her colleague Patricia Ohlott confirmed this.

"We have a mother of two in our group who until recently didn't work full time," said Ohlott, referring to Ruderman, "but she was one of the most productive people here."

The whole experience of becoming a parent had been so positive for Ruderman, personally and professionally, that she was inspired to initiate the study that showed that multiple roles in life do enhance and enrich each other.

Spatial Efficiency

A number of mothers told me that their holistic ability to manage countless details at once extended to geography as well. Rapoport remembers that when she was a medical intern (and the only female in her group of forty-five), she carefully thought through every trip she had to make, both within the hospital and on her way home: stop by the blood bank to pick up a blood sample on the way to the cafeteria, so you won't have to make two trips; get the paper with the lab values on your way back to the ward; go by the laundry and the grocery store on the way home from work. None of the male interns seemed to have these road maps stored in their heads, and often had to make two or more trips around the hospital for every one she made.

"To this day," says Rapoport, "I am still doing this: On my way to your house for this interview I stopped by the liquor store for some wine to marinate the meat I'm serving for dinner this weekend and, when we're finished, I'll go by the supermarket on my way home. No man I know thinks like this."

Focus: The Merits of Distraction

Supposedly one can accomplish more by focusing on a single goal, ignoring all else. Is this really true? As we have seen, effective business managers and life managers alike have to function in the midst of distractions. Mary Catherine Bateson eloquently describes the merits of distractions:

Women have been regarded as unreliable because they are torn by multiple commitments; men become capable of true dedication when they are either celibate, in the old religious model, with no family to distract them, or have families organized to provide support but not distraction, the little woman behind the great man.

But what if we were to recognize the capacity for distraction, the divided will, as representing a higher wisdom? Perhaps Kierkegaard was wrong when he said that "purity is to will one thing." Perhaps . . . sustained attention to diversity and interdependence may offer a different clarity of vision, one that is sensitive to ecological complexity, to the multiple rather than the singular. Perhaps we can discern in women honoring multiple commitments a new level of productivity and new possibilities of learning. . . .

The rejection of ambiguity may be a rejection of the complexity of the real world in favor of some dangerously simple competitive model . . .[19]

Again, the real skill we are talking about here is the ability to manage life—with all its glorious messiness. The new mother's sink-or-swim test is whether she can handle the whole inescapable package, from the sublime to the ridiculous. One of my friends has an extremely talented daughter who clerked for a Supreme Court justice, then held a high-level position in the Justice Department before she became a mother. She wanted to be an involved parent, so she stopped working full time and found a more flexible job as a part-time attorney working on campaign finance reform.

"I will need six uninterrupted hours a day in order to do this job," she informed her mother, and she hired a full-time nanny.

"You'll never in the world get six uninterrupted hours a day with a nursing infant, even with a full-time nanny," my friend thought to herself. Sure enough, soon after the new job started, she went over to her daughter's house and there was Mom at her desk, the baby cradled under one arm guzzling away, while she juggled two manuscripts, pencil editing, and reconciling the differences between the two. The phone was ringing, the place was in disarray, but her pen was busy and her concentration intense. She was functioning in full mother mode, focusing amid a dozen distractions.

Significantly, all four of the outstanding female executives profiled in the 1990 book *The Female Advantage* saw distractions, such as unscheduled encounters and calls, not as interruptions but as opportunities. As Barbara Grogan, then president of an industrial contracting company in Denver, put it, "When something unexpected needs my attention, it just goes to the top of my list. Maybe that comes from being a mom. (Grogan was a divorced mother of two). If a kid suddenly has to go to the doctor, that isn't an interruption—that's a priority! As a mother, you find there's always something new to be fitted in. You learn not to expect to ever completely control your schedule."[20]

The creative industries in particular demand people who can thrive amid distractions. In businesses like advertising and film, a certain amount of chaos is inevitable. It's probably no accident that mothers have done well in these fields.

"The advertising business by its very nature is chaotic . . . things aren't neat and contained or always happening on schedule," says Shelly Lazarus, the CEO of Ogilvy & Mather and one of the top executives in the business. "Having a life as frenzied as mine—with a husband who has his own career (as a physician), three children (two grown, one in middle school), and multiple houses—is perfect training. People who need order and neatness just wouldn't fit in. They restrain creativity. When we meet with our most productive people, it's everyone talking at once, shooting ideas around, interrupting—it's like my dinner table! If you can't handle that . . ."[21]

Lazarus's comments were echoed by a number of mothers in the entertainment industry, who have one other unexpected advantage over others in their business: They are used to getting up early. Lindsay Crouse told me that, when she was shooting a film when her children were little, she was the only person who was cheerful on the set in the morning.[22]

And when Soledad O'Brien had Hootie and the Blowfish on NBC's *Weekend Today* show, she noticed that unlike most rock groups, who look haggard early in the morning, this group of guys looked great. When she complimented them on their appearance, they explained, "We're all parents. We all go to bed by 9:00 P.M."[23]

One of the best descriptions of the merits of distraction is in the beautifully written autobiography of Madeleine Kunin, a former governor of Vermont. In the book, Kunin describes her evolution from Vermont housewife and mother of four to community leader to state representative and finally governor. In retrospect, she sees her ten years at home, full of interruptions and volunteer activities—bringing professional children's theatre to the state, fighting for neighborhood sidewalks, challenging the AMA's opposition to medical reform—as central to her subsequent success. As she writes in *Living a Political Life*:

> *The interruptions of life matter—they may, in fact, be what is most important. Tidiness is not everything. The ability to layer experience, fold one part over another, smooth out the wrinkles, is a survival skill that is essential in both private and public life. And domestic, motherly skills I learned at home have extraordinary usefulness. Counting out strawberries one by one to make certain that exactly the same number of strawberries went into each child's dessert dish taught me how much people care about fairness and how to mediate an argument. Cleaning up the third glass of spilled milk in the course of one meal taught me a great deal about the art of self-control. And where better to learn patience than watching a child learn to tie his shoe?*[24]

These homey lessons stood Kunin—and the people of Vermont—in good stead. By the time she decided not to run for a fourth term as governor, in 1990, the state was ranked first among the states for environmental policy, children's services, including the collection of child support, and mental health. *Fortune* magazine listed Kunin as one of the nation's top ten education governors.

Naomi Foner, a screenwriter and producer in Los Angeles, found that constant interruptions actually taught her an important writing technique. Foner left her career as a producer with Children's Television Workshop after her children were born, and spent many years freelancing at home while the kids were napping or in school. "I got more done in those chaotic family years," Foner told me, "though I often had only two hours without interruption . . . Sometimes I'd have to stop writing just when I was getting into a groove, which was frustrating, but that taught me something important. When I sat down to write the next day, I would always know what I was going to do next—I'd pick up right where I'd left off with a little burst of energy, instead of sitting down and wondering where to start up again. Now I stop writing when I know what I'm going to do next, not when I've 'finished' something."

Foner put a scene from real life into her script for *Running On Empty*. It didn't make the final cut, but maybe we'll see it eventually in some other movie. The family was on vacation, and her son, aged four or so, decided to scratch two words he had just learned on the side of his father's new car. The two words were HOT LOVE.

Foner was inspired to give her script that tentative title. When the real estate agent from whom they rented their vacation house heard that she called and asked Foner if she were writing a porn film.[25]

Set Priorities

You can't successfully multitask unless you set priorities and "just say no" to the nonessential demands on your precious time. You may be able to keep three or four balls in the air at once, but don't even think about more unless you want to be mistaken for the court jester. Former Maryland Republican congresswoman Connie Morella and her husband raised nine children, including the six kids of her late sister. Morella came away from the experience with a set of rules she calls the Four Ds:

1. *Don't* do it unless it's really important, and *has* to be done.
2. *Dovetail* it. Do as many things as you can at the same time, that is, do the ironing while watching that TV show you can't miss.
3. *Delegate* it. I used to think I was the only one who could do anything—no more.
4. *Delay* it.

Don't Sweat the Small Stuff

"This is all a version of don't sweat the small stuff," said Morella over breakfast in a diner in Montgomery county, her old district. "I've used these principles with my staff as well and they work. Basically, you need a sense of humor and a kind of tunnel vision that excludes all the small stuff. I always tell young mothers, just replace all your hundred watt bulbs and put in ten watt bulbs so you can't see the dirt."

While all the kids were at home, Morella organized the household into weekly teams, one to set the table, another to clear the table, another to clean the bathrooms, and so on. Laundry didn't work as a team, because no one could do it to everyone's satisfaction, so each child got his or her own hamper and was responsible for washing his or her own clothes. Ironing didn't work so well either. At one point a pile of unironed clothes sat in the basement for so long that Morella finally let a charity come by and take it away. No one ever noticed.[26]

For Abigail Trafford, a health columnist for the *Washington Post*, eliminating the nonessential meant saying *no* to a dog.

"My daughters were about six and seven," Trafford recalls, "and I was a single mother stretched very thin between work and home in the middle of a marriage breakup. I figured I couldn't handle work, my family, the house, and a dog too. I had to set some priorities."

The girls' disappointment was acute, and they launched an intensive lobbying campaign to overturn the dog ban.

"All the other kids in school have a dog!"

"Pets are good for children."

"How can you be a good mother and not have a dog in the house?"

Trafford stuck to her guns, but a few years later the situation was different. Her life had settled down, the children were more mature, and more able to care for a dog themselves. So one Saturday morning she brought home a golden cocker spaniel puppy.

The lesson here for managers, she believes, is not just that you set priorities and stick to them in the face of opposition, but that priorities change. Good management involves reassessing priorities, just as good parenting requires adjusting family rules as family members change.[27]

Multitasking Children

The things that don't take absolute priority can be delegated. It is often said that behind every successful woman is a supportive husband but, after listening to dozens of mothers tell their stories, I'm convinced that another factor in their success was their insistence that the children pitch in and do their part as well. This seemed to be particularly true of working mothers with three or more children. For them, delegating is a necessity.

Nancy Pelosi, minority party leader in the House of Representatives, raised five children. While still a stay-at-home mother, she began volunteering in state politics and, as she rose to become chair of the Democratic party in California, she trained her children to help out. They stuffed envelopes, answered the door and served hors d'oeuvres at political functions, took phone calls, and helped in campaigns. "It would have been impossible to do it without them," she says. She finally ran for Congress in her forties, when her youngest daughter was in high school.

Supreme Court Justice Sandra Day O'Connor was in the Arizona state senate and eventually became the Republican majority leader while her three sons were still in school. She did her share of multitasking ("I had to be aware of eighty-nine things at once," she told me during an interview in her office in the Supreme Court building) but her boys had to learn how to do at least some daily chores for themselves. They occasionally cooked their own dinner, washed their own

clothes, and even ironed a shirt now and then. The justice still obviously takes pride in their ability to cope, and she told me two stories as
illustration.

On one occasion the family's beloved dog was struck by a car. The
kids remembered that there was a veterinarian's office in a nearby shopping center so they found an old door in the basement, laid the dog on
the door, and the three of them carried the animal to the doctor.

Another time they discovered that a queen bee had made a new
nest right under their house, and a huge swarm of bees was gathering
literally underneath their feet. As O'Connor tells the story, "they
had the presence of mind to look in the *Yellow Pages* and get a bee-
keeper out there. It was a real crisis and they solved it as well as I could
have. . . . My working hard had a spillover effect on the children.
They had to become a little more independent. There were times
when they had to fill in the gaps."

The self-reliance must have stuck. On the day we talked, O'Connor's youngest son was on Mt. Everest, heading for the summit. He
made it.

Crisis Management

It is notable how cool mothers can be when they have to be. Just as
mother rats are braver than other rats, and mother bears are more dangerous than others of their species, human mothers too will fearlessly
put their own lives at risk in defense of their children. It makes one
suspect that the Department of Homeland Security would best be run
by an alert mother. In any event, I heard story after story of mothers
handling crises at work with absolute sangfroid. And why not? After
all, they have faced worse disasters at home!

Sara Eversden of Chandler, Arizona, a senior systems engineer in
the healthcare field and a mother of three, described in an email the
first time she saw a mother in action in a business crisis:

At one of my first jobs out of college I worked for a large consulting firm and was at a client site with a senior manager, a working mother of preteens. About ten minutes before the client presentation I was instructed to make a final copy of the transparencies. I was supposed to make the transparencies out of the stack of slides that had the client's logo on them. Well, guess what? In my haste, I made slides with our firm's logo on them! It was a major deal for this particular presentation. I panicked, told my senior manager what had happened, and suggested we just give the presentation as is and apologize later.

She didn't accept this, and fiddled with the now jammed copy machine. She then decided we didn't have time to unjam a copy machine and rerun the 95 transparencies ourselves. So she quickly located the client's secretary and calmly and politely asked her to make copies of the full presentation with the correct logo. Now she may have been sweating bullets, as I was, but she looked as calm as could be and never showed any sign of the panic I was feeling inside.

I didn't recognize it at the time since I was only twenty-six years old and had no kids. But now I recognize that that was the look of someone who had gone through day-to-day calamities or crises of multiple kinds with children, and who knew how to think on her feet, find a solution to a pressing problem, and keep her head. After parenting for the last five years I know with certainty that I could at least come close to having that same look in my eye, if confronted with a similar challenge in the workplace. That is what being a mother does for you.[28]

My own favorite anecdote about maternal crisis management involved Sally Novetzke, the U.S. ambassador to Malta when George H. W. Bush and Mikail Gorbachev met there for a summit conference in 1989. Novetzke was in charge of the complex arrangements for the high-level meeting, and in one of her interviews with the press, a female correspondent for the *Washington Post* asked her condescendingly, "Isn't it true that this is your first real job? How can you handle all this?"

The ambassador, a mature woman who had earned her post after years of unpaid labor for the Republican Party, looked at the reporter and cooly replied, "My dear, you obviously haven't raised four children."

It Works Both Ways

> "Parenting informs work and work informs parenting. The idea that if you're good at one you're not good at the other, that if you're a good businesswoman you can't be a good mother, is completely wrong."
>
> —Pamela Thomas-Graham,
> president and CEO of CNBC

The transfer of skills from home to office obviously works the other way as well, from office to home. Countless articles have described how formerly employed mothers become *managerial moms*, running their households like line divisions and organizing the kids into non-stop programmed activities. This should come as no surprise, for as women have children later in life, after years of workplace discipline, their approach to parenting will inevitably reflect their earlier training. A person can't check her previous persona at the door just because she has had a baby. As Miriam Sapiro of Washington, D.C., a former international negotiator, put it, "If I can wring a peace treaty out of warring parties in the Balkans, no two-year-old's tantrum is going to ruin an otherwise lovely afternoon."[29]

Pamela Thomas-Graham found that having three small children (twin toddlers and a six-year-old) was "Just like running my company . . . One of the things that helped my husband and I adapt was the thought, 'We're management!' Both at home and in the office we start by looking at the needs people have that are immediate, and who's okay for now; who needs oversight right now and who doesn't need oversight."

Veronica Lopez, an outgoing forty-six-year-old mother of three in

Staten Island, is an explicitly managerial mom. Kids hit Lopez like a freight train, and she survived the impact by consciously applying the lessons she learned as a human resources executive to bringing up the babies.

Lopez was thirty-one, and responsible for personnel training and development at Manufacturer's Hanover Trust in Manhattan when her son was born, followed by identical twin girls two-and-a-half years later. The part-time job she had negotiated was eliminated, and suddenly Veronica was a stay-at-home mother of three infants under the age of three.

She was overwhelmed by the unexpected amount of work involved. Up all night, confronted in the morning by huge piles of laundry, a sink full of dirty dishes, constant diaper changes, and seemingly endless meals to prepare, the one-time bank executive decided that she had to find out "how to communicate effectively instead of following my natural instinct to yell a little louder when things didn't go as planned."

Lopez took several parenting classes and eventually became certified by the archdiocese of New York to teach the classes herself. Parenting education became her new profession. She created a parenting center at Holy Rosary Parish in Staten Island, and for nine years has offered workshops on parenting techniques. Her guidelines reflect her corporate experience, tempered by the familiar principles of the humanistic psychologists.

The family should begin, as in any well-run company, with a *mission statement*, identifying the basic values the parents want their children to learn. This will enable the parents to identify the specific behaviors that they would like to teach.

The next step is to *clarify the children's responsibilities*. In her job in human resources, Lopez had to write job descriptions and develop procedures so that employees knew their responsibilities. She believes that children also need to know exactly what is expected of them. "It is important to tell children specifically how we want them to behave and then hold them accountable," she told me.

Lopez agrees that it is harder to hold children accountable than it is to manage employees, who can be motivated by salary increases, bonuses, promotions, and more meaningful tasks. "If you can motivate a child without yelling and losing your temper, you can certainly manage adults," she says. "You can't fire your children, so you have to use a lot more psychology."

One way to motivate children is to give them *kid reasons*—careful explanations of why it's in their best interest to behave in a certain way. For example, "When you pick up your toys they don't get stepped on and broken," "When you say please and thank you and play nicely at your friend's house you get invited back," "When you brush your teeth you don't get cavities."

Children can also look forward to getting a *promotion* to greater freedom and independence when they show they can be honest and responsible. As they demonstrate good behavior they can gradually earn more privileges.

Lopez's businesslike approach to parenting helped her bring order out of a frightening transition from bank officer to home-based OCE: Officer in Charge of Everything. It also illustrates the fact that work and family are not two clearly distinct and separate spheres, but two parts of a whole, each influencing, informing, and enriching the other.

The classic description of this interplay is *Cheaper by the Dozen*, a book written by two of the twelve children growing up in the eccentric Gilbreth household in Montclair, New Jersey during the 1910s and early twenties. The father, an efficiency expert, and the mother, a psychologist, ran a consulting firm advising manufacturing companies in the United States and Europe. This exceptional pair of parents fully grasped the fact that managing children and managing workers involve many of the same skills, particularly in large families. (In my own interviews people with more than two young children all said that they needed firm rules and businesslike schedules to keep chaos at bay.)

As their family grew, Frank and Lillian Gilbreth decided "to look into the new field of the psychology of management and the old field of psychologically managing a houseful of children," and test the theory that what would work in a factory would work in the home.

The Gilbreths organized their children into production teams that handled household chores, and met in committees to discuss big decisions, like whether to get a dog or a new rug. The kids were encouraged to put out competitive bids for big jobs, and forced to stick to the terms of their contracts. When eight-year-old Lill, for example, put in a bid to paint a long fence for forty-seven cents, she was given the contract, over her mother's objections that her price was too low. The work took ten days. Her hands blistered and some nights she couldn't sleep. But her father insisted she finish the job, to teach her "the value of money and to keep agreements." When she was finally finished she came to him in tears.

"It's done," she said. "I hope you're satisfied. Now can I have my forty-seven cents?"

He counted out the change. Remember, he told her, I made you finish for your own good. Then he told her to go look under her pillow. She ran upstairs and found a pair of roller skates.

Cheaper by the Dozen was published in 1948, and was a runaway bestseller. It was translated into fifty-three languages and in 1950 made into a popular film starring Myrna Loy and Clifton Webb, remade in 2003 as a vehicle for Steve Martin. The Gilbreths' story is usually described as the charming tale of an eccentric scientist who ran his home like an industrial organization. Very little was said about the mother in the family. Looking at their story again more than fifty years later, it is obvious that the Gilbreths probably developed and road-tested many of their management theories at home, later applying those that worked in the household to workers in organizations. The incident with Lucy, for instance, may have taught Frank Gilbreth as much as it taught Lucy about the need to keep up worker morale with generous incentive payments for a job well done.

I also suspect that the mother of this large brood deserves much more of the credit for the Gilbreths' organizational principles than she has been given. One telling indication is the fact that this mother of twelve effortlessly stepped into her husband's shoes after he died suddenly of a heart attack at age fifty-five. Three days after his death she sailed for Europe to deliver two lectures he was scheduled to give in London and Prague, and she went on to become the world's foremost female industrial engineer.

CHAPTER 2

How to Spot a Baby When You See One

"If you just go through life assuming that everybody you meet is about four years old, you can't go wrong."

—Editor at a New York–based
publishing house

"Dealing with three-year-olds is great training for dealing with executives. They all have short attention spans, short fuses, and are prone to pout."

—Female executive at AOL

"When you talk about the men at work, it's as though we were their mothers," says a woman to her friend in Allison Pearson's comic novel, *I Don't Know How She Does It*. "We *are* their mothers," replies her friend, an investment banker. "I have people hanging on to my skirt in the office and then I have them hanging on to my skirt when I go home. You'd better get used to it."

The ability to recognize a baby when you see one, even when the infant is disguised in adult clothing, is one of the great insights gained from parenting. The realization that often very big people can be very small inside dramatically changes the way you view the world. I first realized that I was looking at the world through this maternal lens when my son was about six or seven. One evening, as I was watching CNN and the news of the latest war, James came through the room swinging his terrible swift toy sword. He was playing that favorite boys' game: "Kill the Bad Guys!" The thought was inescapable: The world is run by grown men who think like seven-year-old boys; who see the world in black and white and who think smiting the Evil Ones is the answer.

Countless mothers have had a similar epiphany, and overtly maternal observations on the behavior of world leaders are no longer unusual. How many times have you heard someone say, apropos the government or a crazy company: "The situation is completely out of control . . . there's no adult supervision."

When psychologist Marian Ruderman observed how biologically driven her first infant was, she started to think, "Maybe if someone is snippy at work it may not be anything I did. Maybe she's being driven by feelings she can't control. My daughter was so hard-wired, it made me realize that some adults may be hard-wired too. This has helped me deal with difficult people. If someone is being difficult, that may just be how they are—and there's no reason to take it personally."[1]

A classic example of the grownup infant in action involved Newt Gingrich, the baby-faced former speaker of the House of Representatives. In 1995, Gingrich admitted that he had forced the federal government to shut down just to spite Bill Clinton. Apparently the president had hurt Gingrich's feelings by not inviting him to sit with him during a long plane flight back from Israel. In retaliation, the Republican leader had loaded a critical piece of spending legislation with conditions that he knew Clinton would have to veto, thereby forcing government offices to close their doors.

"This is petty, but I think it is human," whined the powerful politician. Human, perhaps, for a two-year-old.

A number of mothers had no trouble seeing this snit for what it was.

"I think they're just little boys playing their little games," declared an employee for the Federal Centers for Disease Control and Prevention in Atlanta.

Colorado Congresswoman Pat Schroeder, mother of two, had the last word. She held up a model Oscar statuette on the floor of the House and declared that Mr. Gingrich had "sewn up the category of best performance by a child actor this year."[2]

One danger lurking in the maternal ability to see through immature behavior is that it can come across as condescending. There is perhaps a touch of self-satisfaction in the writer Alice McDermott's description of how mothers' wisdom stands out "among a population of adult children and inner children and recovering children." She notes that those who have "spent weeks and months and years considering, living with, responding to all the finer meanings of growth, maturity, reward, punishment, dependence, independence, love . . . see all our bluster, our striving, our frenzies, our dramas as if from a certain height and . . . respond to each of them with a compassionate, knowing, 'Now, boys.' "[3]

This image of Big Mother watching you from on high makes everyone uncomfortable, and mothers ought to avoid taking such a smug stance. But the fact remains that people who've been successful, involved parents are probably better equipped to recognize and handle people with arrested emotional development. Here are a few techniques suggested by the working mothers I interviewed.

Try Humor

A friend of mine tried this out-of-the-box technique on a foulmouthed co-worker who was constantly losing his temper and erupting with the F word. Every time he did it, she'd go "Pluck, pluck, pluck! Listen! There must be a big chicken in here!" She'd learned this trick by pretending that she was a bird, flapping her wings and dancing, to amuse and divert her irritable three-year-old. Sure enough, the ill-tempered oaf in her office got so embarrassed by her chicken routine that he cut out the obscenities.

Ann Moore, CEO of Time Inc., had an amazingly competent mother who turned the toughest family challenges into fun and games. Moore's mother was a military wife with five children who had to move her household around the country frequently. As her daughter described her, she had the ability to convince the kids that it was the most exciting thing in the world to leave their friends, their school, and their familiar neighborhood to embark on an uncertain adventure in another part of the country. Moore, the oldest, remembers that each child would be given a chance to pick the color of their new bedroom. Her brother Andy would pick red and black. Somehow these colors never materialized on any wall, but the children did end up accepting the moves.

"She was a *general*," Moore recalls. "She was a master at making an unpopular choice red hot. That lesson has served me well."[4]

Make It Look Like It Was His Idea

Rita Colwell, head of the National Science Foundation and mother of two grown daughters, told me she frequently utilized this technique in meetings. American scientists can still be notoriously chauvinistic, and Colwell says that early on in her career "I learned to keep quiet and listen, and then make my statements, never trying to command or dominate. Men hate that! Often I'd make some comment and it would be followed by silence. Several seconds later, a man would say the same thing in a slightly different way, and they'd all say 'What a great idea!' I learned I could get my agenda done by making it their agenda."[5]

This is a tried-and-true mommy technique. Kate Reddy, the heroine in *I Don't Know How She Does It*, learned it by reading the baby books:

. . . then Emily hit the Terrible Twos and I bought a book called Toddler Taming. It was a revelation. The advice on how to deal with small angry immature people who have no idea of limits and were constantly testing their mother applied perfectly to my boss. Instead of treating him as a superior, I began handling him as though he were a tricky small boy. Whenever he was about to do something naughty, I would do my best to distract him; if I wanted him to do something, I always made it look like it was his idea.[6]

This brings to mind the old adage, attributed to Harry Truman, that "There is no limit to what you can accomplish in life, provided that you don't mind who gets the credit."

One surefire way to make someone think something is their idea is to set up a choice. This tactic is suggested by Haim Ginott in his classic child-rearing manual *Between Parent and Child.* If you want a child to eat a vegetable, for example, you offer alternatives. You don't say "Eat your spinach!" like the Mom in the old Thurber cartoon. You say, "Honey, would you rather eat spinach, carrots, or squash?" The child gets to pick, buys into his selection, and thinks eating a vegetable was his idea all along. By the same token, never ask open-ended questions, like "What would you like for breakfast?" opening the door to answers like "Cake and ice cream." Just inquire "Do you want your milk in a cup or a mug?"

As Ginott explains, this gives the child the message that he or she "is not just a recipient of orders but a participant in decisions that shape his life."[7]

This trick is was used by Queen Isabella of Castile in the fifteenth century when she wanted to ensure that the Pope appointed the candidate of her choice as archbishop. She sent the pontiff a list of three possible candidates: her loyal servant and two obvious incompetents. Her man got the nod. I wonder if the clever monarch learned this technique from dealing with her five children, one of whom, Catherine of Aragon, became Henry VIII's first wife.

Stay Calm and Pick Your Fights

Immature people are prone to temper tantrums, just like teens and toddlers. Numerous mothers told me they learned to deal with this by simply not reacting. As Cheryl Bachelder put it, "Calm is always the high ground."

Naomi Foner told me that she once pulled into a studio parking lot and inadvertently took the space of a big, self-important executive whose sense of himself was determined by things like his parking space. He threw a full-scale hissy fit that would have made any kiddie proud.

"I thought, 'I'm watching a four-year-old,' " said Foner, "and then I thought 'there's no point talking to him. He needs a time-out.' " She restrained herself from reacting, and eventually she received a call of apology.

Carole Browner ran into plenty of these outbursts while she was head of the Environmental Protection Agency during the Clinton administration. "I saw a number of Congressmen throw temper tantrums," she told me during an interview in her office in Washington, where she works as a consultant. "They'd tell me 'you *have* to do this . . . fix it! I want it fixed!' I'd just ignore it—it was so silly!"

Browner had one memorable run-in with Republican Senator Trent Lott from Mississippi. When he was senate majority leader Lott demanded that she fire a career civil servant in the EPA, an employee four layers down from her office. If she refused, he declared, he would hold up all of her nominees for higher positions. (There was one nomination pending at the time.)

Browner, who had one son in primary school when this incident occurred, explained to Lott that she couldn't reach down into the bureaucracy and do something like that. So she refused. Then, three months later, the person in question quit voluntarily, never having known about Lott's ultimatum. Browner called Lott again and said, "I want you to know that the person has left the agency of their own accord, so I assume my nominee will now be confirmed."

"Like a kid, Lott had been testing me by making an unreasonable demand," she explained. "But I never did engage in battle. That's one thing you learn with a kid. You don't engage in every little silliness that comes along. You just stand firm, explain the limits, and say no."[8]

Parents try to pick their fights, saving their ammunition for really important things like controlled substances. Pauline Schneider, a partner in the Washington office of the prestigious law firm of Hunton & Williams, says the most important lesson she learned from childrearing "is understanding which principles are important enough to stand on, and when you can and cannot be flexible.

"You learn that you simply can't overreact when they do something incredibly foolish. If you react it can turn *you* into a raging idiot," Schneider told me. "I am much more careful to think before I speak and act. I cannot tell you how many times that's helped me, both at home and in the office."[9]

Schneider has a grown son with an MBA in finance, and a daughter who is getting her PhD at Duke. She seems to have learned more about picking her fights from her daughter Suzanne, who was apparently quite the rebellious teenager. Schneider recalls that when Suzanne was sixteen, during the Reagan administration, she and her friends were opposed to Star Wars. One day she asked her mother if she could skip school that day in order to attend a demonstration. Her mother said no, but a few hours later Schneider was called out of a meeting with a client by an emergency telephone call. Her daughter had disobeyed her and gone to the demonstration after all, and was now in police custody. After she hung up and returned to the meeting, everyone eagerly wanted to know if everything was OK. What was the emergency?

Schneider finessed the questions, finished the meeting, went down to the police station, got her daughter out of jail, and saw that the charges were dismissed. On the way home in the car, she said, "I was absolutely silent. She tried to talk and I said 'I do not want to discuss it.' Maybe I should have dealt with it differently, but I had to take a deep breath or I would have overreacted. . . . They will test you. And do they teach you self-control!" Schneider, an obviously well-groomed woman, also had differences with her daughter over matters of dress. "She drove me crazy over her unconventional clothes. She never wanted to wear the clothes I bought for her; she went to the thrift shops instead. But I didn't want to take a stand on something like hair or dress codes. These weren't as important to me as good table manners, for example. So I learned to let some things go."

When Suzanne was sixteen the dress issue came to a head. Schneider's firm needed a part-time receptionist from four o'clock to six thirty every afternoon, and she asked her daughter if she had any friends who might be interested in the job. The girl said that maybe she herself would apply. "I told her I didn't think that would be a good idea; that we shouldn't be working in the same place. She persisted, and I finally said 'OK, if that's what you want to do, but I'm not going to help you.'

"So she called and asked some questions about the job, including the recommended dress. The interviewer told her that since she was the first person that people coming into the office would see, she would have to make a good impression. So she should dress like her mother dresses."

Schneider thought that comment would put an end to it, but after some hesitation, her daughter decided that she did want to try for the job, and so she and her mother went shopping. They were in the dressing room at a well-known department store and the girl took off her clothes to try something on. That's when her mother saw, for the first time, the tattoo on her hip.

"I wanted to *scream*," Schneider laughed, "but it was a public place! Do they ever teach you self-control!" she repeated.

The lesson has been useful professionally. Schneider still occasionally has to deal with people who underestimate her abilities as a black woman, despite her degree from Yale Law School (which she attended while raising two young children) and her expertise in the field of public finance. She described one incident when her firm was competing with another firm to become bond counsel on a deal.

I had drafted the underlying legislation that made this particular transaction work, and some questions had come up about what the legislation meant. I said "I think it means A, B, and C." The other lawyer resisted what I said. He insisted on arguing; in fact, he was extremely argumentative and sure of his position. It was just like when kids insist that they are right. You don't take them on, because you know that they won't listen. So I didn't tell him. Later he came to me and said, "Pauline, about that legislation. I saw . . ." and I said, "Yes, Peter, I wrote it."

Today, if there's one thing I tell our associates, it's learn to pick your fights. You don't give in on ethical issues, or issues that involve our reputation. But you don't have to have a fight over everything.

At an economic summit in the 1980s, Margaret Thatcher, who was chairing the meeting, took a delegate to task for being "out of line." The man vigorously objected, while she remained silent. After the meeting, Ronald Reagan asked her why she had accepted the scolding, particularly since, in his view, she had been right.

"Women know when men are being childish," she explained.

Do Your Homework! No Excuses!

A number of female leaders told me that they hear a lot of "The dog ate my homework" excuses from people who can't seem to understand that grownups, too, have to do their homework. Like children who get in trouble, an employee who drops the ball will often reach for an excuse: "You didn't explain the assignment clearly enough;" "You didn't give me enough coaching or direction;" "I wasn't given enough time to do the assignment;" "I delegated it to someone else, and it's *their* fault that there are so many errors in the report. . . ."

When Patricia Wald was chief judge of the court of appeals for the District of Columbia she found out that even Federal judges on the second highest court in the land often couldn't get their assignments in on time. Wald told me she had learned from dealing with her five children that she should "never assume that something was going to get done, just because it was supposed to. That goes for making sure the kids get their homework done to making sure a judge gets his opinions out on time. By the end of the year each judge here has to produce roughly forty opinions. Some of the judges *just can't do it.* They can't meet deadlines, even knowing that other people are depending on them."[10]

Other mothers I spoke with said they put their foot down and refused to tolerate this kind of shirking. Ann Moore was particularly emphatic.

> *It shocks me to see how some people think they could have my job or get my job done without doing their homework. In middle school my son had a problem with his homework. Two teachers told me he wasn't turning it in. I had to explain to him that homework was what was expected of him, that doing it was not optional.*
>
> *It's black and white. If homework is due, you do it!*
>
> *I'm astounded when I encounter the same attitude in the business world—that assumption that some people have that they don't really have to do it. . . . Well, you do. I like people who don't try to punt it or fake it.*

Give Out Gold Stars

Whether they're five years old or forty, everyone loves recognition for a job well done. No one is ever too old or accomplished to appreciate a compliment, a pat on the back, or public praise for their performance. Michael Fossaceca, thirty-six, a senior vice president at JPMorgan-Chase in New York City, told me that, back in the 1980s when he started his career at Chase Manhattan Bank, he had a hot-shot sales manager who had previously worked for Xerox. She was tough and disciplined, and knew exactly how to motivate people. Every month she would hold a huge meeting, attended by hundreds of people, and she would recognize the top salesperson of the month. They would become the king or queen of the month, and they'd get a big crown, which was displayed prominently for that month.

"People would snicker, and call it corny or cheesy," Fossaceca recalls, "But it gave you the biggest sense of pride to win that crown, and have everyone say, 'That guy's a good salesman; that guy's the best!' No one ever admitted it, but we all wanted to win that crown, and if you lost it, you really wanted to win it back. That recognition in front of your peers was a more important motivator than money. . . . It was like those laminated tombstones that banks give people after they close a big deal. In spite of yourself, your juices start flowing, and you want to do another deal so you can win another tombstone to display on your desk."

"It sounds like awarding kids a gold star," I suggested.

"Come to think of it," Fossaceca suddenly remembered, "That sales manager—Pat O'Grady—was a kindergarten teacher before she went to work at Xerox."[11]

Judith Rapoport, a child psychiatrist, has a professional understanding of why grown people still need gold stars and reassurance that they're doing a good job.

When you become a boss, you become a symbolic parent for your people. Many people come to a workplace from families who haven't met their needs or appreciated them sufficiently. So statements that should seem innocuous might offend or elicit the wrong reaction. If you've raised kids, you realize that you have to qualify everything you say with affectionate, positive statements. You have to do the same thing in the workplace. People bring in their past baggage and open it up, releasing love and hate that gets projected onto their bosses, just as they once felt love and hate for their parents. They see their bosses as gods or devils, or both at different times, and if you've had children, you've been through that before and understand it better. You can de-flect it with affirmative statements added to the critical or corrective ones, such as "This was a really fabulous report. It shows how much research went into it. I just wonder if we should add X and Y. Or change Z to W. Or do a little more looking into this piece of it . . ."

This works infinitely better than just stating what needs fixing in a piece of work.

Babies in Hollywood

No group of working mothers has more grownup infants confronting them than the moms of Hollywood. Everyone in Los Angeles has stories about directors throwing fits like two-year-olds, needy actors obsessing like teenagers over their looks, actresses pouting and refusing to come out of their dressing rooms like kids who won't go to school. One spring break in Los Angeles, I had several amusing lunches with female producers, directors, and actresses who recalled dealings with people who should have been in diapers. A lot of them agreed that mothers have a slight edge in handling the big babies.

"Being a director is like being a child," says Lucy Fisher, a producer and former top studio executive who raised three kids while turning out a string of hit movies, including *The Witches of Eastwick, The Bridges of Madison County,* and *Men In Black.*

Good directors want everything, whatever the cost. They're perfectionists, who care about every little detail. They know the difference between being good and being great is that last one per cent. So they are cunning, manipulative, demanding, even abusive—anything to get what they want. They'll fight for what they want as if their life depended on it, just like a child. A studio executive needs to have ways of dealing with this, and of saying no in a way that lets the other person keep his dignity. It's just like being a parent.

Fisher told me about the time she was supervising production of a major film and was on the phone being screamed at by the director who was known for his terrible temper. He was ranting and raving and hurling insults and if she hadn't had children, Fisher says, she would have been completely offended and totally furious. Instead, she waited until he paused for breath, and snapped, "Cut it out right now. I already have one two-year-old." She says this stopped him cold.[12]

Sarah Pillsbury, a producer, told me she was once on a set in Canada trying to produce a movie and nurse a new baby at the same time. Everyone was acting out and she thought "If only I had 100 pacifiers I could just stick in everyone's mouth and go home to take care of a real baby."[13]

Naomi Foner has witnessed the infantile behavior of actors from the interesting perspective of a director's wife.

In Hollywood you get a lot of people who've been deprived as children. A huge proportion of the people who go into acting are trying to get the attention they never had. So they are extremely demanding. Forget about their fair share—they want it all! During filming, the structure is a lot like a family. The director is the central parent, supported by the producer behind the scenes. The actors are like the kids. As producer I had to learn to sort of give my husband Stephen, as director, over to the kids and take a back seat so the "other parent" could spend time with all these children who needed attention. With actors it's always "Why did you give her that?" or "Why can't I have what he has?" It's exactly the same as with children.

In our line of work, people act out all the time.

Lucy Fisher elaborated:

These are people who are being paid to express their feelings. . . . These are people who suffer more, who feel more deeply, and who are often insecure. Nine-tenths of the time when people are upset it's because they feel insecure. One of my greatest strengths, which comes from being a mom, is that I can see this person in need first. I can go through a lot of aggravation to get to that and address it. My ego isn't involved. The ego thing may be being a woman, but the mother part is my ability to understand that it's okay if someone gets mad.

"We're in a very indulgent business," confirms entertainment lawyer Melanie Cook, who represents such clients as Keanu Reeves; Ed Harris; Sam Mendes, the director of *American Beauty*; and Scott Rudin, who produced *The Hours*. "We'll put up with an enormous amount of bad behavior by talented people who deliver profit."[14]

Infantile Bureaucracy

Katherine Marshall is an official at the World Bank and mother of two: a daughter who graduated from Princeton and a son in middle school. Marshall has thought long and hard about the similarities between dealing with children and dealing with bureaucrats and, at one point, when her daughter was a baby, she actually wrote a little essay on the topic of infantile bureaucracy.

Marshall was teaching her baby to eat solid food when it first hit her that her two jobs—as a bureaucrat and as a mother—had a lot in common. In both instances, when trying to introduce something new, it was better to start with something bland—not too hot, not too cold. And definitely not with anything spicy that might irritate the system.

With both babies and bureaucracies, the unfamiliar must be tried slowly, or mixed with something already known and liked. With both there is also a tendency for certain flavors to be popular for a brief period to the exclusion of all else. With a small child, this might be macaroni and cheese; with an economic development bureaucracy it could be a fad such as microlending. This is not good—a balanced diet and balanced programs are better.

Babies and bureaucracies can also balk at something that is good for them, be it vegetables or diversity. If you try to slip this unpopular item in on them, they may notice immediately, and spit it out with gusto. Screams and tantrums are not unheard of. Whether nurturing an infant or a bureaucracy, you first have to spoon the food in and, when they spit most of it out, you have to scoop it up and push it back in. As a rule, the faster the food goes in, the more will eventually reach its ultimate destination. A pause will give a baby or a bureaucrat time to think and play and spit even more out. Persistence usually pays, and a sense of humor and a relaxed attitude definitely help. With time, there is a clear increase in proficiency. The baby feeder and the bureaucratic innovator learn to get more input into the target audience and learn which substances and methods cause irritable reactions or utter rejection.

The final step is cleaning up. Here, Marshall confesses, she found teaching a baby how to eat solid food was easier than coping with a bureaucracy. Take one wet rag and a washing machine and most evidence of a messy meal disappears. However, in the wake of trying to introduce something new to a bureaucracy, you may have wounded feelings and hurt dignity. Here again, a sense of humor helps.

"The parallels in management of babies and bureaucracies seem striking to a working mother," Marshall concludes. "Child management requires more sophisticated skills than some appreciate, while even a bureaucracy has human foibles."[15]

Is There a Danger in Being Mom at Work?

When faced with childish behavior, is it smart for a female manager to play the role of *mother*, the superior grownup, too overtly? This posture can be more than a little risky, and opinion among the executive women I talked to was divided.

Louise Francesconi, a vice president at Raytheon with a grown son and a stepson, makes no bones about the fact that the men in her very masculine environment often act like selfish babies. "Infantile behavior comes about when an infant isn't mature enough to think about others . . . we see a lot of that in organizations," Francesconi told me in a telephone interview from her office in Phoenix. "You see all this ranting and raving, acting like idiots. If I acted like that they'd think I was an 'emotional woman.' "

Francesconi says she doesn't care if her colleagues see her as an office mom when she just says no to such behavior:

> I'll say "Stop it! Hey! I don't care what happened to you yesterday, cut it out!" They'll get mad and call me Mom . . . But I'm very comfortable using whatever I've learned in the home environment as I relate to people here. . . .
>
> For example, I make an explicit analogy between the welfare of the company and the welfare of a family. Say I'm in a meeting trying to get people to give up some money to spend on some project. Someone will ask, "What's in it for me?"
>
> I'll say, "I'm sure a lot of you are married and have children. If the first thing you say when you walk in the door at night is 'What's in it for me?' they know they're going to have a bad night! If that's your attitude, we'd better just stop now. Let's end the meeting . . ."
>
> They may say "Okay, Mom," but they get it.[16]

Lisa Anderson, dean of the School of International and Public Affairs at Columbia University in New York is also unafraid of being stereotyped as the Mother Hen. As she put it, "There are still so few of us in power that we're going to be stereotyped anyway, and Mom is better than wife or girlfriend."

"I conceptualize interaction differently from many of my male colleagues," Anderson told me. "I see a lot of behavior as bullying, and I ask, how do you deal with a bully? Let's say two professors are fighting with each other. In one such case, a former president of this university referred to them as two stags in a clearing. But I always think of two kids fighting during recess. I spend a lot of time being the recess monitor."[17]

Anderson has a special technique she uses when she needs to lay down the law, which might be called *Mom says*.

I draw on my own mother, who was a great source of pithy little sayings. I'll say, "As my mother always said, 'Just because everybody else does it doesn't make it right.' " I say things like that to my teenaged daughter, and to be able to bring that into the office is useful. When I refer to my mother having said something I'm not saying it. So I can be strict by invoking my mother without causing as much resentment. It permits me to lay down the law in a much less confrontational way. So much of this "Mom says" technique is so easy to understand, so nonoffensive and common sense, that it's not belittling or offensive to use it.

I have never heard any of my male colleagues refer to their mothers—or to lessons learned from their kids. Either they don't draw lessons from home, or they don't think it's appropriate. You'll hear the men say, "These people are behaving like animals*!"*

I'll say, "These people are behaving like children*!"*

Another university administrator, Shirley Kenny, cautions that there is danger in becoming a mother figure to the people you work with. "There could be resentfulness," she explained. "Somehow I think there is more resentment against a mother figure than against other kinds of authority."

I asked her to elaborate on this important point.

"They're not used to dealing with mother figures, so you have to be careful. You can't be heavyhanded. At the same time, we've gotten past the point where you have to be like a man."

Kenny offered this example of a maternal management style that could be resented:

Say a professor wants to get out of teaching an 8:00 A.M. class. So he and a male department chairman might bargain. It will be, "Okay, you can teach the class at 11:00 A.M.," and both will understand that now he owes the chairman one. Or it might be, "No, you can't change that class," and now the two of them will get into a conflict and be enemies.

A woman in authority might make the guy feel he's acting childishly if he's trying to get out of an inconvenient schedule. Mothers work a lot by expectations. These can be stated and unstated, but the kid knows what they are and he or she will try to measure up. So if a maternal authority figure uses this technique the guy can feel belittled. He can't win against an expectation that he will act responsibly or maturely. He may resent an authority figure who holds him to a higher standard. He may feel exposed or embarrassed.[18]

Again, maybe being mom works best when the role is performed with a sense of humor. When attorney Jamie Gorelick, later deputy attorney general in the Clinton administration, became president of the 60,000-member D.C. Bar—that is not a typo; there really are more than 60,000 lawyers in Washington—one of her law partners told her that governing the bar would be just like being the mother of a three-year-old, which she was at the time. He gave her a gavel inscribed Jamie's Law: Because I Said So.[19]

CHAPTER 3

Win–Win Negotiating and the Irrational No!

> "To win one hundred victories in one hundred battles is not the acme of skill. To subdue the enemy without fighting is the acme of skill."
>
> —Chinese General Sun Tzu

Parents are expert negotiators. After all, they have been up against the best in the world: their kids. Diplomats who are parents will readily admit it. Jeanne Kirkpatrick, former U.S. ambassador to the United Nations, reared three sons, and former Secretary of State Madeleine Albright raised three daughters. Both have said that diplomacy was child's play compared with dealing with real children. A high-level Defense Department official during the Reagan administration, no softy, once confided to me over dinner that negotiating with his teenaged daughter taught him more about how to deal with the Soviets than any other training he had ever had. After years of dealing with "Can I stay up late?" "Why can't I go to that movie?" "Can I have the car?" "Why can't we buy that?" talking about the ABM treaty with a grownup in Geneva was relatively easy.

Anita Roddick, founder of the Body Shop, is reported to have said that any mother who has dealt with two kids and one piece of toffee can negotiate any contract in the world.

The average mother is well aware of this. Kate Lauderbaugh, of Evanston, Illinois, a former vice president of technology who is now the mother of two preschoolers, says that trying to get her son from the house to the car is harder than managing sixty-five systems professionals and consultants. "Managing mature adults is a piece of cake, even if they have performance issues, compared with parenting," says Lauderbaugh.[1]

"All you do with children is negotiate constantly," says Lori Okun, a partner at Ernst & Young in New York City and the mother of two school-age children. "You negotiate to get them to eat their breakfast, to get out the door, to do their homework, to take a bath, to go to bed and—finally—to sleep." Ernst & Young recently sent Okun to a two-week executive management program run by the Kellogg School of Management, and the very first day was entirely about negotiation.

"Of course," said Okun, "I already knew how to do it."[2]

Negotiating skills have never been more important than they are today. They are required of everyone, from parents to diplomats to the heads of organizations. This is because the way people relate to each other—in business, in government, in families—is fundamentally changing. Call it democracy, call it a breakdown in respect for authority, call it whatever you like, but increasingly, people simply don't take orders anymore.

It used to be that in the family, mothers would order their children to do something "because I said so." No back talk. The father would come home and lay down the law, and the woman and children obeyed, because the presumption was that Father knows best. An authoritarian hierarchy was accepted in corporations, and in religious institutions like the Catholic Church, which were rigidly controlled from the top down.

No more. Today, husbands, business executives, employers, priests, bishops, prime ministers, and even presidents can no longer simply tell people to do what they want them to do. Leaders have to spend much of their time trying to *persuade* others, rather than *coerce* them, to do their bidding.

Historian Richard E. Neustadt related an anecdote about the limits of presidential authority in his classic book *Presidential Power*. In the early summer of 1952, President Harry Truman was thinking about the problems Gen. Dwight Eisenhower would face if he were to win the forthcoming election (which he did). "He'll sit here," Truman said, tapping his desk for emphasis, "and he'll say, 'Do this! Do that!' *And nothing will happen.* Poor Ike—it won't be a bit like the Army. He'll find it very frustrating. . . . I sit here all day trying to persuade people to do the things they ought to have sense enough to do without my persuading them . . . That's all the powers of the President amount to."[3] Neustadt, a father of two when he wrote this, did not compare the frustrations of a president with those of a parent, but he easily could have.

This gradual, massive shift away from authoritarianism in human organizations, from the family on up, explains why effective negotiation skills have become such a hot topic in recent years. As recently as the 1970s, the subject was hardly a defined field of study or training. Almost no courses were offered in universities. By the 1990s, negotiation and conflict resolution courses were everywhere. They are now taught in most schools of law, business, and government; are offered in large companies and in many government agencies; and are part of the public school curriculum.[4] Books on negotiation are regularly on bestseller lists—the bestselling business book of all time, *Getting to Yes*, is on how to negotiate—and coaching and training of executives has become a new industry.

And what are all these books, coaches, and courses trying to teach us? Here is where it gets interesting.

Reading the Baby Books at Harvard

In the first months after my only child was born, I was an avid reader of *baby books*, those knowing manuals on how to produce a healthy, happy, well-adjusted—not to mention brilliant—child. I gradually noticed a striking similarity between the advice dispensed by these books and the advice contained in management literature. The techniques looked suspiciously similar, though neither the child-rearing manuals nor the business books let on that they might be two sides of the same coin.

In order to test my theory that parenting and management techniques are related, I signed up in the mid-1990s for a three-day seminar at Harvard on the topic of dealing with difficult people. The course was taught by Bill Ury, a co-author of *Getting to Yes* and author of its sequel, *Getting Past No*, and was sponsored by the Program on Negotiation, a multiuniversity consortium based in Cambridge, Massachusetts. The more than 150 people in attendance included senior managers from large corporations, banks, utilities, government agencies, nonprofits, and the military. They had each paid almost two thousand dollars to be there. Only a handful were women.

When I arrived at Pound Hall in the Harvard Law School, where the course was being taught, Ury was warming things up with a series of questions.

"Who do you have difficult negotiations with?" he asked the audience.

"Plaintiffs' lawyers," a voice rang out. "Agents." "Buyers." A dozen more answers followed, including "the opposite sex" and "kids."

"How much time do you spend negotiating with these people?" Ury inquired. "If it's more than 50 percent of your time, raise your hand." Almost everyone's hand went up.

"Of the most important decisions you had to make last year, how many did you have to negotiate?" he continued. "How many here would say at least eight out of ten?"

Almost all hands went up again.

Having established that modern management is virtually synonymous with negotiation, Ury then drove home his principal message: that leadership is more a matter of intelligent bargaining and persuasion than a macho exercise of overt power.

"The most important thing to take out of these three days is to think about the process . . . not just the outcome. I want you to leave here a more reflective negotiator."

A man sitting next to me, who was taking the course for the second time, confirmed that that was the key lesson he had learned. "I used to be really tough," he confided. "My dad was a plant foreman and I used to think I had to be tough or I'd lose. It had to do with my ego— nothing to do with getting results."

Ury's message was that negotiating can and should be a process of mutual gain, not an arm-wrestling contest with a winner and a loser.[5] The way to reach such a win–win outcome, he stressed, begins with taking other people seriously and respecting their point of view. The first step in resolving any conflict is to signal this respect by listening respectfully and actively to the other person's concerns.

Ury gives this example of how to listen actively in *Getting Past No*:

Customer: "I bought this answering machine from you barely six months ago, and now you can scarcely hear the voices. . . . What kind of lousy machines do you sell here?"

Salesperson: "Okay, let me make sure I understand. You bought this machine here six months ago . . . But now you can't hear the voices. You need a working machine . . . Have I got it right?"

Customer: "That's right."

Salesperson: "Let's see what we can do for you."[6]

Anger defused. Onward to mutually agreeable solution.

Already I recognized the familiar set of ideas that govern the most widespread American child-rearing practices. Since the 1950s, mainstream parenting books have been based on an approach first popularized in Dr. Haim Ginott's *Between Parent and Child*. Ginott, a psychotherapist, suggested that instead of issuing commands, parents should make a serious effort to understand their child's feelings, and to search for a win–win solution when conflict arose. The first step, Ginott counselled, is to listen respectfully and actively to your children's concerns. Don't recoil from your children's feelings (i.e., "I don't want to hear this!"). Don't argue with their feelings (i.e., "You shouldn't be frightened"). Instead, reflect their feelings back to them accurately, so that they feel understood and clear about what they feel. The best response to a child who is upset, for example, is to *paraphrase* their sentiment, with a nonjudgmental "I hear you" statement, as in "It sounds as though you are very angry." This confirms the child's feelings, and he will feel safe to express what's troubling him. Then parent and child can proceed to explore why he feels the way he does, and how they might resolve the conflict or deal with whatever is bothering him.

Ginott's basic techniques—avoid direct confrontations, listen carefully, respect the child's feelings, and search for win–win solutions—have been repeated in countless baby books, such as *How to Talk So Kids Will Listen and Listen So Kids Will Talk*, by Adele Faber and Elaine Mazlish, an illustrated primer based on the authors' workshops with Ginott. They have become familiar stuff to mothers, many of whom realize, as *New York Times* columnist Jane Brody recently noted, that they apply "equally to interactions with adults."[7]

But, judging from their rapt attention, the same advice was news to the men attending the workshop. As Ury led them through an exercise on how to deal with angry clients or customers, they had no idea they were learning rules first taught to moms in the 1950s on how to deal with irate tots. I thought this was a fascinating discovery, and I asked Ury about it after the first session of the seminar. "Would you be offended," I inquired, "if I compare what you are teaching to the material in the child-rearing books?"

He smiled. "No, not at all. I read Ginott and Maslow and all that humanistic psychology for *Getting Past No*."

What really intrigued me, though, was that Ury seemed to be taking some pains *not* to reveal his sources. The authorities he cited were impeccably macho: the "eminent Prussian military strategist" Carl von Clausewitz and the great Chinese general Sun Tzu. The midlevel managers at Harvard were led to believe that they were learning the lessons of the battlefield when they were really absorbing the lessons of the therapist in the nursery. They heard quotes from *The Art of War*, but nothing was attributed to *Between Parent and Child*. At no point in his lectures during the three-day seminar did Ury mention Haim Ginott's name. (In *Getting Past No*, Ginott is referred to only once, as an unnamed "leading child psychologist.")[8]

Nor did Ury give any credit to another important disseminator of the communication skills pioneered by Ginott. One of the first people to recognize that parenting techniques could be marketed to managers was Thomas Gordon, the founder of Parent Effectiveness Training. In the early 1960s, Gordon, a clinical psychologist who had studied with Carl Rogers at the University of Chicago, began teaching parent education classes in his own community of Pasadena, California. The classes burgeoned, and eight years later, in 1970, Gordon published *P.E.T. Parent Effectiveness Training: The Tested New Way to Raise Responsible Children*. The book became a bestseller and started a national parent education movement. By the time of his death in 2002, the book had sold more than 5 million copies and P.E.T. courses were being taught in forty countries.

The enthusiasm convinced Gordon that he was onto something even bigger than child-rearing. Numerous parents told him that he had made a mistake in not titling his book *People Effectiveness Training*, because they could apply the skills they learned through P.E.T. with anybody, including employees and associates at work. Clearly the techniques P.E.T. promoted—active listening, I-messages, and no-lose conflict resolution—were applicable to any and all human relationships.

Gordon proceeded to design training programs for teachers, supervisors, managers, executives, and government officials. "It took me far too long to see the almost exact parallel between the parent–child relationship and the boss–subordinate relationship," he wrote. "But after so many fathers taking P.E.T. reported how they were using everything they learned in class in the organization where they worked, I finally got the point."[9]

In 1977, Gordon published L.E.T. *Leadership Effectiveness Training: The No-Lose Way to Release the Productive Potential of People*, another hit that went through eleven printings in its first year and a half. The new book continued P.E.T.'s emphasis on communications skills, and tackled head-on the fundamental issue of the decline of authority in the modern world. As Gordon put it, "being the leader doesn't make you one," because leaders don't automatically earn respect and acceptance. He advised his readers that the trick was "to influence people without using power." He warned that overt attempts to dominate will simply breed resentment and encourage retaliation, in both children and adults.[10]

Or as Sun Tzu put it so well two thousand years ago: "The best general is the one who never fights."[11]

Just as Thomas Gordon's pupils were amazed that his parenting techniques worked in business, Ury told me that his students were always surprised to discover that the same methods of dealing with conflict in the office worked with family members. "I can't count the number of times people have come up to me after a speech and said 'I wish I'd brought my spouse with me, or my teenager,' " said Ury. "I can see that half the people in the audience are applying this to their personal situation."

What Ury's business audiences don't realize, of course, is that the spouse they didn't bring had probably already been using these conflict resolution techniques on the family for years.[12]

One of the few women in the Harvard seminar seemed to get it right away. Kathryn Trickey, the regional manager of a Houston-based uniform-supply company, told me that seven men reported to her at work and two children reported to her at home. To her the parallels were obvious. "Businesses and families aren't all that different," she commented matter of factly.

At one session, we watched a video showing an exchange between a production manager and a sales chief that quickly degenerated into a cockfight. Trickey leaned over to me and whispered, "Those kids aren't playing well together. I'd spank 'em and send them to bed without any dinner."

Diplomatic Relationships

So is there any hard evidence that experienced parents are any better negotiators than other people? This would be hard, if not impossible, to prove. If anything, there is even some evidence that women, with or without children, are *less* effective negotiators than men *when they are negotiating on their own behalf*: for higher salaries, better assignments, promotions, and the like. Women of all ages are far less likely than men to initiate salary negotiations, and are more willing to accept whatever is offered by prospective or current employers.[13] Apparently the social pressure to be accommodating takes its toll on women's ability to advocate forcefully for themselves. A mini-industry of books, training programs, and on-line courses has sprung up to teach women to be more assertive in bargaining, especially with employers.

Interestingly, however, when women are representing a cause other than themselves they do not seem to be similarly handicapped. Female foreign service officers from Norway, Sweden, the United States, and the United Kingdom have all told me that they gained invaluable negotiating skills from dealing with their children. And some of the United States' most successful negotiators have been female diplomats with children.

Doral Cooper, an economist who was chief negotiator of the 1983 U.S.–Israel Free Trade Agreement, was handling that negotiation when her daughter Bergen was born. (She already had a three-year-old son.) One hour after the baby girl arrived, while Cooper was still in the recovery room, she received a call from her Israeli counterpart.

"I know it's a really bad time to call," he said, in a masterpiece of understatement, "but the U.S. government's procurement position doesn't work for us."

"And, fool that I was, I said 'OK, let's talk it through,'" Cooper told me. "My husband is standing there rolling his eyes."

Twenty years later, Cooper said she had become convinced that for whatever reason—gender, culture, or the parental experience—women make better diplomatic negotiators than men. It is no accident she says, that half of the career staff in the Office of the United States Trade Representative are women.

"A successful international negotiation cannot be adversarial, or win–lose," she explained. "Both sides have to come out with something and feel that they won, or at least didn't lose."

Cooper believes that women are more accustomed to compromising, better at not demanding the whole cake, and better at understanding what the other side has to have to do a deal. "Women are much better at sizing up the other side, figuring out what makes them tick."

In 1987, when her two children were six and four, Cooper gave up her high-pressure position as a trade negotiator, with its stress and frequent travel, to start an international trade consulting firm affiliated with a major Washington law firm. Ten of her staff of twelve are women, and all those who are over the age of thirty-five are mothers.

"It really helps," she says. "They know what's important and not important; they don't take themselves too seriously; they can handle crises; and they all know it's sometimes much easier to deal with clients with multibillion-dollar deals on the table than dealing with kids."

The most moving story I heard from a parent-diplomat came from a father, Harold Saunders, a retired foreign service officer who negotiated the historic peace agreement between Israel and Egypt in 1979. (This agreement returned the Sinai and the Gaza Strip to Egypt in return for Egyptian recognition of the state of Israel.)

In Saunders's opinion, although nation states have certain institutional characteristics, "They cannot be considered completely apart from the human beings who influence, make, carry out, and politically sustain their policy." In other words, dealing with states is at bottom dealing with people. If you know something about negotiating with people, you will know something about how to handle international relations—although Saunders dislikes the term "international relations."

"I'm boycotting that phrase," he told me over lunch in Washington several years ago. "It carries all the baggage of the old power politics model. I deliberately say 'international *relationships*.' "

Saunders believes that relationships between nations need to be seen through an entirely new, less abstract lens. As he put it, "Someone thinking or acting in the context of building, nurturing, changing, and conducting a relationship with another country will behave differently from those who are playing power games on a strategic chess board."

These views were profoundly influenced by the veteran diplomat's personal experience. In 1973 his wife died when their two children were only nine and seven years old. Saunders was their sole parent for seventeen years, and was still helping them come to terms with their loss when he became involved in the negotiations between Egyptian president Anwar Sadat and Israeli prime minister Menachem Begin. He told me that his understanding of mourning, in particular, which "is so built into the Jewish past," helped him address Israeli fears and persuade their leaders that they could safely make an exchange of land for peace. Saunders said that he wasn't sure he could have done that if he had not had the parenting experience.

This is a new vision of a skilled diplomatic negotiator: an empathetic, reassuring parental figure. And to this day, the agreement Saunders brokered still stands, despite the violence devouring the Middle East.

Some researchers believe that an ability to manage relationships is more characteristic of female negotiators. Leonard Greenhalgh, a professor of management at the Amos Tuck School of Business Administration at Dartmouth, concluded from his studies on gender differences in negotiating styles that men tended to focus on winning in negotiations; on besting an opponent, as opposed to building a relationship. Women were more likely to treat negotiations within a context of continuing relationships, in which both parties have to keep coming back for more.[14] This may reflect women's greater responsibility for maintaining relationships within a family. They are usually the ones who try to hold things together between people who have to live under the same roof, wake up every morning, and carry on, whatever their differences.

In *Managing Strategic Relationships: The Key to Business Success*, Greenhalgh stresses the value of this ability to manage ongoing relationships in business. Like many others who have studied what managers actually do, he argues that effective executives don't direct or control, but negotiate with and manage internal networks of professionals and external networks of suppliers, customers, regulators, stakeholders, and competitors, among others. Relationships, in short, are everything.[15]

In other words, if you are used to managing relationships at home, you have had a first-rate education on how to manage relationships in business and international affairs. In all cases, the job is much more like bargaining and settling disputes within a family than a one-shot chess match or duel.

The Irrational No

Do parents acquire any other negotiating skills? I heard about one tactic that should help correct the false impression that women are invariably more accommodating negotiators than men. Karen Mills, an investment banker, mother of three, and wife of the president of Bowdoin College, calls this technique the *Irrational No* (as when, at the end of your rope, you bellow "NO!").

"The Irrational No is a very valuable negotiating skill," Mills told me. "And it was not part of my repertoire until I became a mother."[16]

Mills remembers the exact moment in 1993 when she discovered the power of the Irrational No. She was approaching forty, and had a two-and-a-half-year-old, an infant, and was pregnant with a third child. Mills had been a charter member of the superwoman generation: a 1975 graduate of Harvard, and a 1977 graduate of Harvard Business School. As she recalls, "We were the 'we can do it all' generation: 'We're no different from the men,' 'we can do everything as well as they can—or better,' 'we don't need any special treatment. . . .' " She had gone to work for General Foods, then to McKinsey, and by the mid-1980s was in the leveraged buy-out business. She was playing in a tough, competitive, high-stakes game but she retained, she says, a "nice girl" style of negotiating. "I was like, 'I'm a reasonable person, I want to carefully explain to you all the good reasons why you can't have points A or B,' and so on." Very polite and ladylike.

But, in this one particular negotiation in 1993, she was at the height of the sleep-deprived, full-court-stress period of early parenthood. After being up most of the night with one of her children, she was tired, irritable, and in no mood to be civil.

So, when the other side opened the discussion with a list of demands—we want this, we want that—she snapped "No!" When they said, what's more, we also have to have this and that, she barked "No! Absolutely not!" Whatever they said, her reaction was " No! No way! Forget this! We might as well go home!"

The other team asked for a timeout, and stepped out of the room. In a few minutes, they came back in and agreed to all her demands. She had won.

"All week long my terrible two-year-old had been bringing out these no's in me," says Mills.

"It was, 'I want to stay up late!' "

"No!"

"I want more cookies!"

"No! It's time to go to bed!"

"No, I won't!"

"I had been mentally trained to just say no. I was tired and irritated, and these guys were pushing me and irritating me even more. I had gotten used to saying no, and it just came out naturally. At that moment I learned the value of the Irrational No."

A few years later Mills, who now runs Solera Capital, her own investment banking firm, was speaking at the Harvard Business School. When she told this story one of the more famous professors there commented, "That's fascinating. When do men learn the Irrational No?"

A woman piped up and said, "They're born with it!"

CHAPTER 4

The Importance of Listening

"We have two ears and one mouth. Therefore we should listen twice as much as we talk."

—American Indian maxim

"To lead is to heed. This is not the counsel of wimpishness, but of wisdom." So said a prominent German journalist, in advice to American foreign policy makers. As we have seen, listening carefully to others' concerns is the basis of all successful negotiations. *Listening* is also one of the skills parents mention most frequently when asked what they learn from raising children. Few parents seem to have missed the message, spelled out in countless magazines, child-rearing books, and parent education classes, that listening respectfully is the key to being a good parent. Indeed, you can't be a good parent if you don't listen, and the same is true of leaders in every profession.

When I asked former Texas Governor Ann Richards to describe how her twenty years as a stay-at-home mother of four children had affected her leadership style, she said "I guess the most important thing was this: In a family no one can leave the table without feeling like they've been *heard*. We call this *consensus building*, or managing by consensus, but all it really means is that everyone has to believe that they've been *listened to*. . . . When you're dealing with your children, you're very aware of their feelings, and this transfers over to the management of a lot of people."[1]

Listening to the Electorate

In politics, the ability to listen has never been more important. We are living in a time of ethnic pride, raw sensibilities, injured feelings. Experts on terrorism tell us that one of the key factors in producing a terrorist is the feeling that he or she is not being listened to or heard. To lack power is to lack a voice. The original political sin is to *dis* someone—to fail to show proper respect for their person, their ethnic identity, their gender, or for what they have to say. "What every political group in America wants—it is close to a definition of what it means to *be* a political group—is to be taken seriously," Henry Louis Gates of Harvard has written. Political theorist Charles Taylor calls this the "politics of recognition." It means *listening.*

Being heard apparently has a powerful, positive effect on people. Laboratory experiments conducted by social psychologists suggest that when leaders of a group solicit minority opinions, or when a group is instructed to solicit the opinion of everyone in it, the group performs better than groups where the minority was not consulted.[2] A leader who doesn't understand the effect of listening on morale risks failure, and the loss of all ability to lead.

Here's what Ann Richards has to say on the importance of listening to constituents.

> When policy is made in government or in law, when any people whose lives are going to be affected aren't at the table and in on the decisions, the reactions aren't going to be as good. For example, when I was Travis county commissioner in Austin, I had decisions to make about the hospital system. My husband had some strong opinions on the subject, and as he spoke, it dawned on me that he hadn't been in the hospital since he was a child. I'd been in a bunch more

than he had, having four children and a few other things. Now here was a strongly held opinion from someone who'd had essentially no experience being in a hospital. Someone with that experience should be the first person brought in to talk about whatever problems there are.

If you have a decision on mental retardation, you bring in the parents of children with Down's syndrome, and the decisions will be different. The "experts" who are brought in on an issue usually are academics; they aren't people who've had any experience with the issue. So they will leave out an important dimension. I learned from my kids to listen to people's experience before making any decisions that would affect them . . .

So women's presence, and especially the presence of women with children, is essential when decisions are made about child care, medical care, education, mental health, taxes, war and peace. . . . This experiential school we go to, of raising families, is enormously important in any dialogue about public policy.

Helen Miller, a state representative from Fort Dodge, Iowa, won a seat in the state legislature by convincing the public that an energetic, competent mom could understand their concerns better than anyone else. Miller spent thirty years as the wife of an Air Force physician, traveling around the United States and Germany while raising two daughters, now ages thirty-three and twenty-two, and a son, thirty. When her husband retired from the military, this black couple decided to make a completely new life in a small town in rural Iowa, the fifth whitest state in America. Fort Dodge at that time had 27,000 people, including 800 blacks. The Millers made it 802.

Helen, an open and forthright person, says that at age 53, she "hit town, and got involved in everything." Within three years, she was involved in the local art museum, the youth shelter, the library board, and the prison task force, in addition to running an art enrichment program for at-risk children. It didn't take long for the Democratic central committee in the state to approach her and ask her to run for the state legislature. In 2002 she did and she won, with 65 percent of the vote.

Before the election one skeptic asked her what she, a newcomer and a neophyte, "had to offer" the voters.

"I told him, 'a positive attitude.' He said, 'what good is that?' "

"What good is it?" I said. "It's everything!"[3]

Miller has a master's degree in library science and some paid work experience; among other things, she worked as a mediator in the Washington, D.C. Superior Court during a period when her family was based in the nation's capitol. But the primary experience she brought to her job as a legislator was that of a mother and homemaker. And the most relevant skill she learned as a parent, she told me, was an ability to listen to conflicting voices.

"Everybody always tells me I'm such a good listener," she said, during a coffee break in the cafeteria of the ornate old state capitol building in Des Moines. "Well, if you wake up on a Saturday morning and you have a high-school kid who wants to go to the mall, a thirteen-year-old boy who wants a dirt bike, and a six-year-old who wants to go to a puppet show—all at the same time—you go to the puppet show, then the dirt bike store, then the mall, driving around all day, talking, talking, talking, and trying to keep everyone happy. All three of my kids were different, all wanted different things at the same time, and a husband on top of it all. . . . I learned to listen very, very well!"

"Now I get calls and emails from people wanting things who are not even in my jurisdiction. I'm told people feel I'll hear them. I believe you have to listen to your constituents. In this business the customer is always right."

Miller says she listens to lobbyists—another group of people who wants her ear—with a grain of salt. "I'm harassed by them all the time; they're always around, grinning and smiling. . . . You *know* that if you didn't have this office they wouldn't be acting like that."

As governor of Texas, Ann Richards appointed a number of women like Helen Miller to state office and literally changed the face of government. Fifty percent of her appointments were women, more than the presidential record of 44 percent set by Bill Clinton. At one point in the 1980s there were so many women in prominent political positions in Texas, including the mayors of Dallas, Houston, San Antonio, and Corpus Christi, that when Queen Elizabeth and Prince Charles visited the state, and walked down a receiving line of top officials at the state capitol, Charles quipped, "My God, it's a matriarchy!"

Listening to the Consumer

Geraldine Laybourne, head of Oxygen Media, told me that "This is the biggest challenge in business today: who's going to listen to the consumer. If you've had kids, you've had plenty of practice in this."

Laybourne literally built her career on listening to children and responding to what they liked. When she became program manager of the Nickelodeon cable channel in 1980, she brought with her a conviction that one of the problems with children's television was that no one ever asked kids themselves what they wanted to see. She did, and her own two small children became her first collaborators.

"In the early days of Nick, I really needed to hear what kids like and what they had to say," Laybourne told me during a telephone interview. "Before we had a research department, my two kids screened every show I bought. I had crates of tapes in my office, and I would bring a stack home and we'd pull out the couch and we'd all sit down and they'd log in twenty hours watching those tapes on a weekend. It got to be 'Please, Mommy, no more TV!' "[4]

After becoming president of Nickelodeon and Nick at Nite, Laybourne created focus groups of children, something no other television programmer had thought of doing. The kids' comments helped her create such successful shows as *Double Dare*, the first game show for kids, and proof that shaving cream and green slime could create millions of viewers. Later hits followed, including *Rugrats*, *Doug*, and *The Ren and Stimpy Show*. Together, the Nick shows conquered the marketplace for children between six and fifteen years old. Laybourne later told a reporter that she never dreamed that listening to eight-year-olds would change her life.

By the mid-1990s Nickelodeon was reaching more than 20 million children each month and *Time* magazine named Laybourne one of the twenty-five most influential people in America. The channel's estimated profits were almost $100 million per year. One of the most profitable enterprises in television was literally a house that a mother built by listening to kids.

The irony was not lost on Laybourne. "In the 1980s the cable companies hired women not because they thought it would be good for business, but because they thought it would look good," she told me. "No one ever thought Nickelodeon would become such a profitable asset."

One of cable television's rising young executives, Pamela Thomas-Graham of CNBC, doesn't have a kiddie audience but she does pay attention to her children's reactions to the channel's shows. Graham told me that her six-year-old son Gordon really likes *Kudlow & Cramer*, a pair of financial analysts who share a regular program. Gordon isn't particularly interested in their investment tips, but he sees that the two men are having fun and enjoying a lively, high energy conversation. According to Graham, the pace of communication is what captures his attention. Apparently, capturing the attention of a six-year-old is a good litmus test for the entertainment value of an adult show.

At least one other female media executive has fattened her company's bottom line by listening, in this case to other women. When Ann Moore took over as publisher of *People* magazine in 1991, the Time Inc. executive suite was still a men's club, and the corporate hierarchy thought of *People* as a dual-audience (male and female) magazine. An earlier publisher had even described *People* as a "black-and-white news magazine." But Moore was not shy about acknowledging that most readers were women, and she thought she had a better sense of what women wanted. Among other things, she believed that women would prefer seeing the dresses and the people in the magazine in color. So, over multiple objections, she converted *People* to an all-color layout and, sure enough, sales jumped.

When the Consumer Is a Mother

Moore's success illustrates how much easier it is to understand and serve your customers when they resemble you. A guy who loves cycles ought to be the person selling Harley-Davidsons. An avid hunter will make a better gun dealer. Only a golfer can really sell golf clubs. By the same token, a woman who's managed that small production unit called the *home* will clearly have an edge selling consumer products over the guy who never did a load of wash. Women buy 83 percent of all consumer purchases, including 94 percent of home furnishings, 82 percent of groceries, 75 percent of all over-the-counter medications, 60 percent of automobiles, 51 percent of all travel and consumer-electronics purchases, and—are you ready—80 percent of all riding lawn mowers![5] It is estimated that households with preschool children spend more than $100 billion per year.

This is a pretty powerful argument for having women, and mothers in particular, dominating businesses that sell and market to households. As one of the female executives surveyed by researchers at The Center for Creative Leadership, put it, "I am a consumer and I happen to work for a company that sells products that the gatekeeper for, if you will, is me. I may not be typical because of income and position in my job, but . . . if you're looking to appeal to the gatekeeper, to the decision maker in the household, you're looking to appeal to people that think . . . like me."[6]

Deb Henretta of Proctor & Gamble is a good example of a gatekeeper who brought success to her company by heeding consumers like herself. Henretta, who has three children, made her mark in diapers.

In 1999, the Pampers brand of diapers was in trouble. Once the bestselling diaper in the world, Pampers had been losing market share for several years. Proctor & Gamble, the manufacturer, decided to bring in a mother to run the business.

Henretta was thirty-eight at the time, with children ages nine, seven, and two. She had never worked anywhere other than Proctor & Gamble, and had established her reputation by successfully running the company's popular Tide brand, among others. But she hadn't had a chance to get out of "laundry," as she put it. Her appointment as general manager of P & G's North American baby-care business was a major opportunity.

The baby-care business had always been run by men, and it had always been driven by technology. Diapers are made out of paper and plastic, and the paper industry, along with forest products in general, tends to be male-dominated and technically oriented. The guys were proud of their highly complex diaper products, which could both hold liquid and keep babies dry, which is pretty amazing, when you stop to think about it. However, as Henretta tactfully put it in a telephone interview, Pampers were "missing out on some other, nontechnical benefits."[7]

She spotted the problem immediately. Her youngest child was still in diapers, so she had an at-home test market and plenty of experience as a consumer. She knew that some competitors had replaced old-fashioned tape fasteners with Velcro, and had moved away from plastic outer coverings to soft cloth that was pleasing to the touch. On one of her very first days on the job, she told me, she "was sitting in this room, looking at this plastic-y diaper with this loud crackling tape, and thinking, 'Would I buy this?' It was missing the aesthetics."

One of her first decisions was to adopt quiet fasteners and a cloth back sheet for Pampers, and in no time sales took off. Pampers continued to gain market share thanks to a second Henretta innovation. She noticed that the baby books are full of descriptions of the stages of child development and that more and more baby products, from food to toys, are being sold for tots at different stages of development. One product is tailored for infants, another for the early toddler, another for the independent toddler, and on. Why not do this with diapers? she reasoned. Thus, there are now Swaddler Pampers for newborns, Cruiser Pampers for the child who is just beginning to move around on her own, and Easy-Ups, designed to make a more independent toddler feel he's wearing real underpants rather than a babyish "diaper."

Henretta summarizes her innovations as "getting out of the factory and into the nursery." For her success, she was promoted again and is now president of Global Baby Care for P & G and on *Fortune* magazine's list of the fifty top women in American business.

Cheryl Bachelder, the former CEO of Kentucky Fried Chicken and a highly regarded consumer marketer, is another executive whose success owes a great deal to her firsthand knowledge of "what mothers want" and "what kids want." Earlier in her career Bachelder ran the Life Savers division of RJR Nabisco, which included Bubble Yum. "I would have had no idea that kids were eating blue food, like jello, if I hadn't had kids myself," she says, "and it gave me the idea to make blue gum, which turned out to be a big hit. . . . Mothers have great instincts on how to market to kids, and being a mother is a big advantage if you're in new product development or advertising."

When she first took over as CEO of Kentucky Fried Chicken, Bachelder found that the company hadn't used female focus groups for years, although 80 percent of the dinner decisions in America are made by mothers. She changed that in a hurry.

Listening to Your People

Listening to one's own colleagues is as important as listening to customers, particularly for administrators. University president Shirley Strum Kenny notes that people often come into her office with problems they want her to solve, much as a child will. "As they are describing the problem," said Kenny, "if you just listen you will hear them telling you how they would solve it themselves. That's a parenting skill."

Michael Fossaceca, head of JPMorgan Treasury Services, has a quote from Colin Powell framed and hung on his wall: "When people stop bringing you problems you stop being a leader."

"It's the same with kids," says Fossaceca, the father of two young girls. "When they stop bringing you problems you stop being a parent. A big part of your job as a parent or as a manager is solving problems and removing obstacles. If I say to people, it's my way or the highway, they won't come to me. I want to foster an open dialogue. I want them to be comfortable in saying, 'Dad—or Mike—that's not fair.' "

Judy Blades, an executive vice president at The Hartford and one of the most prominent women in the insurance industry, learned the same lesson at home. Growing up in a large, conservative, Catholic family, she saw that there were a lot of things that her brothers and sisters could not tell their parents. An unmarried sister even got pregnant, and told Judy that she was going to have an abortion because she couldn't tell her parents what had happened.

"I decided then and there that I wanted to be the first person my kids came to with their problems. I told them there's nothing that you can't tell me and we'll work it out together. That kind of approachability is also essential in business. I'm told that I am very approachable, and I'm most proud of that. Your people have to feel that you will listen to them. If my direct reports didn't feel that they could come to me we would *never* be a world-class organization." As the person responsible for The Hartford's commercial, personal, and specialty insurance underwriting businesses Blades soon learned that what is true of children—that you can't just order them to do something because you say so—was also true of her salespeople. She once called her entire team into the home office in Hartford, for example, and told them that they had to raise prices. Her message was, in essence, "This is what we expect you to do—now get on out there and do it!"

It didn't happen.

Then Blades realized that when she got out of headquarters, and personally visited the forty-odd field offices, compliance went way up. When she conducted a serious conversation with the sales force, and explained the rising costs of hospital care and prescription drug prices and the soaring numbers of lawsuits, her people finally understood the need for an increase in premiums. Because she had taken the trouble to spell out the company's reasons, and to respond to the concerns of the sales staff, they had the tools they needed to justify the increases to customers and clients.

"You've got to explain your actions, and then listen and get feedback, rather than pronounce from on high," Blades told me. "That works better with everybody."

At least one other parent I talked to found that after having children she became much clearer in her communications with those reporting to her. Marian Ruderman of The Center for Creative Leadership in North Carolina told me that, as soon as she had a baby, her child-care provider became the most important supervisory relationship in her life. A caregiver is to a mother what a big international bank is to the global economy: too important to fail. As Ruderman put it, "I didn't want her to make *any* mistakes! And English wasn't her first language. So I really spelled out what I wanted. . . . I became very clear in my communications. From managing that child-care situation I learned some skills that were very helpful in managing others."

It may not be coincidental that all four outstanding female managers singled out in the influential 1990 book *The Female Advantage* were skilled listeners. All four executives used listening respectfully as an intrinsic element in their management style, both to gather information and to make people in their organizations feel valued. Author Sally Helgesen found that all of them operated through a lateral management style, utilizing a web structure that connected them to every point in their organization. This network gave them better input than would have been possible in more traditional top–down structures. Helgesen dubbed this nonhierarchical style the *female advantage* but, since all four of her subjects were mothers, she might just as well have called it the *maternal advantage*.

For example, Frances Hesselbein, the former national executive director of the Girl Scouts, firmly believed that only a leader who really listened to her people could hope to bring out the best in them. She had a policy of asking every single Girl Scout employee—from mailroom clerks to management—to write her with suggestions. "It doesn't matter if it's just a toaster oven for the seventh floor," she said, "they need to know that somebody cares."[8] Hesselbein, a widow with a grown son, made herself personally available to hear whatever suggestions people wanted to make. Rather than use her staff to shield her from unwanted encounters, Hesselbein saw visitors as conduits who brought her information from within the company. "I'm fortunate to have three secretaries," she remarked. "It means I can keep in contact with more people."

Dorothy Brunson, owner of several black radio and television stations, and the only black woman who owns a broadcast TV station, used listening to pick up clues on how to handle people. A woman who could put on any number of personalities to fit different situations, from charming a client to bargaining hard over a raise with the host of a gospel music show, Brunson used listening to figure out what aspect of herself she should play up in order to gain the greatest advantage.[9]

Nancy Badore of Ford Motor Company was the mother of a toddler when she was director of Ford's Executive Development Center, the unit responsible for retraining the automaker's top 2,000 managers in the wake of a corporate reorganization. In the 1980s, Ford dismantled layers of managerial hierarchy and instituted a team approach focused on quality and customer orientation. Badore, a PhD psychologist, was instrumental in getting old-school division heads to listen to the ideas developed on the plant floor by the new plant-management teams. She then went on to devise programs designed to ensure that top management at the huge company listened to the insights and suggestions of employees with more direct experience in day-to-day operations. Reinventing Ford's corporate culture to make it more responsive to the rank and file was credited with bringing the company back from near-bankruptcy.

According to Helgesen, the very crux of Ford's managerial revolution was "in requiring leaders who had previously been exclusively speakers to *listen* to what their people have to say."[10]

Deb Henretta believes that women have a tendency to listen more to others than do most men. She speculates that this is not hard-wired in females, or necessarily learned from parenting, but may reflect the more careful way women have had to operate as they come up through the ranks of predominantly male organizations. A woman has to make sure that she doesn't step on any toes, embarass herself, or be seen as too aggressive or threatening. Whatever its origins, this behavior has hidden strengths. Henretta found that she was listened to more seriously when she sought to understand others' views before plopping her own on the table.

> In the early days I had to speak a little louder, but I always made sure I had heard everyone's position and taken account of it before I formed my own. If you operate this way, you tend to get to a better answer than when you're thinking in a vacuum. I know that approach benefitted me, because when I spoke I spoke from a broad knowledge. It made it easier to implement my vision, because I had already incorporated other people's views into that vision. If people feel they've contributed to the construction of the goal, they feel more a part of it, and will be much more supportive and productive. The approach that's taken to get to the vision is crucial, and many women's way of getting there is more effective than other approaches.

Therapeutic Listening to Colleagues

In her recent book, *Disappearing Acts: Gender, Power, and Relational Practice at Work*, Joyce K. Fletcher of the Simmons Graduate School of Management in Boston argues that listening to one's colleagues and peers within an organization can be an important element in maintaining morale and productivity. Fletcher's research was based on close observation of the workdays of six female engineers at Digital Equipment Corporation (DEC), a high-tech company near Boston that is now part of Hewlett-Packard. One of the engineers explained at length how she listened to a co-worker's rambling story.

> . . . when a man does have something he wants to talk about he won't go to another man . . . he goes to a woman. I've had men [in

the office] *who I know don't even like me use me to vent about really personal things . . . like the fertility problems he and his wife were having. . . . And I've talked to several women who say that men come in and sit down and talk to them. You don't really have to say anything, just listen . . . it doesn't cost me anything, really, just to listen. But sometimes it just feels like a big responsibility because even if you are not really in the mood, you have to do it.*[11]

This engineer saw her listening as *work*; as a job that had to be done because it enhanced the quality of life in the office.

Fletcher dubs this *therapeutic listening*, and it does closely resemble the work of therapists, counselors, priests, and mothers, all of whom have the job of hearing out others' problems, signaling that their concerns are being taken seriously, providing some constructive feedback, and sending them back out stronger than when they came in. This is hard work, for a serious listener always takes on some of the pain of the person who is unloading his troubles. That transfer of a burden is precisely what makes the speaker feel better, and why even your best friends can't listen to your problems too many times.

Did the women engineers learn this strategy as mothers, who had experience doing the same thing for their children? Or did they listen because, as Henretta suggests, women in male-dominated organizations often feel they have to be accommodating, even at some cost to themselves? It has often been observed that listening is a characteristic of weaker groups, a way of flattering, deferring to, or monitoring the intentions of the higher ranking group. For whatever reason, studies do reveal that men, the socially dominant gender, tend to speak far more than women, and women do far more of the listening in mixed groups.

(On their own home turf, of course, women take up plenty of airtime. One writer jokes that seeing his mother speechless was an event on a par with a burning bush or the parting of the Red Sea.)

Fletcher did not explore the hypothesis that motherhood had influenced the engineers' practice of listening, but she does speculate that it may be learned from the general experience of caring for others, both children and other dependents. She rejects the idea that it is based on women's relative lack of power. In her view, the women at DEC consciously performed this vital function in their company because they knew it improved morale and productivity, even though they also realized that they would not get credit for their efforts.

Listening to Your Kids

The most touching story of how a parent's willingness to listen made her a better professional comes from Linda Chavez-Thompson, executive vice president of the AFL-CIO. Chavez came up the hard way, born in west Texas in 1944 to Mexican-American sharecroppers. The third of eight children, she had to drop out of high school in her second year. Married at twenty, she had her first child, a daughter named Maricela, at twenty-one. Shortly thereafter she began working for a local construction union as a bilingual secretary and, before long, she was working for the AFL-CIO, coordinating disaster relief, organizing, and lobbying for workers in the state legislature. Before she was thirty, Chavez had become a staff representative for AFSCME (American Federation of State, County, and Municipal Employees), a job that demanded continuous travel and a great deal of time away from her family.

During the five years she held the job with AFSCME, Chavez's mother essentially raised Maricela. Even after Chavez quit her demanding post and took a lesser job and a pay cut in order to have more time for her family, her daughter was still angry about her frequent absences, and for a long period remained more deeply attached to her grandmother. During an interview at the AFL-CIO headquarters in downtown Washington, D.C., Chavez recalled those early years with a palpable sense of regret.

"It was ironic," she told me. "Here I was, the union representative, filing grievances against management on behalf of employees, and then going home where I was management and my daughter was the aggrieved employee! I was battling with management by day, and at night I was struggling with managing a seven-year-old. . . . My concept was I was the good guy, and I ended up the bad guy."[12]

The experience obviously gave Chavez a degree of self-awareness that confrontational union representatives and absentee parents may often lack. And she gained an invaluable insight from her dissident, different daughter:

Maricela is a very patient person. She is quite different from me. I'm like a bulldozer. I'm a take-charge, take-no-prisoners kind of person. I thought my job was to represent my membership and I didn't care who thought what about me or who didn't like me as long as I was doing my job. I was always antagonistic. I would push, make demands, yell at the other side, and all that. . . . My mother would've washed my mouth out with soap every day if she had heard me!

Maricela was always telling me, "You're too impatient, Mom. You can do a lot of things, but you've always got to do it now! You could do more if you stepped back and thought about things before you jump in."

I listened to her. I thought maybe if I gave myself more time in certain situations I wouldn't be so rash. And one day I came home and said, "Guess what? Today I pulled a Maricela!"

I had been in a negotiation on behalf of a worker who was going to be suspended for two days for talking back to his supervisor. My first inclination was to jump up and down and give the supervisor hell, to really let him have it. But I didn't. I took a step back and asked if we could have a five-minute recess.

We left the room and the employee asked, "What are we doing?"

"Nothing," I said. "I'm just giving myself a little time to think. I want to think through how we're going to approach this."

"What are you going to do?" he asked. He really wanted me to give it back to that supervisor.

"I don't know," I said. I was thinking.

Finally, I said, "Okay, do you remember exactly what that supervisor said to you?"

"Yes."

"Do you remember how that made you feel?"

"Yes, I was angry, and insulted. I felt humiliated."

"How long have you been doing this job?"

"For twenty-two years."

"So you've gone up from operator one to operator two to operator three, and he insulted your ability to do your job, and you were embarrassed and humiliated. So, naturally you got emotional. Now, let's go back in and you tell them that."

We returned and I asked the supervisor and the company director to let me paint the picture. Here was a guy in his fifties with a clean record who'd been verbally stripped of his dignity. Of course he talked back! Does any supervisor have the right to destroy the dignity of the workers on his crew? Is insulting a worker part of his job description? I was playing on the sympathies of the director against the supervisor.

And it worked! The guy did get a two-day suspension and a reprimand, but the reprimand was removed from his record after six months. I had taken that step back like my daughter said I should and I won!

I learned from my daughter. She taught me to have a little more patience, to stand back, and look before I leap.

CHAPTER 5

Practicing Patience

"Genius is nothing but a great aptitude for patience."
—French naturalist
Comte Georges-Louis Leclerc de Buffon

Children operate on a different system of time. Their clocks run more slowly than ours. Kids are on the liveable hour, not the billable hour. This can be very hard for modern parents to get used to, with their need to make every minute count.

I remember how excruciating it was at first to operate on kid time, shifting from the daily pressures of a newsroom to the leisurely pace of a toddler's day. Taking a deep breath and waiting while James learned to tie his shoes; waiting in the pediatrician's office, where only the doctor's time is worth money; waiting in the line at the library, while the lonely old lady chatted with the clerk; and waiting while James explained the plot of a favorite television show in excruciating detail, in that wonderfully meandering way a child's mind works. It was hard to get over the idea that I was wasting time, as if life itself were a waste.

Living in a child's preindustrial time zone developed muscles I never knew I had, like the muscle that suppresses the urge to get something done every second, and the muscles that force you to sit still, instead of constantly stirring up dust. Other journalists have told me that they too have had to take a deep breath and learn patience in dealing with their toddlers, a group that has no respect for the pressures on their deadline-driven mommies. Soledad O'Brien, cohost of CNN's *American Morning*, and the mother of two small girls, told me that motherhood taught her that "Sometimes you have to go at someone else's pace."

"With a toddler, the more you try to rush them—into their clothes, into bed, through a meal—the more counterproductive it is. You have to slow down and get on their schedule. We learned this especially while Sophia was learning toilet training. You just can't rush it. Every night, after getting into all these layers of clothing, and tucked into bed, she'd say 'Mommy, I got to go pee-pee.' We'd peel off all the clothes and go into the bathroom and nine times out of ten she didn't need to. Then finally, the last time, she went and sat on the potty. She'd learned!"

"And so did I. You need patience if you want to get some things done."

Sit with It

Lisa Anderson sits in her office overlooking the Columbia University campus and laughs about the reactions when she became the first woman to chair the political science department in 1993. Her two boys were ages three and eight at the time. "Everyone asked me why I was taking this on while I had small children at home. I would say, 'Oh, the job is perfect, because I'm still used to tying other people's shoes.' I meant that I had infinitely more patience than I'd ever had before. When I said this, there would be a split second while they'd think about it, and then you could see them conclude, 'Why be offended? It's true!' "

"Being a department chair means you have to deal with people as they face major life transitions, like retirement or trying to decide whether to accept an offer to come live in New York City. In any of these transitions a lot of personal anxiety comes out. People get nutty! It's easy to get impatient with that. You can say, 'You shouldn't let personal anxiety shape your decision,' you can tell people they can handle the decision themselves . . . But often people just need someone to hold their hand, like a child learning how to ride a bicycle. So you assure them that personal transitions are always hard, and help them work through it.

"I have an indulgence, a patience with people that I wouldn't have had if I hadn't had my own experience of transitions. I don't think that necessarily makes me a *better* administrator, but it does make me a more generous one."

Anderson is describing the kind of work that ministers and counselors often do, which is being patient while people sit with their problems before they eventually come to a decision or some resolution. So, it's not surprising that I found women in the clergy who said that the patience required by motherhood closely resembled their religious vocation. Catherine R. Powell, an ordained Episcopal priest in Washington, D.C., was previously a minister in a blue-collar parish in Salem, Massachusetts. When she arrived, the congregation was still "recovering," as she put it, from thirty-five years of authoritarian leadership by a very traditional male priest. At her first meeting with the vestry (the lay church leaders), she found them completely silent. They literally had no ability to communicate after having been dictated to for so many years.

Powell fell back on the skills she had learned as a mom, including her knowledge of child development. She started with such nursery-school tactics as going around the circle and having everyone say what they thought about various issues. "I started teaching them how to 'use your words,' the way you'd teach young children to express their thoughts," she told me over lunch near the girls' school where she is now a chaplain.

The group soon faced a tough decision. A young man, a member of the congregation, was trying to become a painter, and he asked if the church could put on a show of his works. Powell said she would take it to the vestry, and asked him to submit some paintings for them to consider. He turned up with several canvases of rather strange-looking women, with huge bull's eyes for breasts.

"If it had been my decision, I'd have said no way," Powell told me, but she put it to the group to decide. They mulled it over for awhile. They finally agreed that the paintings weren't quite the thing for a church, but they also agreed that the artist was a nice guy, and why not give him a boost? So, this conservative, working-class church hung the pictures and threw a party for the budding artist, who felt like a great success. "Those people really surprised me," Powell said, still full of wonder.

She believes that the successful group decision-making process that gradually developed in her church reflected what she had learned as a parent. As she put it, "In a family, if a problem comes up, you often have to 'sit with it.' You can't just rush in and 'fix it.' You do a lot of sitting with it for awhile, until a solution gradually emerges. This is like patience, but it's actually more than patience—it's a *trust* that things will develop. This is something parents learn. For example, my oldest daughter had some learning disabilities, which she eventually outgrew. This taught me that it is so wrong to make assumptions about what a child can or cannot do. She may be having trouble, and then suddenly everything will just plop into place. She'll come to you, all excited about a book that two years ago she hated, or couldn't read. . . . That vestry was just like that. . . . As a parent, you learn to have faith in the developmental process."[1]

Zenlike Resignation

Patience is a thin word to describe the strength a person has to muster in coping with the frustrations of dealing with a sick, cranky, or distressed child. Perhaps self-possession, or Zenlike resignation, are better terms for what it takes to be the controlled center in the eye of an emotional storm. One of my friends urged me to include in this book the despair that comes over you when a child throws up in your bed in the middle of the night, or dissolves into an hour-long screaming meltdown, and there's nothing you can do to escape the existential disaster. You cope; that's what you do, because you have to, but those are the moments when you think, "If I can do this, I can do anything! I can take anything else that life decides to throw at me."

Lori Okun of Ernst & Young describes a night when she came home to a weeping, hysterical six-year-old who was so tired that she could no longer control her emotions. The nanny didn't know what was wrong, and she gratefully slid out the door leaving Okun, exhausted herself after a long day at the office, with the miserable child. We all know what Mom's emotions were at that point:

"I wanted to strangle her . . ." Okun told me. " It took every ounce of strength I had to stay calm, to work on soothing her down, to hold myself together without losing it myself. Adults can be a pain in the neck, they can complain about you behind your back, manipulate you, and all the rest, but I can handle that. All that's easy in comparison."

The high degree of self-control it takes to practice this kind of patience and forbearance is reflected in this story from actress Lindsay Crouse about her daughter Willa:

When Willa was five, we were living in Vermont. I was about to deliver Zosia, my youngest daughter, and one day I was struggling to get Willa into her snow suit. She was resisting and I was having a hard time, being very pregnant, and I felt this rage. I just wanted to say, "You will do this or you don't get to go out and play all day!" But I controlled myself and talked reasonably to her, saying "Honey, I bought this outfit especially for you at a very nice store and look! It's pink, your favorite color!"

She looked at me and said, "It's for girls? You bought it at a store?"

"Yes, honey, why do you ask?"

"I thought it was the kind of hood bad men wear when the police come and take them away."

She'd seen that on TV and was terrified. That really was the first moment I began to construct my own mothering style; to see how I did it, and to see that I was doing fine. That's when I began to get confidence as a mother. The bottom line I took away from that incident was the realization that at any given moment the child is doing her best. Your job is to try to understand what that means.

You can certainly extrapolate that to working with adults. Once I was on a film and the director and I had a very different vision of the character I was playing. I was resisting, digging in my heels, being opinionated. It never occurred to me until I remembered that incident with Willa that there might be something I could take from someone else's idea about the part. So I adopted a listening quality instead of a resisting quality.

I devised this technique: I imagined that my character had a three-dimensional life that came before and would continue after the particular scene we were shooting. I imagined that the scene was simply an interruption of that life. This helped me take weight off the scene. Rather than insisting on my way, or withdrawing, I thought, "If I pay attention and really listen to this director, something good will come of it." And what came was an enlarged vision of the character.

I now teach this quality of adaptation in my classes. I teach graduate directors at USC Film School how to work with actors, and I teach actors here in my home. I tell them they have to learn how to adapt to different ways of doing things. And a lot of it I learned from my kids.

For example, another time I was making a peanut-butter-and-jelly sandwich for Zosia when she was about three and I cut it on the diagonal. She crumbled to the floor in tears. I thought, "What is going on? Hummm, I don't usually cut her sandwiches on the diagonal." So, I asked her, "Are you upset because of the way I cut the sandwich?"

"Yes!" (Sobbing.)

Again, a mother's choice. I could make her eat it or else. Or I *could say what I did say: "Okay, I'll make another one and I'll eat this one."*

It's just plain old adaptation because someone is upset.[2]

Take the Time to Explain

Okun is one of a number of women at Ernst & Young who made part-ner while working a four-day week, and she obviously enjoys the family-friendly environment at the firm.[3] As I was leaving her office, I noticed a tee shirt on display in a bookcase. Emblazoned across the front in bold letters was THE EVOLUTION OF AUTHORITY, and under-neath were four footprints: of an ape, a human foot, a male shoe, and a spike heel.

Okun believes that what she calls the *patience factor* is one of the advantages that she, as a mother, brings to her work with clients.

I'm used to finding creative ways of convincing people to do things. At home I have to tell the children what I need from them in three or four different ways. For example, my older daughter is in first grade and I often have to get her to sit down and do her homework. First, I'll say, "Do your homework."

"No!"

Then I try, "Let's look at these new words."

"No!"

Finally I think of something like, "Oh, look, you get to figure out what word fits in here—what a fun puzzle!"

And she gets interested in doing the homework.

It's the same with a client. I can bring up an issue and if it hasn't struck home the first time, I have to go into more detail. For exam-ple, I specialize in financial services. The financial companies I deal with have quantitative models that produce values for their prod-ucts, such as derivatives. In order to make sure that the models are

reasonable and accurate you have to have someone outside the com-
pany look at them. So, I may have to explain why they need to have
independent model validation. First, I might try to tell them what it
means to have an independent validation. They will say, "Why do
we need it?" Then I explain that they need to document their as-
sumptions so that others will understand them. They'll say, "Why,
why, why, Laurie?" They will need several good explanations before
they agree, because what they are really thinking is, "This is going to
cost us a lot of money." It's just like children. Why, Laurie? Why,
Mommy?

Nancy Drozdow, a Philadelphia-based management consultant who
has a ten-year-old daughter and two grown stepchildren, agrees that
patience with children has applicability in the business world. She
cites as an example the parent whose child has difficulty with math.

"It's a *struggle* to figure out how to take a simple math problem apart
so that they can understand it, step by step. It's a struggle of wanting to
help, and not knowing exactly how to help, but patiently sticking with
it, to that a-ha! when the child finally gets it.

"This experience of working with a child can be valuable in dealing
with subordinates. For example, when there's a new role for them to
play, and they don't have a clue how to do it, a superior can't just order
them to do it. She or he can't just say increase your profitability ten
percent and it happens. She has to explain why the new goals have
been set, and show how they can be met. There's a period of guidance
that has to be gone through. It's exactly the same as breaking down a
math problem."

Drozdow's firm, which helps companies devise business strategies,
has discovered that companies often fail to provide this kind of guidance to their employees when they reorganize or undertake a new
strategy:

We see that when a top team devises a new strategy for, say, how to
compete more effectively, and they need to roll it out, the notion of

*bringing people along and getting them on board is often lost. I see
this all the time—the people who come up with the strategy think that
everyone else is just going to get it when they announce it, as if
everyone's been reading their mind.*

*That's where we come in. We help them make the new approach
work by making it come alive to the people who have to carry it out.
This involves explaining the purpose of the new strategy, explaining
that if you do things this way, that good things will happen. . . . We
stress the need to tell all your employees, like bank tellers and others,
that if they do things differently it will truly make a difference.*

*This is commonsensical. But it is also very hard. It takes time and
it takes patience. It's much easier to be top–down and just order people to do things in a certain way. In companies that have had real difficulty in previous years and may be losing money, which are often
the very ones developing new strategies, the executives may feel they
don't have the luxury of time. They have a hard time with this approach because it does take time. It's difficult to make things move as
fast as they would like. These companies might revert to the old command and control management style.*

*Stressed companies, like stressed parents, revert to more primitive
methods.*

This is why it must be said that not all parents, not even all good
parents, acquire patience. (Remember the Irrational No.) Although
Soledad O'Brien told me that patience was one of the lessons she
learned from her children, she is also in an extremely high-pressure
business, and it sounds like she's also learned a form of impatience
from her children:

"My toddler taught me how to issue little ultimatums to move people along," O'Brien says. "You have to set limits or issue orders with a
small child, like 'You do not hit your sister;' 'you do not put food in
your hair.' Now I use the same technique at work. I have to leave the
office at 5:00 P.M. because my nanny has to go home. So, I make it
clear that I have to have my scripts ready by five. If something's not

ready, you'll have to jump through the hoops to messenger it over to me. . . . You have to figure out how to do it. I'm clear now on what's my problem and what's so *not* my problem. It's your problem if the script isn't ready! Before I had kids it was harder for me to lay out rules, and be clear about what I needed."

Sandra Day O'Connor actually scoffed at the idea that children teach patience. "I was always impatient," she told me during a conversation in her chambers at the Supreme Court. Her husband, sitting beside her, agreed, and made a chop-chop motion in the air with his hands. "With three kids, she had to be organized," he said, with a neat karate chop. I got the message, and I'm sure the kids did too.

Patient Statesmanship

A final comment on the uses of patience by political leaders.

Volumes have been written about how the wise exercise of leadership requires patience. "Our patience will achieve more than our force," admonished Edmund Burke, the eighteenth-century British statesman who opposed the war against the American colonists. French General Charles de Gaulle was an exemplar of the patient leader, with his historic ability to say *non*; to simply refuse to take what he thought was unwise action in the face of enormous pressure. This strength enabled de Gaulle to just say no to France's colonial past in Algeria, by withdrawing French forces, and to resist joining the NATO alliance, in defiance of the United States. De Gaulle taught that great leadership sometimes means *not* doing something, or doing it deliberately, as opposed to action for the sake of action. He was a master of patience, disproving the old adage, "Patience is a virtue, possess it if you can, seldom found in women, never found in man!"

CHAPTER 6

Empathy: The E.Q. Factor

"To ensure that their young are cared for, women have evolved a powerful capacity to feel and express empathy."
—Anthropologist Helen Fisher, in *The First Sex*

I was struck during my interviews with how many people told me that they had become much more empathetic after they had children. They believed that their E.Q., *empathy quotient*, shot up after they had been intimately involved in nurturing a child. Empathy is usually defined as a sensitivity to others' feelings and the ability to respond sympathetically and appropriately. Several people referred to their enhanced capacity for empathy as *courage*, the courage to give enough of yourself to connect with another person on a deep level.

The Courage of Empathy

Gillian Moorhead is a former theater director who is now in the business of preparing people to testify at trial. She is hired by law firms to coach defendants and witnesses on how to make the most convincing impression on a jury. This can range from advice on what to wear to techniques for conveying character.

For years Moorhead, a brisk, confident woman in her forties, thought that her skills in this area came from her experience in the theater, coaxing powerful performances out of actors. But, increasingly, she realizes that her work has been most enriched by the experience of being a mother, particularly the mother of two teenagers. (She had a fourteen-year-old daughter and a twelve-year-old son when we spoke.)

I realize now that my work with witnesses is not that different from sitting with my daughter in the kitchen, as she tells me she's so very lonely in school. I sit with witnesses who are often at the edge of their lives. One man, for example, a teacher, was facing two years in prison for allegedly fondling a child in his classroom, and his career had been ruined.

In working with defendants like this, I look them in the eye and try to find their inner truth, what's really bothering them. Only if they dig deep and get in touch with their own deepest truths can people become good witnesses for themselves. It's exactly what you do with your teenaged child. You sit there, believing in their essential goodness, trying to get to the bottom of whatever the problem is.

In the case of this schoolteacher, he finally told me what had really happened. He had told a girl in the class, in front of the whole class, that if she didn't do her homework, people would think she was stupid. He had humiliated her in front of her peers.

The kids in the class had already found out that he was gay and had been teasing him, and after this incident the girl and a friend concocted a story. They decided to say that the teacher was molesting one of the boys. And because the teacher was ashamed of what he had said, because he didn't want to admit he had been a bad teacher, he was facing a prison sentence! I told him, "You're on trial unfairly because you humiliated that girl!"

Now he has a chance of acquittal because we've found the motive for the story. Before, there was no motivation for those two kids to have made up a story. We found it—in his truth, not his lawyer's

truth or the prosecutor's or the school's. For me it was just like find-
ing those moments of truth from your child. It took a sort of dogged-
ness that only a mother has. I know I'm better at this than I was ten
years ago before my kids were this age.[1]

Moorhead thinks she now brings to her work the same kind of emotional covenant she has with her children: She can send an emotional
signal to the other person that they are still lovable, no matter what
they may have done, and that they can be perfectly honest without
fear of rejection. In another recent criminal case, her team was defending a tall, imposing black woman doctor. Her own attorney, a
white male Southerner, described her to Moorhead as difficult and ar-
rogant. She was a person who was apparently hard to love, and perhaps hard to defend. But operating on her theory, derived from her
experience with her children, that you can't get someone to open up
unless you love them, Moorhead started talking to the woman about
religion. It soon became clear that everything had changed for this
woman when she found religious faith. So, Moorhead told her about a
recent experience in her own church, where she had found enormous
relief from something that had been troubling her after members of
the congregation had put their hands on her and prayed for her.

"She felt seen and heard in that witness prep, and our conversation
gave her the emotional courage to bring her whole person into the
courtroom, " Moorhead told me. "When she goes into that courtroom
she will now be able to show them who she is, that she is a healer.
Ironically, if I had asked her lawyer if I could talk to her about faith he
would have said no!"

Moorhead is sure that she didn't get this capacity to reach people
from the theater, which she left when her oldest child was about
seven. In the theater, she explained, "There is a magical, stark truth in
the middle of each scene. . . . Plays are built moment to moment, from
one emotional, decision-making moment to another. These moments
only work when something really honest happens between people. I

was good at getting this out of actors, but I got that result by pushing, demanding, bossing them around, and so on. I didn't love them enough to get results any other way. I was impatient, imperious, and deeply selfish, in the sense of being all about myself, rather than them.

"Because of motherhood, I know this thing about people—that they all have this deep inner core we can love. I have more openness and accessibility, and the courage to take emotional risks. Motherhood has made me brave!"

For some parents, tragically, the courage to connect with others on a deep level comes not with having a child, but after losing one. After his son's death at age fourteen, Rabbi Harold Kushner produced a best-selling book called *When Bad Things Happen to Good People*. "I am a more sensitive person, a more effective pastor, a more sympathetic counselor because of Aaron's life and death than I would have ever been," he wrote in 1981. "And I would give up all of those gains in a second if I could have my son back. If I could choose, I would forego all the spiritual growth and depth which has come my way because of our experiences, and be what I was fifteen years ago, an average rabbi, an indifferent counselor, helping some people and unable to help others, and the father of a bright, happy boy."[2]

But Kushner had no choice. He had to accept the wisdom that had come to him so painfully.

Patty Dietch, a mental-health nurse in eastern Canada, says she had a similar experience after losing her eighteen-year-old son in a fiery automobile accident five-and-a-half years ago. Dietch is writing a master's thesis called "Living in the Presence of Its Absence," in which she explains how, after her son's death, she was able to bring a greater degree of empathy to her counseling. Like Moorhead, she describes it as courage. Perhaps it is the courage that comes from having nothing left to lose.

"I graduated from nursing school thirty years ago," she told me in a telephone interview from her home in rural New Brunswick. "And for years I thought I was bringing the Mom in me to work. During my first job interview, for example, I had breakfast banana mashed on my sleeve, and I told the guy that my baby would be coming in on my lunch break. I thought I was bringing motherhood to work with me. Now I know I only really did that after Jeremiah was killed."

After the accident I had to reinvent myself. And gradually my counseling changed. My ears were more open, I was more attentive to what was really being said, more responsive to body language. I was listening with my heart rather than just my head. Before during my counseling, it was always which approach or which model will work in this case and so on. Afterwards, I was using wisdom that came from within. I was more unafraid.

For example, I work with adolescents. It's a small community here, and one day a sixteen-year-old girl came in who had known my son. Her father was an alcoholic, her mother was in an abusive relationship, and she herself had been abused from eleven to thirteen. She was very angry, and she told me that she had torn her dad's house apart. He'd told her he was going to charge her for the damage.

I looked at her and said, "Honey, do you ever cry?"

I moved slightly toward her and she was suddenly in my arms, sobbing. I thought, "This kid, who's loved her? Nobody has."

Jeremiah told me once that "If everyone had a mother like you it would be a better world." That was such a gift. I've carried that with me and it has given me courage. I think, "that's the one thing I've done right." The most creative parts of me were involved with my mothering and now I can bring that to others.[3]

Is Empathy Hardwired?

Some researchers believe that women are hardwired for empathy. In *The Essential Difference*, Simon Baron-Cohen argues that ". . . on average, females spontaneously empathize to a greater degree than do males."[4] As evidence, he cites the fact that women score better than men on a test to describe what a person is thinking or feeling when all they have to go by is a picture of their eyes. On another questionnaire, women are on average more likely to value empathizing and intimacy in friendships while men are more likely to value shared interests.[5] Similar sex differences have been detected immediately after birth. Experiments on day-old babies have found that the girls looked longer at a human face, while the boys gazed longer at a mechanical mobile.[6]

Mothers also demonstrate more empathetic parenting styles. Mothers more often hold an infant in a face-to-face position, enabling them to exchange more emotional information. Mothers fine-tune their speech more often to help the child understand what they are saying. And mothers are more likely to follow a child's choice of play, while fathers are more likely to impose their own play agenda.[7]

It has been theorized that the female's relatively greater ability to empathize coevolved with primate parental investment. Female investment of time and energy in the young is extremely high in the great apes and in humans, and empathetic mothering is also notably higher in humans and great apes than in other mammals. A mother who is empathetic will be better at picking up on her baby's needs and feelings and less likely to be neglectful, thereby ensuring her offspring a better chance at survival.[8]

Much more research needs to be done in this area (among other issues, it is hard to see how teenaged girls' behavior toward each another could be characterized as highly empathetic). For now, suffice it to say that many mothers and some fathers report that their capacity for empathy was triggered by or increased after the experience of giving birth and raising a child. The constant practice of nurturing seems to be a catalyst.

As Leslie Gaines-Ross of Burston-Marsteller put it, "When a child can't talk, you've got to figure out what they're communicating to you . . . This gives you the ability to read feelings as well as facts. A male-dominated society discounts anything but facts and numbers, but a lot more is communicated among human beings than facts and numbers.

"You know how you develop this sense about your kids; that when something doesn't seem right, it probably isn't? Your intuitive skills really get sharpened. Especially with babies, who can't talk, you have to pick up nonverbal cues. In a similar way, I'm very sensitive to the feelings and moods of colleagues. In meetings of our senior staff, I can pick up body language, tone of voice, and so on, and tell when something's wrong. Last week, for example, a fellow went to pitch a client and the client came back to us and reported that the chemistry wasn't right; that they preferred not to work with that guy. At a subsequent meeting the fellow was very quiet. I called him later and asked him if something was wrong. He told me he hadn't been able to shake the feeling that things hadn't gone well with that client, and then I realized that he was *hurt*. Like a kid. It was taking him a long time to get over that hurt feeling."9

Lisa Anderson, the dean at Columbia, also told me that she believed she was much quicker than most male deans in picking up emotional signals about issues and problems that were not being verbalized. When she is interviewing a candidate for a job in her department, for example, she can read the emotional subtext in their comments, the part they don't dare or can't quite articulate. The candidate may be talking about the teaching load, for example, but she can sense that they are really thinking, "I wonder if I can live in an apartment in New York City, where would my kids go to school, where can they cross Broadway. . . ."

"I'll go ahead and talk about the personal part of life at the university. I'll ask them, 'Would you be more comfortable living in the suburbs?' This is partly because this is lived experience for me; I don't have a wife at home, so I have to deal with these kinds of issues. Some of the men here do live it too, they share the chores at home, but they are not sure that it's 'professional' to talk about such personal things."

The Empathetic Office Mom

Management experts are familiar with the phenomenon of the *office mom*, a senior or older woman who props people up when they need support, helps them work out interpersonal problems, and smooths over conflicts; all the background relational work that keeps things running smoothly within an organization. Gaines-Ross, for example, is fully aware that she is looked to as a sort of mother confessor, perhaps because so many of her fellow workers are much younger and have no children of their own.

"People talk to me about issues that are bothering them, and I help them go through back channels to resolve it. A person who was very mad came to me not long ago, saying they wanted to quit. They told me why they were leaving, and poured out a litany on why the company had failed them. I helped defuse that anger. I pointed out that all companies, like all families, are at least a little dysfunctional. There's no such thing as the perfect family or the perfect company. I said, look at it for what it's given you: a good start to your career, a good name on your resume, and so on. I said it's important to leave on good terms; you never know when circumstances change and you might want to come back."

The office mom can find herself working two jobs: the one that she is paid to do, and another that comes to be expected of her. She is, in effect, providing the company with the same kind of emotional, empathetic support that mothers provide at home. And, although this labor is just as important in a corporate setting, it is often even more taken for granted. The work may be the emotional glue that holds the organization together, but it's still largely invisible and unrewarded.

This is precisely the service that the female engineers at DEC performed for their company in the 1980s and 1990s. A number of years ago I interviewed a former DEC employee who described the process. She explained that when a project was cancelled, for example, the female managers would engineer the equivalent of grieving. They would talk to team members, help put the loss of the project in perspective, deal with wounded feelings, and so on, until people felt better and could get back up to speed at work. They recognized that the disappointed workers were like kids who had been hurt and needed a little TLC.

The male managers, in contrast, tended to move immediately on to a new project, without doing any of that emotional work. The bruised feelings would remain repressed, until they popped up somewhere else in the form of lower morale, sloppy work, or a loss of productivity. Yet the female or, perhaps more accurately, maternal, work that allowed those feelings to be expressed and finally put to rest was never acknowledged or appreciated.

Management expert Joyce Fletcher examines why these relational practices tend to be devalued in male-dominated organizations, even though they serve the organization's interests. She thinks it is because men assume that women who take the trouble to be empathetic are simply being nice and sypathetic, rather than smart. A female boss who takes the time to debrief an employee who misses a meeting, or a superior who consoles the feelings of a subordinate, may be seen as nurturing rather than someone concerned with productivity. By the same token, coaching and encouraging people is frequently taken as a sign of motherly behavior, rather than good business practice. And when a female manager tries to make people think something was their own idea in order to get them to buy into it, her action can be taken as evidence that she has no big strategic vision of her own.

In short, blinded by stereotypical thinking, men may see an office mom when what is in front of their nose is an effective, clever executive.

This is obviously a no-win situation for many competent managers. Fletcher told me about one female executive within DEC who was a senior engineer and project leader on a technical assignment. She worked directly under a man who was supposed to be the supervisor, with responsibility to resolve all personal differences and other relationship issues. But the members of the team preferred to take their issues to her instead. For a while she complied, but then realized that if she continued she would not get promoted, because the relational work was eating up much of the time she needed to devote to her other responsibilities.

She tried to withdraw from the role of office peacemaker/troubleshooter/mom. And everyone responded with indignation. She heard comments like "What's wrong with you? Is it that time of the month?"[10]

Her empathetic work wasn't valued highly by her male supervisor, but she also got slapped down for *not* performing it. This is very familiar territory to most parents. I'm reminded of a friend who once complained that she and her husband could stay home every night for six nights straight, and on the seventh night, as they dressed to go out, the children would wail, "Oh, Mom, you're *never* home!"

Creative Empathy

Actors, directors, screen writers, and journalists often say they have access to a broader range of emotions for having been parents. Television producer John Romano, who has written and produced numerous successful shows, including *Hill Street Blues*, admits that he didn't know girls were people until he had daughters. "I *loved* girls but I had seen them as the Other," he explained during an interview at his studio in Hollywood. "Having daughters, and diapering them, and seeing everything they go through, you realize that it's a full human being here. . . ."[11]

(Romano's comment reminded me of that writer in a movie who was asked, How could he create such realistic female characters? "It's easy," he responded. "I just think of a man, and then I take away reason and accountability.")

Romano put his new sensitivity to good use when he was one of the producers of a show called *Party of Five*, in which a couple with five children is killed, leaving the kids to raise themselves. He had to write scenes for teenaged girls and, because he had his own, he knew how deep those characters' feelings and anger could be. "It was a cure for that condescension that often creeps into writing about teenagers," he told me.

Another writer, a mother of two who works with Romano on *American Dreams*, summed it up: "Having children is a whole human experience that you can't imagine. The only way to imagine it is to live it. As a writer, that's invaluable."

It is just as invaluable in journalism. I noticed that Katie Couric showed extraordinary empathy in her interviews with the widows of the World Trade Center. Couric had lost her own husband to cancer, and was able to talk with more recent widows as if she were literally inside their grief.

Soledad O'Brien, the perky television anchor, has not experienced such a personal tragedy, but she too feels a particular empathy for grieving parents now that she has children of her own. O'Brien has had to interview four or five couples whose children were missing, including the parents of Elizabeth Smart, the Salt Lake City teenager who was whisked out of her bedroom one night by a delusional drifter and fortunately found unharmed several months later.

"When you have children you look at those parents and all you can think to say is 'How do you get out of bed in the morning? How do you not end your life?'" O'Brien commented. "Before I had children of course I knew that it was horrible to lose a child, but having a child of your own opens up a whole new realm of feeling. You understand fully what they're going through."

For an actress, maternal empathy can add an extra dimension to one's understanding of a character. Lindsay Crouse, who was nominated for the Academy Award for her performance in *Places in the Heart*, once played a cop on a segment of the television show *NYPD Blue*. Her character was the head of intelligence, in charge of running the undercover police in the city. She was a sort of den mother, a sympathetic figure people turned to when they needed to talk, and who could sense when to pull someone out of undercover work before they got sucked into the criminal underworld themselves.

When Crouse arrived on the set and went into costume, on her rack were two severely tailored jackets. She knew immediately that they were all wrong for her character, who would have worn something more informal and earthy. She prevailed, and got to wear a sweater in her scenes.

Film producer Lucy Fisher saved a major project from disaster thanks to her insight as a mom. One of the first things Fisher did when she became vice chairman of Sony's Columbia TriStar Motion Picture Group in 1996 was to tell the people making *Jerry Maguire* that they should fire the child actor who was originally cast as Renee Zellweger's son. Fisher recalls telling director Cameron Crowe: "You worked for four years and it's going to be ruined . . . The movie depends on [Tom] Cruise falling in love with the boy, and he's not even making eye contact with Cruise . . ."

"They said 'It's too late, we already shot three days.' But I said, 'We don't care, we'll reshoot, because you can do better.' "

They found a new kid, and the movie was a hit.

Empathy and Power

Empathy is an essential element in political leadership and a characteristic of all truly great leaders. The supreme example in American public life is probably Franklin Delano Roosevelt, who gained empathy after he was paralyzed by polio in 1921. According to writer Garry Wills, Roosevelt's affliction enabled him to forge a powerful emotional bond with a nation that was afflicted by the poverty and despair of the Depression. Roosevelt understood what it meant to say, "The only thing we have to fear is fear itself." He unleashed a blizzard of government projects to make the country feel hopeful that better days were on the way. The public, according to Wills, never knew the full extent of Roosevelt's impairment, but "it knew enough to feel that if he could go on as he did, gaily despite loss, so might they."[12] Loss and empathy, in this case, produced a perfect leader for troubled times. (One wonders if Bill Clinton's "I feel your pain" was a conscious effort to revive Roosevelt's amazing connection with voters. Clinton's empathy, which stemmed in large part from his loss-ridden childhood, was also politically effective.)

Empathy is equally important in international relations. Robert McNamara, one of the architects of the Vietnam war, speculated in *The Fog of War*, an Academy Award–winning documentary, that it was a lack of empathy on the part of American leaders that caused the United States to become so deeply embroiled in that bloody conflict. According to McNamara, who was secretary of defense under Presidents Kennedy and Johnson, the men in power simply had no understanding of the feelings and motives of the Vietnamese. A failure of empathy was responsible for deaths of millions, and for the greatest foreign policy disaster in American history—prompting one to ask, where were our maternal leaders when we needed them?

On a brighter note, McNamara also revealed that President Kennedy's ability to empathize with Soviet leader Nikita S. Krushchev during the Cuban missile crisis helped save the world from nuclear war. Imagining himself in Krushchev's shoes, Kennedy decided that the Russian wanted to find a way to avert war without losing face. So, the American president ignored the advice of the American joint chiefs of staff to bomb Cuba, and war was avoided.

Film maker Errol Morris has drawn from McNamara's vivid memories eleven lessons for world leaders. The first is "Empathize with your enemy." Empathy is particularly necessary in a guerilla war, when one's enemy can be the very people one is fighting amongst. I was struck by a journalist's observation about the situation in Iraq in late 2003. In a country neither at war nor at peace, he wrote, "Firepower and good intentions would be less important than learning to read the signs."[13] Reading people—their thoughts, emotions, resentments, and dreams—had become more crucial to postwar stability than all the F-16 fighter-bombers, AC-130 gun ships, or 2,000 pound bombs that money could buy.

Would mothers be any better at reading the signs? Are political leaders with direct child-rearing experience more likely to demonstrate empathy than other people? Research on this is as sparse as the number of women who have held high office, and those few who have do not encourage any such generalizations. Margaret Thatcher, a mother, was surely one of Britain's least empathetic modern leaders. But Thatcher notwithstanding, some researchers have found that female politicians on the whole tend to support a broader social agenda than males do.[14] A study by the Center for the American Woman and Politics at Rutgers University, for example, concluded that female legislators, whatever their political orientation, were more likely than men to give top priority to public policies supporting children, families, and health care. Many male legislators support the same causes, but as Madeleine Kunin, the former governor of Vermont wrote in her autobiography, women often bring an extra degree of intensity to these issues because they've lived them.[15]

One indicator of the difference between male and female legislators is to look at the voting record of female Republicans in Congress, who have often parted company with their male colleagues over issues of importance to mothers and children. Connie Morella of Maryland, who spent sixteen years in the House of Representatives, is one of the best examples. Morella cosponsored legislation to put value on unpaid work in the home, was one of the major supporters of the Violence Against Women Act, and was a staunch advocate of Federal support for child care. When her first child was two and a half, she had to go back to work as a public-school teacher, and she knew firsthand how important quality care is for working mothers. She later started a bipartisan child care caucus in Congress and successfully pushed for legislation allowing Federal agencies to provide child care for their employees, and for college campuses to subsidize child care for low-income students.

Morella also put her convictions into practice in her own office, unlike some other female members of Congress. In the early 1990s, after her legislative aide Cindy Hall had a baby, Morella not only gave Hall a four-day workweek, she brought in electricians and wired up a room to accommodate a breast pump. The Capital Hill electricians had never had a call like that before.

"Milk Is Food!"

One of the funnier stories I heard about empathy in a powerful mother came from an acquaintance who was a senior executive at Bechtel, the huge, San Francisco–based construction company. For years she had put off having children but, when her twins were born, she suddenly became aware of all of the obstacles to motherhood at Bechtel. There she was, in her glamorous corner office, madly pumping breast milk while her secretary fended off people trying to come in the door. "What do those women in the secretarial pool do?" my newly empathetic friend wondered. "How do they have any privacy at all?"

She made some inquiries, and discovered that lower-level women in the company were ducking into broom closets, stairways, and other hidden nooks and crannies to perform their pumping in semiprivacy. Something has to be done, she thought, and she sent a memo to the person in charge of facilities, suggesting that an appropriate space be made available where nursing mothers could breast pump.

He sent back an email dismissing the idea, proposing that they do what they had to do in the bathroom.

"In the bathroom!" she furiously emailed back. "I don't think you want to put something like that in writing. Breast milk is food! You're suggesting that our employees prepare *food* in the *bathroom?*"

A proper space for nursing moms was promptly created.[16]

CHAPTER 7

Appreciating Differences

"Going by the baby" is better than "going by the book."
—Penelope Leach,
British child-rearing expert

Numerous parents in all walks of life told me that they had learned to appreciate and be more tolerant of individual differences after having children who were different from one another. One executive who had a large blended family, including stepchildren and adopted children, said that they had taught her that there is no one right way to do anything. She subsequently became known as the person in her organization who could work with anyone.[1]

Everyone Is Good at Something

Louise Francesconi of Raytheon has achieved enormous success in the very masculine world of defense contracting. Like several of the executive mothers I interviewed, including Ann Moore, Shelly Lazarus, Jamie Gorelick, and Deb Henretta, Francesconi regularly turns up on *Fortune* magazine's list of the fifty most powerful women in American business. One of the key rules she follows as a manager, she told me, came from the experience of having two very different sons.

When we spoke by telephone in 2003, Francesconi had one step-son, thirty-one, and another son who was a nineteen-year-old college student. "One is really smart and a valedictorian and the other is aver-age," she told me. The challenge, she said, was to do what the schools had failed to do: Teach each of them to understand what they were good at, for *everyone is good at something.*

"We worked to encourage them to think of themselves as a skill set," says Francesconi, "and to focus on and develop their own strengths. As a result, the child that was struggling academically didn't feel like a failure. He knew what his strengths were, including a strong work ethic. He discovered what turns him on, and when you see that in your children, you encourage it. You water that plant."

Francesconi believes that clarity about her own strengths has been one of the factors in her success. As she put it, "I've turned down jobs that didn't water my plant." She spent twenty-four years of her career at Hughes Aircraft, where she started in a summer job while her father worked there. She rose to become president of Hughes Missile Systems Company, which merged with Raytheon in 1998. Four years later, she was named president of the combined companies' missile systems, the largest in the world.

"With kids and in work, the job is the same," says this female weap-ons maker. "It's to get people to *know* themselves and to feel good about themselves. An ability to do that—to have that conversation both at home and in a work environment—is a fundamental part of being a good leader. One of the biggest things I bring to the job is my ability to make sure that people are in the right jobs. The thing that has shocked me over the years is how many people don't seem to know what they are good at. I can act as a mentor and help them discover their strengths."

She cited the example of a young black woman from the deep South who came out of a highly technical mathematical background. She had allowed herself to be moved from job to job based on where the company wanted her to be, not where she herself felt she belonged.

"She felt really lost. She finally came to me and said 'Louise, I need some career advice.' So I gave her an assignment. I told her to write down all the things she felt successful at; all the things she did better than anyone else. I told her not to put down any jobs, just skills. When she came back, I was able to sit down with her and look at her list, and explain how this particular job would call for this, or what that position would do for her, given her strengths. She's beginning to see that she has some control over her career, which will be much better for her and for the company."

Linda Juergens could not be in a more different field than Louise Francesconi. Juergens is executive director of the National Association of Mothers' Centers, a mothers' support organization based in Levittown, New York. She too believes that the differences in her two children enhanced her ability to evaluate people's unique strengths. Whether you are working with mothers or missiles, the useful lesson is the same. "You learn so much about human nature when you raise a human being," as Juergens puts it.

Her own two daughters are as different as night and day. One is soft-spoken and a bit shy, like Linda herself, and the other is much more adventurous, assertive, and challenging. "They rearranged my thinking on gender differences," says Juergens. "If my second daughter had been a boy, we would have assumed she was the way she was because of her sex." Juergens and her husband, like Francesconi, were forced to learn how to deal with two very distinct personalities, each with her own unique mixture of strengths and weaknesses. It was an excellent training ground for dealing with differences in adults.

In her first job, Juergens had to manage a group of volunteers. In such a situation, she explains, "You can't make people do anything, so you have to carefully assess each person's strengths. You have to find out what they do well, and what they will enjoy doing. You have to make sure that the work they can do well is work they can do without supervision."

"Because of my daughters' differences, I feel more at ease with the fact that people have very different strengths and deficiencies," says Juergens. "They've given me a way of being more positive in approaching people, in focusing on what they can do and not dwelling on what they can't do. I think that prior to having children I wasn't as tolerant or flexible. And I can't think of any situation where the ability to be flexible is not an asset."[2]

Psychiatrist Judith Rapoport has two children, sons now in their thirties, who also have very different temperaments. The first was more like Rapoport and her husband: a very good student, intense about his work, accomplished in everything he tried. Stuart, her second son, was never a candidate for a fellowship at Harvard or Yale, as Rapoport put it. But he had an easygoing personality, a sunny disposition, and enormous amounts of what is now called emotional intelligence.

"He became a model for all of us," she said. "You know the saying, 'let a thousand flowers bloom'? Our second son taught us a visceral understanding of that. We learned a lot about the different ways that people can succeed in life. Sometimes, when my husband and I are discussing a new employee, one of us will say 'I just hired a Stuart.' We mean someone who has good basic skills, but who will above all bring enormous value to a team in terms of enthusiasm and helping everyone work together harmoniously. . . . Children make you realize how many different ways there are to live a life. You wouldn't want all Type-A personalities on a team. You need facilitating types."

Rapoport herself has achieved distinction with well-regarded work on children's hyperactivity and obsessive-compulsive behavior. She is currently studying children with very early onset schizophrenia, and has teams of junior scientists fresh out of graduate school working in her lab. She sees a corollary between nurturing them in their careers and the generative sense of giving that goes with raising a child. She learned from her son Stuart how to appreciate the Stuarts of this world, the people who are fun to work with and fun to be around. She feels this has made her a better team manager and a better mentor.

Other educators confirm that the parental insight that "everybody's different" is particularly valuable. Rabbi Margaret Wenig, a professor of homiletics at Hebrew Union in New York City, says "My children had very different personalities at birth. It would have been absurd to force them to jump through the same hoops at the same pace . . . I've carried that over into my teaching. Now I pass out a form after every class asking the students if there was anything they didn't understand, that might threaten their performance at the school. I tell them I'm willing to meet with them, one on one, to be sure that they get out of the class what they need. . . . My kids have forced me to treat students as individuals, rather than a class."

One can learn this important lesson from teaching itself. Television executive Gerry Laybourne told me that her appreciation of individual differences actually grew out of her early experience as a Montessori teacher. "I came from elementary education, where I was an open classroom teacher," Laybourne explained, "and my management philosophy was based upon those same principles: finding out what is good in each individual around you and helping them express it or achieve it. This is very different from the approach that would create a corporate structure, analyze its skill base, and then find the individuals with those skills and fit them into it.

"Parents will ask 'What's this kid good at, and how can I help her or him to develop that talent?' Being a parent . . . you're so much on their side, and rooting for them. If you can transfer that feeling to the people who work for you, you are a manager."

Goodness of Fit

This parental wisdom—that everyone is different, and that difference must be respected—was first articulated by Stella Chess and Alexander Thomas, a husband-and-wife team of child psychiatrists who had four children and saw, to their surprise, that each child was "born different." Their subsequent research established that no child is a *tabula rasa*, or blank slate, on which parents could inscribe the personality and traits they desired. Every child has a unique personality, and good

outcomes depend heavily on how well parents adapt to their children's particular characteristics. The key was what Chess called *goodness of fit*. If the parents' expectations and demands fit with the child's
own capacities and temperament, then the baby will enjoy optimal
development.[3]

In an organization, it's a bit different. Obviously the individual's capabilities and goals have to be in line with the employer's needs and
overall mission. No one can be successful if their skills or goals are mis-
aligned with the needs and goals of their organization. That said, a
manager still has to respect and know how to utilize every employee's
unique talents. As Herb Kelleher, the chairman of Southwest Airlines
and one of the most admired CEOs in American business, says, "I've
always felt that you shouldn't have to change your personality when
you come to work. So we decided that we were going to hire good people and let them be themselves . . . People work better and are more
productive if they enjoy what they are doing."[4]

Marcus Buckingham, a popular management guru, tells business audiences much the same thing: The key to harnessing the talents of
your best people is a willingness to treat each employee as an individual. Employees are not interchangeable parts, and good managers,
according to Buckingham, understand that people are for the most
part who they are, not who a boss might want them to be. Like competent parents, the best managers encourage the talents that are there,
rather than trying to make people into something they are not.

Buckingham, a consultant with The Gallup Organization and co-
author with Curt Coffman of *First, Break All the Rules*, offers these tips,
among others, for bosses:

* Capitalize on the diversity within your workforce. Focus on
  people's *strengths* rather than their weaknesses.
* Don't promote people out of jobs they love and do well. Many
  bosses reward outstanding people with a promotion into a different job. Why not give them increased pay and recognition
  instead, if they are happy where they are?

* Recognize that managers' *relationship* skills are crucial. An individual worker's performance is directly related to the relationship with their immediate superior. (In other words, to the
  goodness of fit.)[5]

At this point I'd like to share a personal story.

By the time our son was in middle school, it was very apparent that
he was not going to be an A student. He had difficulty reading, and his
difficulties had gotten him into an endless cycle of testing, tutoring,
anxious school conferences, and nagging and stress at home. He became increasingly turned off at school and disillusioned with all things
academic. At the same time, he was obviously highly creative. He had
turned his room into a starship, with an aluminum-foil ceiling, purple
walls, and strings of tiny blinking lights. His clothes were a symphony
of style: fuzzy gorilla coats and velvet jackets, and a collection of pants
that included faux fur, polyester prints, and silver vinyl. (Once, when I
ran into a girl from his school at a party I asked her if she had seen
James's silver pants. "I know all James's pants," she murmured).

He began composing computer music and shooting experimental
videos. At this point, my husband said "Why are we focusing on his
weaknesses? Let's go with his strengths."

This child was different—from us and from most of his classmates—
so why were we trying to force him into some cookie cutter? We
started supporting him in what *he* was interested in. We purchased the
video equipment he needed and allowed him, with the school's permission, to take outside, for-credit professional courses in film editing on AVID systems, and MIDI computer music composition. By the
time he graduated from high school he was a competent cameraman
and editor, and was getting paid professional assignments from independent film producers around town.

He took a gap year after high school to do freelance work with two
documentary producers, and he ended that year with a trip to Greece
and Turkey to shoot footage for a documentary of his own. Among our
friends, not everyone got it. "Who's paying for his trip?," we were

asked, by people who had spent four times as much money to send their children to college for a semester. "What program is James on?" another acquaintance asked.

"James is on his own program," my husband replied proudly.

James is now a university undergraduate in Montreal, a budding filmmaker, and best of all, a self-confident young man who knows a lot about the world and himself. I'm not a manager of people, but James's experience has convinced me that the only way people can get to that next step in competence or confidence is to be allowed to take that step themselves, with our encouragement and support.

"It's very easy to coach children toward what *we* wish for them, but when we stop transmitting and start listening, our kids start sharing what *they* wish for," says Shaunna Sowell, an engineer who runs a $1 billion operating division of Texas Instruments in Dallas, Texas. "Early on, I made the mistake of pushing and directing my kids toward a goal. As I got wiser, I came to understand that my job was to help reveal the beauty inside them. My job is to help them understand that they are unique; different from anyone else on the planet, and different from me."[6]

In other words, what Mr. Rogers always said was right: "Children do best at the things they are able to do well."

So do grownups.

CHAPTER 8

Growing Human Capabilities

"Leadership is not just about delegating power, it's *growing human capabilities*. This is exactly what we do when we raise children."

—Shaunna Sowell,
Senior Vice President, Texas Instruments

Empowering people, by motivating, mentoring, and encouraging them to be the best they can be, was frequently mentioned as an approach to management that grew out of the practice of child-rearing. This was the most explicitly maternal skill that parents reported. And what Shaunna Sowell calls "growing human capabilities" also happens to be a hallmark of the very best kind of leadership.

James MacGregor Burns, the grand old man of leadership theory, developed a concept he called *transforming* leadership. This is the inspiring, life-changing kind of leadership that lifts people out of their daily concerns and inspires them to seek something higher than narrow self-interest. "That people can be lifted *into* their better selves is the secret of transforming leadership," Burns wrote.[1]

Transforming leadership is quite different from coercion or the mere holding of power. Most relations between leaders and followers, bosses and employees, and in traditional cultures, between parents and children, are semicoercive or *transactional*, an exchange of one thing for another: taxes for public services, votes for jobs, work for wages, obedience for support. These trades are the daily bread and butter of most of our interactions with authority. But some leaders go further, and are able to sense and articulate peoples' deepest needs, aspirations, and values. They hold people to a high standard, and can convince their followers that together they can reach a higher level. Abraham Lincoln, Susan B. Anthony, Martin Luther King, and Nelson Mandela were all quintessential transformational leaders. So was the young Napoleon, who summed it up best: "A leader is a dealer in hope."

The analogy with the good parent is obvious. What *is* a good parent if not a hope dealer? What could be a greater transformational act than turning a drooling, demanding baby into a thinking, compassionate, hard-working, law-abiding adult? Clearly the parents who accomplish this, who help a child develop his or her fullest potential, are the original transformative leaders. Strong mothers, in the words of legal scholar Patricia Collins, have the transformative power to "bring people along." Even Burns saw this, referring to the parent–child relationship as "the initial act of leadership." He deplored the "false conception of leadership as mere command or control," which he said reflected a male bias. "As leadership comes properly to be seen as a process of leaders engaging and mobilizing the human needs and aspirations of followers, women will be more readily recognized as leaders and men will change their own leadership styles."[2]

It is not fashionable these days to extol the power or the leadership qualities of mothers, for fear of reinforcing the idea that the highest, most suitable role for women is motherhood—the old power behind the throne idea, with the emphasis on *behind*. But pick up almost any biography and you'll find that every great man had at least one devoted individual—usually his mother—who made him what he was. The list of outstanding "Mama's boys" includes such titans of industry, politics, and the military as John D. Rockefeller, Franklin Roosevelt, Gen. Douglas MacArthur, Frank Lloyd Wright, Yitzak Rabin, Bill Clinton, Gen. Wesley Clark, and Jack Welch, the tough former

CEO of General Electric Co., who has said that his mother was his chief mentor, closest confidante, and the principle reason for his success.

Even among sports figures, the mother is often the more influential parent. Bud Selig, the current commissioner of major league baseball, credits his mother, a schoolteacher, with instilling his love of the sport by taking him to games beginning at age three. And sports psychologist Robert Rotella told my husband that many of the best American golfers had confided to him that their mother, not their father, was the person most responsible for their success. The time has come to acknowledge that being a mother or a father is one of the most powerful and deeply satisfying roles a person can have in life. No other leadership position offers anything like the opportunity to influence another person—for better or for worse.

So, what specifically do conscientious parents who are managers do to bring people along? What tools do they use to motivate their co-workers and employees? How do they help others reach their full potential? Here are some of the things parent managers say they do to grow human capabilities.

Use Positive Reinforcement

Brian Baxter, president of Baxter's Books, a large store in Indianapolis that specializes in business books, claims that when his clients ask for the best business book in his store, he directs them to *The Little Engine That Could*, in the children's section.

"Remember what the little train said?" asks Baxter. " 'I think I can, I think I can.' Live like that, work like that, and you'll be a success."

The best parents *believe in* their children. They understand that positive reinforcement is a self-fulfilling prophecy. If you tell a child often enough that he or she can do anything, they are likely to believe it. Most of the outstanding people I have known have had at least one parent who gave them that kind of confidence. My husband is one of them. His mother not only told her beloved only child that he could be anything he wanted to be when he grew up, she served him iced tea in a glass twice as big as everyone else's. He got the message. Many years later, when he was starting a new company, a corporate chieftain interrupted his enthusiastic description of its prospects with a question: "John, what is the basis for your confidence?" He paused, and remembered that big glass.

Numerous studies have confirmed these *expectation effects*, also known as the *Pygmalion effect*. When teachers, athletic coaches, judges, and work supervisors expect people to excel, performance soars. High expectations by teachers can raise students' scores by as much as 30 percent. Greater expectations can even enhance the performance of rats. In one set of studies, a group of rats performed 65 percent better at maze learning than another group of identical animals, after researchers were told that those in the first group were a genius strain and the second were dolts.[3]

Great leaders, like great teachers and parents, signal their belief in their people. "A good leader, like a good parent, assumes that a person has an innate drive to be worthy or successful," says Shaunna Sowell of Texas Instruments. "And our job as leaders is to help remove the external and the internal barriers to that striving to be excellent. This is a mentoring role, not a checking role. I contrast it with the command and control style, which assumes that people have to *prove* their worthiness."

Positive reinforcement is particularly important in government and the nonprofit sector, because it is one of the few motivational tools that managers have. Jamie Gorelick says she realized this when she became the second highest official in the Justice Department. "My daughter needs a lot of reinforcement, and so do many employees. This was especially true at Justice. We had none of the tools that corporations have, like money and perquisites, so we had to motivate people just by sheer force of personality. We managed by modeling behavior, by inspiring, by appealing to mutual beliefs, through praise and approbation—all the same tools that a parent uses."

Articulate Values, Vision, and a Common Mission

"If as a leader or a parent you can't articulate a clear direction, you've got no followers."

—Judy Blades, senior vice president,
The Hartford Financial Services Group

In addition to conveying a belief in their people's capacity to excel, good parents and good leaders point the way. As Shaunna Sowell puts it, "a key role of a parent is to teach *values*, or how we expect you to behave in your striving to be excellent. This is equally important in an organization, as its members strive to achieve success. The leadership *vision* is the glue that holds the group together. We may all have very different styles and approaches to life, but in a successful family or organization there will typically be commonly shared values."

According to Sowell, who manages 800 employees, all high-performance organizations have an environment of shared vision and close teamwork, and all, not by accident, speak the language of family. This was true of the Manhattan Project, the crash program to build the first atomic bomb; the famous Lockheed Skunkworks, which produced many of the prominent aircraft of the Cold War, including the famous U-2 spy plane; and the early Disney teams. The leadership of all these groups created a sense of comraderie, like a family on a mission against impossible odds, and in a relatively short time they all did accomplish tremendously ambitious goals.

It doesn't even matter what the family or organization's specific vision is, says Sowell. Parents may stress the value of achievement, creativity, unselfishness, and service to others, or devotion to a religious cause. But rare is the parent who has no dream whatsoever for his or her offspring; or even rarer, who appeals to his or her child's worst instincts.

By the same token, an organization can be about any number of things: a superior product, technical preeminence, community service, outstanding productivity, or exceptional profitability. But whatever it is, the vision has to represent *something* that is a call to people to excel and to express their better nature. Today we are seeing what can happen when companies have no vision and offer no common purpose that transcends each employee's narrow self-interest. Corporate leaders who have no dreams for their people other than self-aggrandizement are like bad parents who provide no moral compass. Both leave demoralization and damage in their wake.

Sowell, and many of the other parents in business whom I interviewed, thought that as parents, they had an especially clear understanding of the need for vision. Mike Fossaceca told me that, in his fairly traditional Catholic family, "We had a common purpose. We were all moving in the same direction, toward getting a good education, having fun together, supporting each other, and so on. It's the same thing at work. You have to have that sense of a common purpose that everyone is committed to. Leadership is not about rewards, salary, money. It comes down to wanting to make your father, mother, boss proud. This is what really drives people. It's like my four-year-old daughter [who] can't wait to come home from school to show me all the things she did that day. Making me proud is what motivates her."

Persuade Others to Share the Vision

The best way to get people to buy into a vision is to let them take part in its creation. In practice, this can be done by signaling that we're all in this together, and together, we can do what has to be done.

"One of the things I learned from my kids was that positive energy always gets more of what I want than negative," says Cheryl Bachelder. " 'Go clean up your room or I'll kill you' doesn't work as well as 'Let's set aside an hour on Sunday and I'll help you clean up your room.'

"At work this translates into what I call *shared accountability*. I make it clear that I don't have all the answers so we need to put all our bright minds together and we'll craft a business strategy and move forward. This participatory way of managing teaches personal account-ability, because the boss is not solving the problem for you."

"I had three coaching sessions today—one-on-one with my executives—and you'd be surprised to see how often senior vice presi-dents come in and say 'What do you want me to do?' I say, 'I want you to lead!' Get out of that kid mode!"

Mike Fossaceca suspects that he became a real leader at JPMorgan-Chase only after he enabled his salespeople to become stakeholders in a common endeavor. "When I first started this job the turning point came after about five months. Things had been going OK, people ac-cepted me, but I hadn't conveyed any particular vision.

"An edict came down, and I gathered together the sales people who headed up the various industry divisions and told them that we had to go for a 10 percent growth in sales that year. Typically, the growth rate is 3 or 4 percent, and we were at about 5 or 6 percent at that time. I suggested that we let each division team set their own goal. We got all the sales people together for a day, and spent the day team building. Each group discussed its products, its own strengths and weaknesses, its possible opportunities, and so on, in a very unstructured way. Then I asked them, if we did everything we've talked about, what could we get in terms of growth? I let them tell me what they thought was pos-sible, although if they came up with a target that was lower than the 10 percent goal that the organization had set, I'd have been in big trouble!" (Fossaceca added that no one in top management had given him a chance to say what growth rate *he* thought was appropriate for his portfolio.)

"Anyway, anonymously they were to put down the growth rate they thought they could realistically accomplish and put it in a box. When we looked at the estimates, they had come up with a 12 percent target on their own. Only a couple of teams had put in a number below dou-ble digits. I then assigned them to come up with ways of handling the key things that would enable them to make it happen, and they did. That year we exceeded that 12 percent by a little bit."

Fossaceca believes that this was his coming-out party as a leader:

"In my mind it was different after that. People looked at me for the first time as a guy that was really leading them. Interestingly, that was not one of the outcomes I had been looking for."

While she was running Nickelodeon, Gerry Laybourne was an expert at inviting everyone in the organization to take ownership in its mission. When she first took command of the struggling children's cable channel in 1984, it was a money-losing operation with an uncertain future. She called in a management coach who gave her this advice: Just concentrate on making Nickelodeon a good place for people to work. She did this in part by encouraging bright ideas from everyone, whatever their job description, and honoring those who showed creativity. The first show created under her leadership, *Double Dare*, was thought up by the receptionist and two on-air promotion producers. It became a hit and, in five or six months, Nickelodeon's ratings more than doubled, with very little extra spending.

This participatory approach has been shown to be highly effective all across corporate America. In *The Five Patterns of Extraordinary Careers*, based on research and surveys of 2,000 executives, James M. Citrin and Richard A. Smith of the executive search firm of Stuart Spencer found that "Extraordinary success is achieved by making those around you successful." Citrin and Smith argue that the best corporate leaders practice "benevolent leadership." In a passage that seems to have had Laybourne, Bachelder, and Fossaseca in mind, they define the benevolent leader as someone who "maximizes performance through facilitation. She eliminates barriers for subordinates and leads with authority, even though at times appearing one of the pack."[4]

Unfortunately, so many organizations still ignore this wisdom, by encouraging a competitive, every-man-for-himself ethic, that it is often hard for managers to practice a benevolent participatory strategy. In those environments, management expert Joyce Fletcher suggests a few subtle ways to make what she calls *mutual empowering* more visible.

She describes a team leader who gave a presentation to top management on her team's project using the pronoun "we." The woman was later taken aside by a superior and warned that she should stop the "we stuff" or she'd never get ahead. So, the next time this engineer was called on to describe her team's effort she still used the "we" rather than the "me" word, but announced that she was using "we" deliberately, to indicate that she had put together a collaborative effort that was able to draw on the talents and initiative of a number of different people, with great results. She thus called attention to her skills as a manager who could inspire first-rate work in others, while at the same time calling attention to the importance of collaborative effort, and giving credit to everyone who had contributed.[5]

CHAPTER 9

Letting Go

> "... we must let our children meet their own difficulties, find their own solutions to knotty problems and gain experience for themselves. It may seem hard but what a sense of satisfaction there is when one feels sure of the ability in oneself to meet a difficulty...."
>
> —Eleanor Roosevelt,
> in "Building Character"[1]

The final, most important step in empowering others is learning to let them go. The parental condition itself is an exercise in letting go. You have to let your children grow and leave, not just once, but again and again at every crucial stage of their development. These *necessary losses*, as author Judith Viorst calls them, are just that, the inevitable loosening of bonds and constraints that are no longer needed, so that new and more mature connections may take their place.

It's nature's little irony that we spend twenty years learning to be a constant presence for a child, and then we have to switch gears, turn around, and learn to let them go.

Parents who resist this process hamper their offspring's growth. No one can remain a baby, or a compliant preteen, or a dependent teenager forever. Life is all about change, and trying to freeze a child at a certain stage of development is like trying to preserve one's own youth. The effort is bound to end in failure and disappointment. Let it go, let them go, gracefully.

Managers have to learn the same lesson. I heard this again and again from working mothers in myriad different fields, from insurance and high technology to advertising and accounting. "With talented people, you set the priorities, and then grant them the freedom to execute," says Shelly Lazarus, advertising executive. "You can't be hovering over them all the time . . . Creative people won't work for you if you do that. . . . You have to just say, tell me what you need and get out of their way."

Judith Rapoport sees the similarities between her postdoctoral students and her own children as teenagers. "Postdocs are very dependent on you the first two years, pleased to be working with you the second two years, and then they really want to go out on their own," said Rapoport, who is engaged in basic research at the National Institute of Mental Health. "It's what they're supposed to do, and it's a feather in your cap if they get a good appointment somewhere. But as they leave, you almost feel it as a slight. Having children prepares you for accepting that process."

Let People Make Their Own Mistakes

No organization can continually grow unless the collective capacity of its individuals grows over time. Successful companies can only assure this will happen if they take risks, and let their people occasionally make mistakes, says Shaunna Sowell. "If people learn that their superiors will permit thoughtful risks and tolerate reasonable mistakes, they will have the freedom to grow. If the company can deal with mistakes without having it be a catastrophe, everyone benefits." This is a lesson Sowell learned directly from her children.

"Part of being a steward of your children's growth is letting them go. You have to let them take risks, and when they fail—and they occasionally will—you have to be there as their safety net and help them learn from those mistakes. This is the only way they can learn how to do things differently next time."

Sowell explained how this worked in practice with her teenaged daughter. When the girl was fifteen, Sowell gave her a $150 monthly allowance, paid into a bank account. She gave her daughter a check-book, an ATM card, and a credit card with a $1,000 limit, with in-structions to live within the limits of that $150 monthly allowance, except for school-related expenses and major purchases, like a winter coat or ski equipment.

The goal was to teach her daughter how to manage her finances while she was still within the security of her home. Sowell remem-bered that when she herself had been an undergraduate counselor at the University of Texas in the mid-1970s, she had students come to her room distraught because they'd run up huge bank overdrafts. Some had no idea how this could have happened, because they still had checks in their checkbook! She wanted her daughter to avoid that kind of financial incompetence, and to learn how to manage the se-duction of a credit card.

She knew that initially the girl would fail and, sure enough, for the first few months she always ran over her budget, had debt on her credit card, and overdrafts on her bank account. But there was the safety net of the $1,000 limit on the card and overdraft protection at the bank. Sowell paid the charges and let the girl work off the debt she owed with hours of service at home. After a year or so, she finally got her fi-nancial act together. By the time I met Sowell her daughter was a freshman in college, managing her bank account down to the penny.

"She's definitely not the bookkeeper type, but she can tell me at any time the exact amount in her account," her proud mother told me. "And she is so grateful that something she now takes for granted other freshmen are still struggling with."

The process is the same in an organization. "At TI we've developed what we call a *spider web*—a safety net of support that allows people to take chances without jeopardizing their careers or the company. If they succeed, they can go on to assume more authority and responsibility. If they fail, we have a coaching session and discuss what they have learned and what they might do differently next time. The point is, it's not the failure but what you've learned that is important."

Sowell gave me a specific example of how this human risk management is tested at TI. She is the operations manager for a manufacturing plant that produces semiconductor chips, the integrated circuit chips that go into cell phones, pagers, CD players, hard disk drives, sensors, and the like. Her plant runs a full production line: It makes the chips, tests them for quality, and ships them. One chip can go through as many as five hundred steps during manufacturing, which is basically a chemical engineering process. Recently, a relatively new engineer was copying one of the chip recipes from a six-inch wafer to an eight-inch wafer. He got all of the steps right but one. It so happened that a major computer manufacturer was anticipating increased demand for a new laptop, and consequently for these chips. As Sowell's plant was gearing up for that big order, managers discovered the neophyte's mistake. As she describes it, "We came very close to disrupting this very important customer's manufacturing line, because we couldn't ship the product we had. We almost caused a line-down and a major revenue loss for our customer."

Top management didn't want to react to this serious near miss by sending the wrong message to its engineers. A common response in many companies would be to overcorrect by telling the junior man that a senior manager would henceforth have to review all of his work, thereby stifling him, or by decreeing that all managers would have to review all work, thereby stifling everyone. So the response was to add a routine review of this specific task by a midlevel manager: an additional safeguard, an extra strand in that spider web, but not a statement that a disaster had almost occurred.

Judy Blades of The Hartford sees the same connection between letting children grow up and giving employees leeway to make their own mistakes. At one point Blades and her husband were having communications difficulties with their youngest daughter. A friend, a child psychologist, taught the couple the importance of empowering her, a lesson Blades saw was equally applicable to adult employees.

"The issue between my daughter and my husband was a rule we had that the kids could not go out on school nights. This daughter was an excellent student, and a few times she had said, 'I've finished my homework and I'd like to go out with So-and-So.' My husband would always say 'No, it's a school night.' She would always respond with 'So what? I've got my work done!' They were at an impasse."

The psychologist said, 'Why don't you let her go out? The rule only makes sense if she hasn't finished her work. Shouldn't there be some sort of reward for her being a good student?'

"We thought rules and boundaries were good, but we weren't giving her any positive reinforcement for her good work, or crediting her with any judgment of her own," Blades said.

She sees the analogy with hidebound rules in an office setting, particularly in large bureaucracies like The Hartford. "I've got some folks in my office who have been in the business for thirty years and think that the way they get from Point A to Point B is the *only* way to get there. They are very directive of their employees. . . . But people don't learn from that. They learn from trial and error . . . You have to give people an opportunity to fail; we learn from our failures. But this puts you as a manager at risk."

In the service industries, like accounting, giving people the freedom to grow is critical. As Lori Okun of Ernst & Young put it, "We have a people-first culture. Our revenues derive from our people. You have to give them room to develop—or hang themselves—by giving them challenging assignments without breathing down their neck. People are so much more motivated with this approach than if you said, 'Do this report, take these steps in this order, and so on.' They can come up with more creative ways of doing things than I could have ever thought of.

"This is exactly how you help children grow and learn," Okun went on. "My first grader is now learning to spell; she has homework of six new words a week. I won't correct everything she does wrong; it would beat her down if I pointed out every time she got a letter wrong. She can learn from her mistakes."

"I never just give a person the 'answer,'" says another mother who works as a trainer in a telephone company. "I show them how to find the answers for themselves, step by step building up their competence."

Nancy Graver, publisher of the girl's magazine *New Moon*, says that the key to managing her staff of thirteen employees is identical to her approach to child-rearing: "Help them develop in ways that don't belittle them; let them take risks and make mistakes and recover. Then when they succeed, they can take the credit!"[2]

Sometimes working mothers allow their staff this kind of freedom out of necessity, because they simply don't have time to micromanage everyone. One prominent Washington attorney told me that before she had a baby she tended to do all the work on a big case, leaving her associates with a much more menial role. But now that she has to get home at a reasonable hour, she delegates more, and gives her associates much more running room. She discovered that not only is she happier, but the associates are flourishing, because they can finally show their stuff.

Provide Feedback and Boundaries

The trick in giving people enough autonomy to learn from their own mistakes is providing the guidance and feedback they need to succeed. Just turning people loose with no guidelines or course correction when they start to stumble won't work. Providing this feedback and setting the proper boundaries is tough. As a childless friend of mine who is a devoted godmother sagely remarked recently, "How in the world did the image of the soft, mushy mother ever develop? You have to be so *tough* to keep a child on the straight and narrow!"

It's hard to tell your children or family members about the wrong decisions and thoughtless things they do. It's equally tough to give employees really firm but compassionate feedback about wrong choices. That's why some mothers, like Catherine Powell, an Episcopal minister, think that people who've raised children may actually be tougher, more decisive managers than many other people, precisely because they have learned how important it is to draw the line.

Many members of the clergy, for example, "bend over backwards to be gentle, accepting, and understanding, to the extent of almost being feminine in their ministry," Powell confided during an interview in Washington, D.C. "But I suspect that those of us who have been real parents know that you can go only so far with that. You have to set some limits. I remember one colleague at our school worrying about pressure from the parents over some issue, and I told her, 'if the parents are complaining, so what? Let it go!' "

Nancy Drozdow, a business consultant, says that companies have learned that setting boundaries for employees is as important as setting them for children. "We've been through the first phase of getting away from strict command and control management styles," she says, "which was letting everyone operate in self-directed teams. But we have learned that you can't leave people on their own. Like children, if they have no boundaries they're likely to get into trouble. Now we're in the second phase, of giving employees the right *kind* of guidance. The idea is to be *clear* about what the rules are; what's the right way and the wrong way to do something . . . and when someone makes a mistake, you go over it again. . . ."

Michael Fossaceca says he has learned, both as a parent and a boss, that it's better to provide this corrective feedback as soon as possible, right after a misstep occurs. As he explains, "You can't watch a kid throw a temper tantrum in someone's house and talk about it later. You have to calm them down right then and there. It's exactly the same with adults. You have to say something to someone right away after they've messed up. This is very hard to do, but not doing it was a mistake I made when I started this job. Someone would do something that was incorrect, and I would mention it much later, during a performance review. They would get defensive, go into denial. . . . It's much better to say right away, 'I've noticed this behavior; this is what I'm seeing; you need to change this.' Now, when I come out of a sales call with someone, I say 'This is what you did right; this is what you did wrong.' "

Several parents also said that setting boundaries and standards doesn't work unless you stick to your guns and follow through with discipline if need be. Cheryl Bachelder says this is one of the great lessons she's learned: "Parents and leaders both have to hold to their principles to have an impact."

Bachelder noticed that when she told one of her daughters to do something, they would wait to see how serious she was. They wouldn't do anything until she brought it up again. "Kids do this all the time. And my team members—that's what I call our employees—do the same thing. I'll say I want something done, and often nothing gets done. They're waiting to see if I'll bring it up again. They're testing my conviction; seeing if I'll follow through and put pressure on people. I have to say everything at least three times.

"One of my daughters had a friend whose mother was always saying I'm going to ground you, but she never did. She'd threaten grounding almost every hour, and she never did anything! My husband is very strict, and we would always ground our kids if we said we were going to. One day my daughter said, 'You know what Rachel needs? Parents who follow through!' And I thought, wow, it works!"

Be an Adversarial Advocate

Film producer Lucy Fisher actually heard from her own child that she needed to exercise her authority more forcefully. Fisher's sixteen-year-old daughter was getting B+'s and A-'s in a competitive high school without studying very much, and although Fisher and her husband did tell her that her options would be greater if she worked harder, they implied that whether she did so or not was her decision. One day her daughter came home from school and complained, "You don't put enough pressure on me! My friends' parents are all over them to make good grades, and their grades are better than mine. Why didn't you put more pressure on me?"

This comment reminded Fisher of an incident that had influenced her early in her career. She was a studio vice president in her twenties working for Alan Ladd, Jr. at Twentieth Century Fox, and one day she overheard an argument between Ladd and Mel Brooks over the marketing of Brooks' latest film, *Young Frankenstein*. Brooks was yelling and screaming and demanding that things be done *his* way, and finally Ladd gave in. The next week, Brooks was back in the office, yelling at Ladd again, this time all upset at the way things were going. "But I did exactly what you told me to do," Ladd protested. Brooks replied indignantly, "Well, *you're* the head of the studio, why'd you listen to *me?*"

"Brooks was being childish, and wasn't taking responsibility for his own mistakes," says Fisher. "But he was also saying that had you been stronger and acted like the adult it would've been better for both of us. . . . I often use this story, and the story about my daughter, when I'm involved in a dispute with a director or an actor, to explain that ultimately I'm in charge. I have to do what I think is right, whatever you may think or do. My job is not to make you like me; it's to make the best decision I can for both of us.

"You know," she added thoughtfully, "when you're a parent, you have to be both an adversary of and an advocate for your child. If in business you could be like that—both advocate and adversary—you'd be unbeatable!"

Domination Is Destruction

The obverse of empowering others by letting them go is trying to dominate and control. Loni Hancock, a California assemblywoman and the former mayor of Berkeley, once told me that the main thing she had learned as a parent that carried over into her political life was the lesson that "Domination is destruction." By this she meant that excessive control can crush people. You can bend a child, a student, or a subordinate to your will, but something in them is destroyed in the process, be it their trust, their confidence, their productivity, or their very spirit. As Hancock put it, "You can force a child into submission, and still not get what you want, which is a healthy, strong, autonomous person. There is no doubt that institutions need this perspective."[3]

Actress and playwright Eve Ensler, author of *The Vagina Monologues* puts it so well: "We have to change the verbs from obliterate, dominate, humiliate to liberate, appreciate, celebrate."

Allowing people autonomy is important in every field, from politics and business to education, where rigid control in the classroom can smother curiosity and creativity. Even in philanthropy, excessive control can kill innovation. All too many foundations impose their agenda, or the latest fashion in giving, on the nonprofit organizations they support. This forces recipients to bend themselves into the shape of the next new thing rather than stick to their original, heartfelt mission. Donors need to let the beneficiaries of their gifts decide how best to use them. Sarah Pillsbury, a producer of *Desperately Seeking Susan*, among other films, is also one of the founders of Liberty Hill, a Los Angeles–based foundation. Liberty Hill, which supports local environmental and community groups, has always been run by women. According to Pillsbury, one secret of its effectiveness is that the board and staff know better than to try to impose their agenda on anyone. The foundation's mission is social change, but it allows the groups it supports to decide how to accomplish that goal. "We say, 'You do your thing and we'll back you if it fits our mission,' " says Pillsbury. "This is very successful because groups know that when they are asked to the table, we really want to know what they have to say. If we had our own agenda, we'd miss out on the creativity and the real world experience that can make things happen."

By letting go, wise philanthropists, like good parents, get back more than they give.

The Value of Playfulness

A number of working mothers told me that one of the most valuable things they learned from their children was the need to let go of their own sober side. Children can teach you to loosen up, have a little fun, and occasionally relinquish that all-business, adult persona that we think is necessary if we are to be taken seriously.

"My kids taught me playfulness," says Gerry Laybourne. "When I was at Nickelodeon we used to do a lot of game playing: charades, Monopoly with the rules changed, football with our own rules. It helped me realize that it is possible to create a workplace in which people can have fun. When we were trying out games for shows at Nickelodeon, I'd have us play them in the office.

"Play loosens people up, gets them out of the box and helps them think *creatively*. Your best ideas happen when you're playing, laughing, goofing around," Laybourne says. She learned this in part from her background as a teacher, where she saw the value of recess. Some time after she was made president of Nickelodeon, one of her team decided that there were too many meetings going on, and too many people taking themselves too seriously. So they instituted recess. Every day at 3:00 P.M. everyone was supposed to be mingling in the hallways, taking a break. She even had buckets of plastic goop around the office that people could play with during meetings.

I got the point when the cable industry executive sent me a tape of herself and as I slipped it into the VCR I was anticipating a speech or a boring panel discussion. What I got was a closeup shot of Ms. Laybourne, with her short blonde hair and big horn-rimmed glasses, saying "People ask how I can run such a fun network, and to their question I just have to say, 'I don't know.' " At which point a torrent of green slime poured over her head. End of tape.

Pamela Thomas-Graham, another prominent woman in cable

(continued)

television, could not be more different from Gerry Laybourne. "When I grew up everything was so *serious*," says Thomas-Graham, whose resume hints at a lifetime of head down, hard work. Before she was tapped to head CNBC in 2001, Thomas-Graham had earned three Harvard degrees, been the first black woman partner at the management consulting firm of McKinsey & Co., and, in her spare time, had written two bestselling mystery novels with Ivy League settings: *A Darker Shade of Crimson* (Harvard), and *Blue Blood* (Yale). A third, *Orange Crush* (Princeton), was subsequently published in the summer of 2004. This was not the track record of someone who had spent a lot of time exploring her silly side.

"Playfulness is just not a Harvard MBA kind of thing. Or a quality you'd know to look for in an employee," said Thomas-Graham, who admitted that having children had made her more appreciative of the importance of playfulness in a creative business. As she put it, "Having kids makes you realize that you really do need people who can say, why *can't* we wear a sock over our head?"

Cheryl Bachelder is another executive who says that her children taught her the value of the light touch:

> *I've always been a real serious, intense person. . . .*
>
> *My kids taught me how to lighten up . . . to play, to laugh, to bring humor to a situation. I guess you could say they taught me joy. When my daughter Kate was little, after dinner she'd say "Let's dance!" When she got older, it was "Let's do karaoke!" It's very hard to be serious while singing karaoke.*
>
> *I learned to take that sense of play with me back into the office. For example, at one team meeting, I came in and said we were all going to play a game. I gave everyone a "voice," and I gave each of them a toy representing their voice. One person was the customer, and they got a chicken, another was the quality person, and she got a diamond, the building guy got a little house, and so on. I kept everyone's toy, with their name on it, around for a whole*

(continued)

quarter. It made for more playful, lighthearted meetings, and loos-
ened everyone up.

I definitely attribute my ability to do that to my kids, and to a
book I read while my daughters were younger, on how to teach
children joy. Some of this came from that as well.

CHAPTER 10

Habits of Integrity

"Integrity is the essence of everything successful."
—Buckminster Fuller

Ultimately, the most important lessons learned from child-rearing are what Brigham Young University political science professor Valerie Hudson calls *habits of integrity*. As parents, we live our lives in front of our children. The conscientious parent is always aware that his or her actions take place under the steady gaze of an impressionable child. Whether we like it or not, we are constantly setting an example, and modeling the behavior that our children will integrate into their own repertoire. In this sense, parents can never avoid being on stage for the most attentive audience in the world: their own children.

As Hudson, a devout Mormon and mother of six, puts it, "Mothers have to craft a life that their kids can emulate. They are fully visible to their kids. Sometimes I'll think maybe I can cut a corner here or there and do something an easier way, and then I'll think, no, they are fully aware of what I do, and I always have to be setting that example."[1]

Kids may fail to listen to you, but they will never fail to imitate you. And when they're calling "Look at me! Look at me!" never doubt whom *they* are watching like a hawk. You.

If our thinking is shaped by the practices in which we engage, then years of trying to be positive role models for our children, day in and day out, may well develop certain patterns of thought and behavior. Hudson speculates that perhaps it is no accident that many of the major whistle-blowers in recent years have been mothers. All three of *Time* magazine's "Persons of the Year" in 2002—Sharron Watkins of Enron, Cynthia Cooper of World Com, and Colleen Rowley of the Federal Bureau of Investigation—were mothers with young children at home. "Maybe their integrity stemmed from their practice as mothers," Hudson suggests. After all, if you are a conscientious role model, the last thing you want your impressionable children to see is you on television, being frog-marched into a police van with your hands cuffed behind your back.

I have to admit I have my doubts. None of the women honored by *Time* have ever implied that being a parent had anything to do with their actions. Rowley and Cooper have also denied that gender played any role. As Rowley, the primary breadwinner in her family for twenty-two years, said, quite correctly, "There are plenty of women who've been co-opted, who don't do the right thing, and plenty of men who do."

Underscoring her point, a few months later it emerged that the Pentagon official who supervised an extremely lucrative and controversial $23 billion contract for the Boeing Co. was a woman, Darlene Druyan, who was subsequently rewarded with a high-paying job at Boeing. Druyan's daughter, a Boeing employee, had arranged her mother's initial employment discussions with the company. Both Druyan and Boeing's chief financial officer were fired when the embarrassing facts were revealed and Druyan later pleaded guilty to conspiracy to defraud taxpayers. So much for maternal rectitude. It's pretty clear that mothers don't have a special brain chip that inhibits them from unethical behavior.

Whistle-blower Sharron Watkins did have this to say about her actions, however. She explained that many organizations, including Enron, still resemble men's clubs whose members put their buddies ahead of any higher standards. "I am really uncomfortable with making general statements," Watkins told *Time*, "but men are reluctant to put their friends in jeopardy. I don't necessarily want friends in the workplace. I think most men have no friendships outside the workplace. [Also] society doesn't ask women what you do for a living. Your ego or self-worth isn't [as] tied to what you do."

That's not quite true. Women's self-worth *is* tied to what they do. They just define what they do more broadly, to include their parental identity. It was telling that when *Time* asked the three women what they did to help cope with the stress in the aftermath of their revelations of wrongdoing and ineptitude, they all referred to the joys and comforts of children. "You come home, and you almost have to put that away because they're wanting books read, games played," said Watkins, who had a three-year-old at the time. Cooper said she went home and got hugs from her two girls and her husband. And Rowley told this story: "When Congress leaked my memos and it was all over the news, we would be watching and Marion [her three-year-old daughter] was getting so bored with it. My husband said we wanted to watch the news, and she piped up, 'Well, how about some Elmo news?' "

These mothers could put their work lives in perspective. They had other priorities, including being a positive influence and a reliable presence in their children's lives. It's not that mothers have a corner on morality or that being a good parent automatically makes a person a good citizen. But people who try hard to be good parents do have an extra dimension to their lives that counteracts any tendency to do "anything" it takes to succeed in their paying job. They have a kind of "checking" reflex that kicks in with this calculation: "What is the action or reaction in this situation that would be best for my child?"

If a person responds to the small temptations regularly with this reflex, and regularly does the "right thing," can that develop habits of integrity that come into play when serious temptations come along? I don't know the answer, but the question is worth posing. And the comments from many of the successful mothers I interviewed did suggest a certain parental ethics at work.

Laurel Cutler, one of the most successful female advertising executives in U.S. history, once told me that her children literally kept her
honest. Like every other attentive parent, Cutler learned that kids will
always do as you do, not as you say. They can smell any deviation between the talk and the walk like a shark smells blood. She concluded
that honesty is always the best policy, and that became her business
philosophy as well. She told me that she advised her corporate clients
that the best way to maintain their reputation was with deeds, not
words or images. The best ad campaign in the world cannot erase
the reality of a corporation's behavior. This may seem strange advice
coming from an expert in manipulating public opinion, but Cutler
knows what she's talking about: "I always say it doesn't matter what we
say; it only matters what we do. It's my motto. I hope it goes on my
tombstone."[2]

Being There

In my conversations with parents, several habits of integrity emerged.
The first, and I believe the foremost, is being there for the people who
count on you.

When asked, what is the most important thing you do for your children, mothers always say "I'm *there* for them." By this they mean assuring their children that they come first; that someone will always be
there when they call for help or cry out for comfort and consolation.
Parents try to be there when disaster strikes or is imagined; they're the
ones who reassure us that there's no need to fear the dark.

Anyone who claims to be a leader has to *be there* as well, whether it
is working late along with the team, rushing to the scene of a disaster,
visiting the troops in time of war, or showing courage under fire. Interestingly, the supreme example of such courage in recent years may
have been set by a woman, Margaret Thatcher, former prime minister
of the United Kingdom. Thatcher was in the bathroom when an IRA
bomb went off in her hotel. The unflappable Iron Lady finished her

toilette and proceeded straight to her scheduled speech, where she gave a powerful denunciation of the Irish terrorists—thereby giving new meaning to the concept of nanny government.[3]

A more recent demonstration of a leader being there was the performance of New York Mayor Rudy Guiliani in the days following the deadly destruction of 9/11. The feisty and controversial mayor won over all hearts with his ability to be there for the wounded city. He was in the streets, at the funerals, sharing the grief, saying all the right comforting things; he personified the good leader, who in times of crisis embodies the good father or mother who is always there when you need them.

Being there does not have to mean being physically present. It can mean everything from always taking the call when the child telephones the office to running to the scene when there is an accident or a high fever. Will and Jada Plunkett Smith were being there when they rushed home from the Academy Awards after getting a call that their toddler had a temperature of 101 degrees. Early in his career as premier of Russia, Vladimir Putin failed to understand the being-there aspect of leadership when he decided not to interrupt a vacation to fly to the scene of a nuclear submarine accident. For days he *wasn't there*, and paid a high price in popularity.

I once asked the woman who had started the Army's excellent child-care program what her own personal parenting tips were. She said that her grown daughters had told her that they most appreciated the fact that she had *always let them leave first*. By this they meant she was always there when they left the house. She was careful to let them think that they were leaving *her*. She tried to never give them the anxious feeling that they were the ones being left behind. This is very subtle stuff, but it is part of every sensitive parent's repertoire.[4]

Being There for Grown-Ups

Even grown children—and which of us isn't one?—still need to know the parent is there, always at their disposal. My son calls me from college and once accused me of not being home when he called unexpectedly. These kinds of feelings are not uncommon in the office. Mothers in corporations often note the similarities between the need to be there for their kids and their employees. When I interviewed Mary Lou Boccio and Mavis Osomobor at TIAA-CREF, the giant pension and insurance company, both executives remarked on this. They each had to travel frequently and, when they did, they would hear the very same comments they heard at home. When they left, it was, "Why do you have to go?" When they returned, it was, "You've been gone a long time!"

Osomobor, forty-six, an African-American who is married to an African businessman, is in charge of training for the New York region. She has triplets who turned four in the fall of 2003. In order to prevent separation anxiety, she carefully plans her departure on business trips, telling the kids that she will be leaving tomorrow, that Daddy will get them up and dressed, and put them to bed. She promises to call every night before they have supper, while Daddy is reading to them. She tries to create the impression that she is still reliably *there*, as part of their daily routine, as much as possible.

She has learned to take similar precautions at work. When she goes on vacation for a week, everything is fine, but if she takes two weeks, she had better call home to the office, and assure everyone that she is thinking about them, and wondering if everything is going well. "This was a big eye opener for me," she says. "I learned that I had to set up some mechanisms to be in touch with my people while I am gone . . . It is very much like what I do with the children."[5]

Boccio, the director of national training for TIAA-CREF, is the stepmother of two teenagers and an eight-year-old. In 2001, when her mother died and her nanny arrangements fell apart, she wasn't able to be as available as usual to her staff. At the time, her people were going through their annual performance appraisals, so there was an extra level of trepidation in the office. She got feedback that people were unhappy that she wasn't *there* for them when they needed her.

"I wasn't there enough to hold their hands or advocate for them, and they were upset," said Boccio. "I was expected to be there for them, just as I was expected to be there for my mother and my kids."[6]

Boccio had her own get-away-from-home techniques as well, which included laying out the youngest child's clothes for every day she was away. One morning, a kindergarten teacher called her cell phone and asked if everything was all right at home. It turned out that her daughter, then aged five, had gone to school wearing three days' worth of clothing. Boccio's husband had dressed her in all of the clothes his wife had laid out for the entire duration of her trip.

Being There Implies Unconditional Love

According to Shelly Lazarus, what employees often need from her is just what children want from a parent: unconditional love. In other words, being there for them.

"Unconditional love is a management concept," Lazarus told me in an interview in her spacious Manhattan office. "To most CEOs this is a foreign concept. It's 'you're only as good as what you did for me yesterday.' They don't understand that unconditional support is a wonderful management tool.

"Life in the commercial world is really tough," she explained. "There are some people on your team who need to know you're there for them. It gives them the courage they need to go out and do what's right. They're braver if they know they've got you behind them; that you won't withdraw your love and respect if they make a mistake."

According to Sarah Pillsbury, supporting the team is especially important on a film project. The enforced intimacy of film-making is something like the enforced intimacy of a family. "You often have to act as if you love the other people, or at least like them," she explains, "because you have to keep working with them day after day, and letting off steam would only destroy what everyone is trying to produce. . . . The only way I can not be angry sometimes is to have as much compassion as I possibly can. . . . telling myself things like 'they're doing the best they can.' It's hard—unconditional love is tough work, whether it's in a family or a production."

Being there is definitely not easy. It takes tremendous discipline to get up several times in the middle of the night to tend to a hungry or cranky baby. It takes enormous self-control to sit through a toddler's temper tantrum, calmly waiting it out without losing it yourself. It takes strength to turn down a fun evening because a young child has lately shown signs of neediness, and raw courage to relinquish a career one loves, but mothers do all this and more all the time.

One of the biggest surprises to many new parents is the enormous amount of renunciation involved. One simply cannot be a decent parent without relinquishing at least part of one's own agenda for the sake of another person. This routine acceptance of life's inevitable tradeoffs is what people mean when they refer to being *grown-up*. Good parents are grown-ups. They are old hands at accepting the fact that you can't have it all at once, and that some gratifications have to be delayed or totally forsaken.

You Can't Be There in Two Places at Once

One of the most excruciating conflicts for working mothers is the impossibility of being there at all times for both your children and your job. Here are three stories, of three different mothers who happen to live in Brooklyn, all of whom had to face the toughest decisions mothers have to face.

Ann Moore, the chairman of Time Inc., has one child, a son born in 1984. On September 11, 2001 he was a seventeen-year-old student at Stuyvesant High School in lower Manhattan, located literally in the shadow of the World Trade Center. Moore was sitting in her midtown office in the Time-Life Building when the first fateful crash occurred. She had no way of reaching her child—it was the one day that he had not taken his BlackBerry with him to school. And she absolutely had to stay at her post. Both *Time* and *People* magazines reported to her, the company had stopped the presses, photographers and reporters were rushing to the scene, and Moore was expected to manage the pandemonium.

What did she do? She called her housekeeper, instructed her to stay by the phone, and to stay calm. She figured Brendan, her son, would get in touch as soon as he could. And she stayed at her desk while the towers collapsed and debris rained down all around her son's school. The children were let out, one at a time, and told to run north, while the others stood horrified by the classroom windows and watched as people jumped out of the burning buildings.

"It was the most emotional, stressful day of my life," Moore recalls, "but I was not able to worry about Brendan. *You only worry about the things you can control.* I had to tell my own staff, including those who were parents, that they had to stay here. How could I have left? I had to be here for them, for those photographers as they came back from Ground Zero, shaken from what they had seen. And where would I have gone? I couldn't have gotten through to the school. I couldn't have found Brendan on the streets of downtown Manhattan. I just had to trust that he was old enough to have the presence of mind to get out safely and to call us when he could."

At 1:00 P.M. the police announced that the Rockefeller Center area had to be closed off, and Time Inc. was ordered to evacuate. All nonessential staff was sent home. The executives, including Moore, remained, and finally she received a call from another mother, telling her that Brendan had escaped with her son and was safe, although he was unable to make his way home to Brooklyn Heights across the Brooklyn Bridge.

Did she make the right decision? Did she have any choice? Do we even have a right to ask, not having been in her shoes? Did she herself have any second thoughts? It seemed to me that by telling this story almost as soon as our conversation began, Moore was still wrestling with the cruelest, most insolvable dilemma of the conscientious working parent. How can you be there in two places at once, when both your child and your employer have immediate and simultaneous needs? You can't.

Millions of mothers have resolved this conflict by giving up their paid employment, including many who loved the work they were doing and the income, independence, friends, respect, and satisfaction it gave them. Let no one denigrate this decision by implying it is easy, or just another lifestyle choice.

Rabbi Margaret Moers Wenig of Brooklyn is one of those mothers who made the difficult decision to give up at least temporarily her life-time work. She was ordained as a rabbi in 1984, soon after her first daughter was born; twelve years after the first woman was ordained by the Reform Jewish movement.[7] A few years later, she and her husband had a second daughter. From then on, it was twelve-hour days and a constant struggle to fulfill all her obligations, including teaching at Hebrew Union College Jewish Institute of Religion. Often, she told me, "There was no food on the table, a mound of laundry to do, and every time a child was sick my husband and I had to negotiate who would stay home. . . ." After twelve years the marriage ended, and Wenig later took a female partner, another prominent rabbi in New York. (She jokes that her kids have two Jewish mothers and are there-fore doubly oppressed.) But the pressures continued. Like countless other mothers working full-time, she felt that she was always failing in some aspect of her life, feeling that she was cheating her kids, or her partner, or her work. Finally, in 2000, when both of her daughters were in high school, she gave up her congregation and retained only her part-time work as an instructor at Hebrew Union.

Wenig left her congregation when her oldest daughter was a senior in high school, and she was in the the process of learning how to let go of her first born. The experience prepared her to let go of a congrega-tion she had been nurturing for an equally long time—more than six-teen years.

"Having kids teaches you that you can't have everything, at least not all at once," she declared over lunch at a restaurant in Greenwich Vil-lage, near the seminary. "When you have children at home, your life, your body, your weekends, and your nights are no longer your own. . . . Life *is* about making choices, and choices require compromises."

But even these hard compromises pale in comparison to the dilem-mas of the mothers who have no choice but to work full-time, leaving young children vulnerable to dangers in the streets, accidents in empty apartments, erratic or neglectful caregivers, or worse. The worst that can happen did happen to a third mother who lives in very different circumstances from those of Ann Moore and Rabbi Wenig.

Kim Brathwaite, a single mother, had succeeded in getting off welfare and became an assistant manager at McDonald's, working irregular hours that were beyond her control, and that made reliable childcare virtually impossible on her modest wages. One night in October 2003, her babysitter failed to show up and she faced an excruciating decision: stay home with her nine-year-old daughter and one-year-old baby and get fired, or leave the children home alone. She went to work, and kept in touch with the older girl by phone. After the restaurant closed, she went home and discovered that her ground floor apartment was ablaze with the two children trapped inside. They both perished in the fire.

The authorities were not outraged that millions of mothers have to work those kinds of hours, forcing them to leave their children in hazardous situations. They were not outraged that children have to be left alone because there is no reliable, affordable child care for working families in America. But they *were* outraged that this particular mother had gone to work that night. Despite several neighbors' statements that she was a good, loving mother, Kim Brathwaite was arrested for recklessly endangering her children, a charge that could bring up to 16 years in prison.

This is a true story. Apparently, the state of New York takes literally the old Jewish saying: "God could not be everywhere; therefore He made mothers." This woman's crime was that she was not more omnipresent than God. God could not be there, everywhere, at all times, but this poor mother was supposed to be. In the face of this cruelty, words fail.[8]

Such a Pathetic Life!

I have to share my favorite family story about being there.

When my son James was fifteen, and going through the Mom-can-do-no-right teen years, he came into my home office one day and declared, "You live such a pathetic life! You just sit in front of a computer all day. I'd rather be dead than lead a life like yours!"

This ungracious moment occurred while I was in the middle of a long and difficult book project with an unsure outcome. I had been sidelined first by a ski accident and knee surgery and, then, a year later, by a bike accident that fractured an elbow and required another operation and months of physical therapy. The book manuscript was delayed, resulting in a cancellation of my contract. So, in addition to the usual writer's uncertainty of who would read the book, I had to spend several more years finishing the manuscript while wondering who was going publish it. This involved gritting my teeth, smiling, and lying at cocktail parties whenever anyone asked, "Who's publishing your book?" A lot of people asked.

So, I was vulnerable to the suspicion that maybe my son was right. My life was a little pathetic. But he had no right to say such a thing. What I was tempted to say to him was, "You little %#*&! Because of you I gave up a prestigious job at the *New York Times* and now here I am, sitting in front of this computer instead of traveling all over the world, meeting fascinating people, winning awards, and earning a reasonable amount of money. I gave all that up so you would have at least one parent at home who would be there for you and make sure you didn't turn out pathetic! If I have a pathetic life, it's all because of you!"

But I didn't say any of that. Feeling like a saint, I simply said, "What I'm doing is important! Just you wait and see."

Flash forward three years. I got another contract with an outstanding publisher and a better editor and the book, *The Price of Motherhood,* came out to critical acclaim and extensive reviews. I had my first reading at Politics and Prose, a bookstore in Washington, D.C., that was voted the best independent bookstore in the nation a few years earlier. A big crowd gathered, there was excitement in the air, and after my talk the store sold more books than it had ever sold at a reading before. James, now eighteen, was there, videotaping the whole thing.

The next morning he came into my office where there I was as usual, pathetically sitting in front of my computer. He said, "You know Mom, you worked really hard. You never gave up. And it paid off! I'm really proud of you."

My first thought was, I'm so proud of you for being able to say that. And my second thought was, "I can die now. I've taught him the best lesson I had to teach."

Being there never felt so good.

Being There for the Greater Good

Joyce Fletcher, an authority on gender differences in management, has observed in working women an ability to put a project first, and do whatever it takes to get the job done. She calls this a preserving skill and compares it explicitly to maternal behavior. Just as the best mothers are concerned about all aspects of their children's well-being—physical, emotional, and intellectual—the best workers accept responsibility for the success of a project as a whole, not just the one small part that may technically be their job.

In observing the female engineers at DEC Fletcher noticed that they expressly felt that they had to be there for the projects for which they were responsible. They expressed disdain for fellow engineers who turned their back on work that might be construed as beneath them or who let substandard products go out the door because fixing the problem wasn't in their job description. They were also very clear that their own practice of putting a project's needs ahead of their own status or self-promotion was not a sign of selflessness but a sign of competence and commitment. Being there was, to them, a mark of strength, not a sign of weakness.

One serious problem with work this subtle is that it often goes unnoticed. People who operate in a mature, supportive manner may be the secret ingredient in a project's success but, if others don't understand the importance of what they are doing, their vital contributions may go unappreciated. The women at DEC told Fletcher that many of their male coworkers thought that if a female was helpful, she was probably naive and could even be taken advantage of. The women had to develop strategies to assure that their assistance to colleagues would be reciprocated and not exploited.

As one of the women put it, "If you try to nurture, they just don't get it. They don't understand that is what you are doing. They see it as a weakness . . . or that they've gotten something over on you . . . I've gotten so that now I say, 'Okay, look, I'll help you out on this one. *But you owe me one.'* "[9]

Even in medicine, a profession in which being there for a patient can mean the difference between life or death, preserving work, and being there for others, can be devalued. Dr. Rita Colwell of the National Science Foundation told me this story:

"When one of my daughters was doing her medical clerkship at a Veterans' Administration hospital, she always made time to talk with an elderly fellow who was dying of lung cancer. One day the chief resident dressed her down for 'wasting time.' 'He's going to die anyway,' he said. She fought back tears and ducked into a nursing station, where a nurse hugged and comforted her, and then she called me. She asked me what she should do. I told her not to rat on him, but to continue doing the best job she could, as she thought best."

Colwell's daughter now teaches at the Dartmouth Medical School. Who do you think is making a greater contribution to the healing art of medicine: the professor or that former resident?

CHAPTER 11

A Sense of Perspective

"A weak mind blows fleas into elephants, and shrinks elephants into fleas. A strong mind sees things in their true perspective."

—Lord Chesterfield,
in his letters to his son

Children totally reorder your priorities, whether you are an average Jane or Joe or a presidential candidate. They bring you face to face with what is truly important in life. A therapist once told an acquaintance that if he didn't go into therapy, he'd better have a serious love affair or a child, because only then would he be asked to decide what really mattered to him. My reaction was, having a child *is* a serious love affair, and nothing else can come close to helping you realize what matters.

A child's accident or illness, in particular, can make it clear that nothing else in life can compete with their well-being. Shirley Strum Kenny says that, "This is the most important lesson of family life." Years ago, Kenny applied for a White House fellowship. The long-awaited letter arrived on a day when one of the children was running a dangerously high fever. The envelope from Washington went unread for hours; by the time it was opened, she says, "the rejection didn't matter."

Congressman Dick Gephardt said almost the very same thing in his concession speech in Iowa in early 2004, after his poor showing in a crucial Presidential primary effectively ended his distinguished political career. "I've been in tougher fights," said the longtime representative from Missouri. "When you've watched your two-year-old son fight terminal cancer and win, it puts everything in perspective."

Judge Patricia Wald, a former Federal judge and mother of five who now sits on the presidential commission on intelligence, tells a similar story. "One of our children almost died of a staph infection," she told me, "and one of us had to stay at the hospital for twenty-four hours a day for a month. We had to send our other children to their grandmother's. Out of that, I had a sense that nothing was more important. I knew that those kids meant more to me than anything, including my profession."

Working mothers of all stripes told me that their children gave them this kind of grounding, and a healthy detachment from their work. Naomi Foner, the screenwriter of such films as *Running On Empty*, said she might be upset about something that happened at work, "and they couldn't care less—they succeeded in shaking me out of it. And they were right. What I was concerned about would be trivial compared to their needs. I'd come home from a script meeting with notes decimating what I had written, and they were hungry! It was very clear: What was important to them was much more important in the great scheme of things."

An executive in a large manufacturing company put it in almost the same language: "Kids live in the here and now. It's all about *them*; it's not about you. They view life as much simpler. Going home to them gives me objectivity. Many of my women friends who for one reason or another didn't have children don't have that objectivity— that understanding that life is not all about selling whatever it is you sell, and that work is not worth losing your mind, or your husband, or your health over. My children provide me with this kind of balance every night. I'll come home thinking about our stock price, and they'll want to know what's for dinner."

Lessons in Humility

A friend of mine recently remarked that "Parenthood is the greatest exercise in ego deflation in the world." It is impossible to be self-important in the face of such observations as "Are you really going to wear *that?*" Or, " Mom, that lipstick looks *horrible!*" Children are like Old Testament prophets, ruthlessly hammering any trace of pride or pomposity out of their people. There is probably no mother on earth who doesn't have her own favorite lesson-in-humility story.

One of the funniest is described in Madeleine Kunin's autobiography. Kunin's four children made sure that she never drifted off into the thin air of self-importance as she rose in state government. They started in as soon as she was elected to her first political office, as state representative for the Burlington area. After she recorded her first solo half-hour interview on Vermont public television, she rushed home, fixed dinner, and, at the appointed hour of 8:00 P.M., gathered the children around the set to watch Mommy. But they wanted to watch something else. As she describes the scene:

> "No," I said, "keep still. I want to watch my interview."
> "Please, please, we want to watch . . ."
> "Shut up."
> "Oh, gee, come on, Mom."
> "Keep quiet."
> There on the screen was an intelligent, attractive, articulate, and self-possessed woman, holding forth on the issues of the day. Back in the living room there was this:
> "Boring, it's so boring."
> My voice rose. "Keep still, please. I mean it, I really, really mean it."

My television voice continued uninterrupted. On camera I smiled, nodded, and smiled again.

Who is this woman? I asked myself admiringly, talking so skillfully, so unperturbed?

"Now can we switch the channel?"

"He hit me."

"She started it."

"I did not."

"Stop, both of you!" I yelled above the din. "I want to listen to myself. I can't hear a thing with all your fighting!"

"Aw, Mom, we've watched enough."[1]

Cheryl Bachelder had a similar ego balloon-popping experience as she began her corporate rise. "Before I had kids, like all grown-ups I paid close attention to titles, money, recognition, magazine covers, and all that," Bachelder confided. "But I'll never forget the first time I got promoted to vice president at RJR Nabisco. It was a big deal. I was showered with congratulations, presented with bottles of champagne, and so on. Later I went home, walked into my house and there was my daughter Tracy, who was about two and a half at the time.

"I said, 'Tracy! I was promoted to vice president today!'

"She looked at me, and said, 'You know what? I got a card with a reindeer on it!' And I thought, 'You know, that's more important.'"

Reality Checks

When Jamie Gorelick was in the Pentagon, as general counsel for the Department of Defense, she held the rank of a four-star general. This meant that when she walked into a room, everyone stood up. Later, at the Justice Department, she was second in command of an agency with an operating budget of $18 billion and almost one hundred thousand employees.

"This was big stuff," she recalled. "And at very senior levels, you risk taking yourself overly seriously. A lot of people are constantly telling you you're terrific. Your children help you keep your bearings. They keep you real. They make you roll on the floor, draw you into 'normal' everyday activities, like going to the grocery store, going on class trips. If one of their bikes breaks down, you don't have your colonel there to fix it, you have to get down on your knees and see if you can do something about it yourself. If the dog poops on the rug, you have to clean it up. If they need help with their math homework, you do it."

Insightful parents appreciate these reality checks, and understand that they are better people and often more successful because of them. As Gorelick spoke, I was reminded of the famous gaffe made by the first President Bush during the campaign of 1992. He went into a supermarket and marveled when a check-out clerk swiped a bar code. He had never seen that before, signaling that he never went grocery shopping, an everyday activity that is part of almost everyone's life. The incident reinforced the image of Bush as an out-of-touch patrician, and he lost the election to Bill Clinton, who definitely had a common touch.

A Down-to-Earth Perspective

Lindsay Crouse, a veteran actress of stage, screen, and television, is aware that her children have given her a grounding that can be quite rare in Hollywood. (In 2003, her oldest daughter, twenty, was an undergraduate at Brown University, her youngest was fifteen, and her stepson was thirteen.) As she puts it, "You can get cocky in this business, or at least you feel maybe you should get cocky and demanding. You wonder, Should I act entitled? If I don't, am I a bozo? But children remind you that all that's really an illusion. You're just an actor, and you never graduate from that.

"This grounding comes in part from literally being *on the ground* with them—a little grubby, a little like *The Velveteen Rabbit*. I was once all dressed up to go to an audition, in a wonderful beige suede skirt, and my daughter Willa, who was about three or four, saw me going out and cried, 'Mommy, you look so beautiful!' She ran over and grabbed me around the legs to give me a hug, smearing peanut butter and jelly all over the skirt. Of course, I had to change clothes. In such a situation, you have to think, it's only a skirt, an outfit doesn't matter . . . You have to keep your eye on what's really important here. This can spare you from a certain kind of arrogance."

Crouse has turned down roles that conflicted with the demands of her family, taking valuable years out of her career while her children were growing up. (Once a gas station attendant gave her an inquiring look and asked, "Are you somebody?") Nevertheless, she has starred in such films as *The Verdict, House of Games,* and *Places in the Heart,* which earned her a nomination for an Academy Award. She is a warm, unpretentious woman who could pass for any other upper-middle-class American mom with a comfortable house, a large furry dog, and a nanny popping in and out as we had lunch in her bright, color-filled kitchen in Pacific Palisades. She told me people are always telling her husband, a television producer, that "Your wife seems so *normal* for an actress!"

Carole Browner, who had a three-year-old when she was named head of the Environmental Protection Agency in 1993, also found that being a mom was a sanity check. Browner and her husband made a conscious decision not to hire a live-in nanny for their son Zachary. They relied on college students who came in during the afternoon, an arrangement that forced them to be home in time for dinner.

Browner, a tall, slender woman with an open, forthright manner, believes that this decision to play an active part in her young child's life made her a *better* manager. The EPA is a huge agency, with a $7 billion budget, 18,000 employees, and countless controversial issues to confront. "You could stay there twenty-four hours a day," Browner says, "and still have work to do. But kids don't care if you're running a huge budget; they want to see you, talk to you. . . . I could have this hellacious day, and then go home and be forced to set it aside, because here was this rightfully demanding child. It definitely forces you to keep it all in perspective. . . . I also think it helped that people at the agency could see the similarities between my life and their own lives.

They could see I might have some insight into their own concerns as parents."

Above all, Browner and other parents told me that their children gave them the ability to communicate in simple, concrete language that anyone could understand. As one prominent parent put it, "Children link us to so many eternal and everyday truths. They enable us to speak to people where they are living, rather than where we think they should be living."

In Browner's case, this meant being able to convey the importance of a clean environment in terms that are meaningful to the average person. "My son enabled me to talk from the perspective of being a mother about air pollution, food safety, and other issues," she said. "Historically, the EPA had preached to converted environmentalists. It was also a hunkered-down agency, somewhat on the defensive, so it tried to explain everything it was doing in very careful, technical terms. I realized that if we wanted public support, we would have to show people the benefits of what we did in very simple ways. And as a mother, I saw that we could speak in very concrete ways to women about their concerns for their children."

Browner began to talk about air pollution, food safety, and clean water in terms of the air our kids breathe, the food our kids eat, and the water our families drink—a language that came directly out of her experience as a mother.

"I had to learn how to explain to a six-year-old what I did at work. So if I said, 'We're taking toxics out of the water,' and he asked why, I learned to say something like, 'Because fish live in that water, and you eat the fish.' "

Browner told me about the time her husband and her son, then age five, got in a taxi and the driver asked, "Where's your mom?"

"She's at work," Zack replied.

"What does she do?"

"She saves things."

"What does she save?"

"Bananas."

She later put that exchange into a speech on food safety.

"All this reminded me of what was important about the job we did—and I got it from a five-year-old!"

Browner believes that this ability to tell the EPA's story in concrete personal terms enabled the agency to withstand the assaults that came after the Republicans took control of the House of Representatives in 1994. At one point, the administration confronted a proposed law that contained sixteen different initiatives to limit the EPA's ability to enforce the nation's existing environmental regulations. According to Browner, "We forced them to rewrite that bill, and we got every one of those restrictions lifted out of it. This was after we had already started our efforts to engage the public."

In other words, she believes that the nation's environmental protections were saved—for at least a few years—with the help of a small boy who kept asking his mother to explain what she did when she went to the office.

I heard a similar story about kids giving adults the power of down-to-earth speech while in Sweden. Gregor Hatt, a former adviser and speech writer to Prime Minister Ingvar Carlsson, is an active coparent of three children. Hatt, whom I met while on a reporting trip to Stockholm in the late 1990s, told me that the best ideas he ever had as a speech writer came to him while he was sitting in the playground. "If you are only inside looking out you only have the metaphors of power," he said. "But if you have everyday experiences you can find the everyday metaphors that speak to people."

In 1993, Carlsson was trying to convince his colleagues in the Socialist Party that Sweden ought to join the European Common Market. In a major speech before the party Congress, Carlsson planned to make the point that political institutions have to grow and evolve when economic, financial, and other links expand. To illustrate the idea, Carlsson used simple, concrete language written by Hatt. "There's no going back to the nation state," he declared. "You can't put the clothes of a one-year-old on a three-year-old."

This image had come to Hatt at a time when his son Christopher, aged three, was outgrowing all his clothes.

"That speech was reported to be the thing that turned public opinion in favor of Sweden joining the Common Market, which in turn was Carlsson's greatest legacy," Hatt proudly related.[2]

Nobody's Perfect

When I was raising my son, I was frequently aware—and he made me aware—of my shortcomings as a parent. These come frighteningly close to one's shortcomings as a person. I think the most common phrase out of my mouth while James was growing up was "Nobody's perfect." I meant me, of course, but the whole experience of being a mother made me more conscious of the fact that people do try to do the best they can, and that it is unreasonable to expect perfection out of anybody, be it a spouse, a coworker, a presidential candidate, or even the Department of Motor Vehicles.

This acceptance of one's own and others' limitations is not resignation; it is the beginning of wisdom and newfound strength. In their study of high-achieving women, Marian Ruderman and Patricia Ohlott of the Center for Creative Leadership found that "Letting go of the ideal of perfection often seems to be the key to success in feeling whole."[3] The women who had given up on the superwoman ideal, of trying to do everything and be all things to all people, felt more centered. And only when a person feels whole can all the parts of her being work together, rather than at cross purposes. Paradoxically, it seems that we can accomplish more when we realize that we can't do it all.

Many mothers told me that the struggles of child-rearing had helped them come to this realization. Children help parents put their mistakes and everyday disasters in perspective—maybe because they live through so many!

Leslie Gaines-Ross, an executive at the public relations firm of Burston-Marsteller in New York City, says her tough experiences as a single working mother made her much more philosophical about mistakes that happened at work. "It's hard for me to get really angry and frustrated, after what I've been through. When people make mistakes in the office—and there are always mistakes—I can look at it in a broader context, and think, everyone has these experiences."

Gaines-Ross was married soon after college to Jim Gaines, who later became editor-in-chief of *People*, *Life*, and *Time* magazines. They had one daughter, Alison, who is now twenty-eight. The marriage ended in divorce when Alison was three and Leslie was working on her doctorate at New York University. She had to go back to work. There she was with a toddler, trying to finish her PhD at night after the baby was asleep, and working full-time during the day for minimum wages.

One day her ceiling fell in, and she thought, "This says it all. The sky is falling. A perfect metaphor for my life!"

She eventually worked her way up in market research, ending up in a job as marketing and communications director at *Fortune* magazine, where she was employed from 1988 to 1997. (She also remarried and had two more children, a second daughter who is now attending Brown University, and a son who is in high school.)

Once, while she was at *Fortune*, the magazine got a new managing editor, and Gaines-Ross had to put out a promotional piece about him. The person in charge of the material said it had been checked thoroughly for typos, so out it went, to more than one thousand clients and media people—with a typo on the first page! Gaines-Ross had to go in and tell the editor.

"My first thought was, this is horrible! I was incredibly ashamed of what had happened. But then I thought, 'This is not the end of the world. There is life and death, and my children, and there's this. There's no comparison.' I don't know if I could've come back to work the next day if I hadn't had that perspective."

Extrapolate this story into all the other kinds of things that can go wrong in an organization—corrupt leadership, treacherous colleagues, product failures, lawsuits, loss of customers or clients, harassment, layoffs—and imagine how useful an ability to put things in perspective can be.

Margaret Moers Wenig, the former congregational rabbi, also discovered that motherhood made her much more tolerant of others' failings, including her own. Several years ago, when she was pregnant for the second time, she was extremely anxious and fearful that somehow the baby would be born with birth defects. One night she had a dream in which the baby was deformed. The child then spoke to her: "I love you anyway, Mommy."

"My fears were about failing as a parent, and in the dream she was accepting me," Wenig explained. "She was saying it's all right, Mommy, I love you unconditionally. After that dream, my fear went away completely."

Children also make it easier to forgive one's parents. Wenig confided that before she had children, she had mentioned to her father that a classmate was planning to see a psychiatrist. His comment was "If you ever see a psychiatrist, don't blame me, I did the best I could." At the time, she thought he was trying to evade any responsibility for whatever problems she might have. After she had her own family, and could consider his remark in a new light, she found it very liberating. Whatever their failings, she realized, parents by and large do try to do the best they can. Not one of us is perfect. And our strengths are not cancelled out by our weaknesses.

"This has very much affected the way I write eulogies," says Wenig. "I usually speak about the person's weaknesses as well as his strengths. The one doesn't cancel out the other. In fact a person's weaknesses and strengths are often flip sides of the same coin.

"Being a parent is a very humbling thing. You make mistakes all the time. Years later, your child will tell you about something you did that had a searing effect, and you don't even remember it. Or things can go wrong even if you did everything right. Things are not always under your control. The experience has made me much more forgiving of other people's weaknesses. When you become a parent, an involved parent, you really understand that nobody's perfect."

Many mothers learn that lesson. Would that the rest of the world could accept it about mothers!

The Power of Authenticity

Perhaps the most valuable perspective that children can give you is an unclouded view of yourself. Not perfect, humbling, but in the end, *real*. Numerous mothers discover that after their children are born they are finally able to say, "That's it! This is what I really value, this is who I am, and I'm done trying to be someone I'm not!"

This epiphany occurs most often to women who work in male-dominated institutions. Being a female executive in much of corporate America means that you are still something of an outsider. When you're an outsider you can do one of two things: take on the protective coloration of the dominant culture (i.e., wear tailored suits, use sports metaphors, put work above everything else in life) or acknowledge that you are different and proud of it. When women choose the latter, they often discover the paradox: By being themselves, and asserting their own priorities, they gain more power and respect than they had when they were trying to conform to norms that didn't feel authentic.

Shaunna Sowell of Texas Instruments, an engineer in her late forties, describes how this can happen:

> Corporate America is a white male majority culture. When you come into such a culture it already has its template for success. Had I chosen to say that my definition of success was the same as that of my male peers, I would have been a complete failure. My definition of success included being a good mom, a good friend, a good daughter, a spiritually healthy person. I was married for seventeen years

but, for the past eight years I've been single, raising children. Most of my peers have stay-at-home spouses, and are able to be married to their jobs. If I had tried to do the same, I would have failed in every other part of my life. So, my definition of success did not include climbing up the corporate ladder. If someone called a 6:00 P.M. meeting, I had to say, "I have to leave at 5:45," and be comfortable with that. This was being authentic, and you only get the guts to do that by being very clear about your own definition of success.

As it turned out, I earned respect for having that clarity. That ability to be authentic, to be true to your own values, is not seen as frequently as conforming behavior. So it was viewed as courageous— though the irony is that the easiest thing to be is yourself. Trying to conform to a model that is not who you are is very difficult.

The difficulty of maintaining an inauthentic persona helps explain why so many highly educated professional women decide to chuck it, and leave their jobs altogether. On top of the grueling, unpredictable hours demanded by most high-paying jobs, they are asked to be some-one they are not, and simply can't keep up the pretense. This is what happened to Tracy Delgado, a former trial attorney who is now a stay-at-home mother and a member of the national support group Mothers and More. In the early stages of her career, as she gained responsibility, Delgado modeled her management style and behavior on her fellow attorneys, the vast majority of whom were men. Both the men and the women in her field were aggressive and gruff, they used profanity to emphasize points, and took hard-line stances on every issue, posturing at every opportunity.

As she moved up the ladder at her firm, Delgado became more and more unhappy in her work, feeling that she was playing a role that didn't fit her true nature. She and her husband joked when she occasionally used her lawyer voice at home. Eventually, after they had a family, she quit the firm.

Now, as a stay-at-home mother, Delgado's swearing is limited to *fiddlesticks*. She has more patience than she ever thought possible and has found that she takes a hard line only on the most important issues. This change feels much more authentic, and she believes that she is just beginning to find her true self. As she put it, she has finally found the confidence to pull off being just herself.

She has also noticed a curious thing. Her new style is much more effective than her previous one. Among other things, she has gotten much better customer service from utility companies by being polite and saying please and thank you—just as she is teaching her children to do—than by pulling out her lawyer voice and trying to intimidate. This discovery has reminded her of the female partner in a prestigious southern law firm whom she occasionally ran into while working on a national product liability litigation.

At the time the woman had seemed an anomaly. She was soft-spoken, never interrupted other attorneys, and the strongest language she ever used was "my foot!" Delgado had assumed that her success was due to her connections, and that her southern-belle manner was an old-fashioned sellout. In retrospect, she wishes she had taken a closer look at the woman and perhaps seen her as a mentor; as one of the truly self-confident and authentic female leaders out there. Like Shaunna Sowell, Delgado now speculates that to be truly successful, you have to be true to your own personal style and beliefs.

CHAPTER 12

Playing Fair

Ruth Messinger, former Manhattan borough president, once told a reporter that, "Everything I needed to learn about politics I mastered by being a mother to my three children." Among the thousands of lessons she learned, she said, being fair was one of the most important.

Messenger's fairness formula: If you have two children arguing over a single remaining cookie, you give one child responsibility for breaking the cookie in two, and the other child the right to choose first.

As anyone who has ever doled out unequal portions of birthday cake can tell you, children are hard-wired for fairness. This probably has evolutionary origins in sibling rivalry, and the bad old days when parental partiality could be fatal to the less-favored child. (I never understood the truly frightening aspect of parental partiality until I visited the Galapagos Islands, and observed the parenting practices of the blue-footed booby. This gimlet-eyed bird hatches two eggs, observes which of the newborn chicks is the sturdiest and most likely to survive, then boots the other out of the nest to die. It was just a spare.)

Small children view any trace of parental favoritism with the same panic that must be felt by the luckless booby chick. Every parent has heard the anguished cries: "Her piece is bigger than mine!" "I want one just like Johnny's!" "You love him better than me!" Unfairness can feel like a matter of life and death and, at one time, it probably was. That's why conscientious parents try very hard not to show any favoritism, even if they secretly feel it.

Barbara Mossberg, now a dean at California State University at Monterey Bay, has said that she learned, as the parent of a six-year-old and a sixteen-year-old, that everyone's voice had to be equally heard and everyone had to get a turn, despite the discrepancy in maturity, in making such family decisions as what to do about dinner. Anyone in authority, from a parent to a national leader, must play the unique role of being on everyone's side, according to Mossberg, citing Meryl Streep's character in the film *The River Wild*. When accused of favoring one child over another, she said "I am not on anybody's side. I'm a mother. I'm on *everybody's* side."[1]

Children's passion for equal treatment may be genetic, as many parents suspect. Researchers have recently found that capuchin monkeys have a sense of fairness, suggesting that human demands to be treated fairly go back into the evolutionary past of all social primates. Drs. Sarah F. Brosnan and Frans B. M. De Waal of Yerkes National Primate Research Center at Emory University trained pairs of monkeys to trade a pebble for a slice of cucumber. When one suddenly got a grape in return for her pebble, and her neighbor got the less desirable cucumber, the shortchanged monkey would angrily slam her pebble down on the floor, or refuse to eat the cucumber. Forty percent of the angry primates stopped trading altogether. When one monkey in each pair got a grape for nothing, the other monkeys went ballistic. Some threw cucumbers and pebbles out of their cages, and eighty percent stopped trading. Their outrage over being treated unfairly was greater than their own self-interest in getting at least a piece of cucumber.[2]

The monkeys' behavior is not all that different from our own, as reflected in a well-known experiment in behavioral economics called the *ultimatum game*. One person is given a sum of money, say one hundred dollars, and asked to divide it (50-50, 60-40, 70-30, or however).

A second person has a choice: He can take the percentage that's offered to him, or reject the offer altogether. If he rejects the offer, both players walk away with nothing.

This procedure is obviously not fair, but it does offer both parties something, even if the split is 99-1. Yet lowball offers are almost always rejected. Like capuchin monkeys, people would rather have nothing than see someone get away with an unfair share. In practice, the split in the ultimatum game is usually fairly equitable, say 60-40, to ensure that it's accepted.

The capacity for outrage over unfairness may lie dormant in adult humans for long periods, but when a generalized feeling of unfairness breaks out, watch out. This is the emotional fuel for all reform movements, insurrections, and revolutions. Leaders ignore at their peril the deep and apparently innate demand for fairness. As St. Augustine noted long ago, even a band of robbers has to be fair with one other.

In 2003, we were treated to three good examples of what can happen to a leader when people believe that they have been given short shrift, or that someone else has gotten away with an unfair deal. The most recent was the sudden and spectacular fall of Richard Grasso, who lost his job as head of the New York Stock Exchange, not for any malfeasance, but for being paid too much. Unlike heart-melting movie stars, or athletes who perform brilliantly, or risk-takers who build major corporations, Grasso did nothing in particular to earn his unimaginable pay package—$139.5 million for an essentially bureaucratic job. He was like the monkey who undeservedly got a grape. When his pay was revealed, sheer public outrage forced him out of his job.

Grasso wasn't the only CEO to run afoul of the fairness gene in 2003. Early the same year, American Airlines was teetering on the edge of bankruptcy. The pilots, mechanics, and flight attendants had just agreed to hefty wage and benefit concessions in order to save the company when their unions found out that top management had secretly awarded themselves huge cash bonuses, not to mention a $41 million trust fund to protect their pensions in case the company did go under. To make matters worse, when news of the lavish perks came out, an American spokesman told a reporter that union leaders had known about the perks all along but hadn't told their members. Outraged, the employees' representatives moved to take back their concessions and demanded blood. Within days, the chairman and chief executive of American, Donald J. Carty, was forced to resign. The airline did not disclose his termination package.

The same fate befell another top manager who failed to heed what every mother knows: treat all the kids fairly. This story began with revelations that a young reporter at The New York Times had falsified many of the articles carrying his byline. Jayson Blair had filed his fictions ostensibly from all over the country, but he had actually never left his neighborhood. His stories were full of made-up anonymous quotes, faked interviews, stolen stories from other newspapers. All in all, he had broken virtually all the rules of journalism.

As the details of Blair's behavior emerged, it came out that Blair's shortcomings had been overlooked by a couple of top editors, including executive editor Howell Raines, despite warnings by other editors that the twenty-seven-year-old was not equipped to handle the challenging national assignments he was being given. Raines later admitted that if Blair, who is black, had been white, he might have paid more attention to the flashing red lights. But, as a white southerner who was committed to the cause of racial equality, he had ignored the warnings.

Among other things, Raines had never asked Blair to name his sources for some of his more sensational scoops. In sharp contrast, Raines had demanded that the talented business writer Gretchen Morgenson reveal her sources for a breakthrough story on Enron's misdeeds. When the veteran reporter demurred, on the grounds that she had promised confidentiality in order to get the goods, Raines killed her article. The blatant discrepancy did not go unnoticed, particularly among the Times's female reporters.

Gradually, it emerged that the Blair episode was simply the most egregious example of the partiality Raines had shown toward a few reporters all through his career. Years earlier, while head of the paper's Washington bureau, Raines had a habit of calling his favorites into his office toward the end of the day, where they would all sit and drink and have a jolly time, while the rest of the newsroom sat outside and seethed. The late Michael Kelly, who was one of Raines's golden boys, told a friend that while it was wonderful being in that inner circle, it also made him uncomfortable. Kelly worried how the other reporters must feel being so ostentatiously excluded from the boss's little club.

Well, now we know how they felt. Bad and mad. A few weeks after the Blair debacle, someone leaked the fact that another of Raines' fair-haired boys, fellow southerner Rick Bragg, used another reporter, or stringer, to report a story that carried his byline. Bragg had apparently flown into a city to file a story he had written on the plane. His colorful prose made it sound like he was right there on the scene, when all he had really seen was the airport. With that revelation, the *Times*'s newsroom broke out into open revolt. The staff's pent-up anger spilled over onto the Web for all the world to read. The extraordinary spectacle of rank-and-file reporters openly challenging their top editor was described by *The Washington Post* as "akin to soldiers bouncing turnips off the visor of a general."

In fact, it was more like children denouncing a parent for unfairly favoring some kids over others. By failing to treat the *Times*'s talented reporters fairly, Raines had struck a raw nerve, and now had to pay the price for the primal rage he had engendered. A few weeks after the Blair episode came to light, Raines and national editor Gerald Boyd were asked to resign.

At the height of the furor at the paper, I remembered what one friend had told me about her family. Growing up, she had been her mother's favorite but, like Michael Kelly, she had worried about the discrepancy between the way she and her older sister were treated. Her sister was punished for behavior that she got away with, and harshly criticized for failings my friend knew were hers as well. Instead of feeling good about all this, she felt uneasy and vulnerable. Her thinking was, "If that can happen to my sister, it can happen to me." And, on top of everything else, of course, her sister bitterly resented her.

Children and employees alike absorb everything, especially the way you treat others. If you are not impartial and fair even your favorites will suffer, and you, of course, could even lose your job.

Treating people fairly, however, doesn't mean you have to treat them equally. People's different abilities and experience levels require different treatment. As psychologist Marian Ruderman put it, "When my infant son still had a bottle, my three-year-old daughter had a cup; because a three-year-old doesn't need a bottle anymore. That brought home to me the realization that when an employee says why haven't you given me the same treatment or opportunity as someone else, and that someone else is a person who's been there five years longer, I can explain that you have to create opportunities for people that are appropriate to their level. It's okay to treat people differently. Fairness does not mean identical treatment. Sometimes, it is like giving every child an equal piece of cake. But sometimes it isn't, like the bottle and the cup."

The key is make certain that differentials in salaries, benefits, and perks are open and transparent and based on objective criteria. People can accept inequality if they are persuaded that those who are better treated really are in some way their betters: more experienced, higher-performing individuals who seem to have truly earned their promotions, bonuses and stock options, bigger offices, and the rest. If this isn't clear, there'll be trouble.

A lack of clarity about rewards was the problem at Fannie Mae when Jamie Gorelick first arrived as vice chair. As she explains it, the organization had a fairly mysterious method by which people moved into the upper ranks. There was no clear meritocracy. No one knew exactly what it took to rise. There was no objective criteria for promotion, no explanation for decisions on compensation, no *process*. The system was potentially unfair. As a result, morale was being undermined.

Gorelick, the mother of two children, could see the problem for what it was. "It was just like at home," she said. " 'Why did Dan get that and I didn't?' 'Why do you always pick on me and not Dan?' 'Why do I always get blamed?' The situation was creating sucking-up behavior on the one hand, and demoralizing people on the other.

"You can go too far, and create too many rules and get too bureaucratic," she continued, "but you do need clear rules giving people re-sponsibility and authority if you want to create a sense of fairness. An organization is just like a household in this respect. In business senior management loves to get in a closed room and move all these little boxes around. But it's bad management. I set up a more open system at Fannie Mae."

As noted, people can accept a lesser status if they can be convinced that the more fortunate are more deserving or are in another category altogether. This helps explain why so many women still swallow a great deal of economic and social inequality. They look around and compare their lot with that of other women, and not with that of com-parable men. This may be beginning to change. Ruth Harkin of United Technologies told me that the women in her office in Washing-ton, D.C. are bringing up the fairness issue quite a bit. "They look around, and compare themselves to others, and see that they may not have the same salary or arrangement as many of the men. When they complain, I say, 'But this is the deal you negotiated.' That's a man thing—the deal you negotiated. But the women will say, 'But it's not *fair*! I'm doing the same work for much less money!' "

Women need to learn to ask what men as well as women are get-ting, in all aspects of life, and settle for nothing less. I bring this up be-cause I made the same mistake as the women at United Technologies in my first job as a writer. I was hired by *Newsweek* in 1971 to become one of the magazines first women writers since World War II. I knew as much as Snow White about how to negotiate compensation, and dur-ing my interviews I timidly asked for $15,000 a year—$1,000 more than I had been making in my previous job as a researcher at *Fortune* magazine. Needless to say, the editors thought I was a splendid bar-gain, and I was hired right away.

I hadn't been in my new office more than a few days when I discov-ered that the man I had replaced had been earning a $26,000 salary for the exact same job. To say I thought this was unfair was putting it mildly. I bided my time and after a couple of months I requested a meeting with Lester Bernstein, the managing editor. I explained why I thought I deserved a raise. He readily agreed. I'll never forget what he said next.

"We are so happy," he smiled, "that this experiment has worked."

The experiment was hiring a woman writer! Forget Jane Austen, George Eliot, Virginia Woolf. A female writer for a weekly news magazine was considered a radical experiment thirty years ago. The funny part is, I was deeply grateful for my raise—to $17,000—and convinced that my bosses were generous, fair-minded men.

CHAPTER 13

The Future Matters

A friend once told me that the best thing about having children was that she was always looking forward to something: the next birthday, Halloween, the end of the science project. . . . This is a special source of joy for older parents, for just at a time when the past might begin to outweigh the future, along comes someone who is all anticipation. I still can't get over the fact that my son will be a member of the college class of '07. His future, stretching out far beyond my own, gives me an exciting, long-term perspective on life.

Children take us back as well as forward, to the leisurely time horizons of an earlier period, when people could and did plan for posterity. At Blenheim and other great English estates, the grand landscapes were planted to come to maturity decades after their original owners had passed from the scene. Parents are like those grandees, imagining what they have seeded coming into its own long after they are gone. And children are like those landscapes, created for posterity.

This long-term outlook can be the best vantage point in business. Gerry Laybourne claims that when she sees women looking at a big problem in business, "I rarely see them looking at the short-term solution, and that may relate to the mothering experience. As a mother you're not just trying to get your kid through the terrible twos or the troublesome threes; you're trying to set the stage for a whole lifetime. You're trying to get them through school, expose them to the influences that will give them a good start. . . . You're thinking about the end result that you're building towards. This is a very healthy optic, rather than how can you screw another nickel out of this year."

A concern with posterity can also shade into a concern for the environment. According to Canadian environmentalist David Suzuki, a professor of zoology at the University of British Columbia, women are the most committed environmentalists. "If you look at people who start environmental organizations, who become often the leaders, but also the workhorses, invariably they are women," he once told a reporter. When asked why this was so, he replied, "Women think about children, and they think about the future."[1]

One of the worrisome trends in the industrialized world is that fewer and fewer adults have any contact with children. Of the 100 million households in the U.S., only one-quarter consist of couples with children. And relatively few business or political leaders, including many highly successful women, have had much day-to-day exposure to children. Could this disconnect from the future help explain why so many companies have been taken over by a there's-no-tomorrow mentality? Why have the *apres moi, le deluge* ethics of Enron, Arthur Andersen, WorldCom, and so many firms on Wall Street become so common? It's much easier to believe there's no tomorrow if children don't play a part in your life. And it's much harder to think that today is all that matters when you're trying to create a world your children can inherit.

Whatever we invest in our children's future, they repay with interest. Shirley Kenny says that, whenever she gives a speech, she is invariably introduced as someone who has produced five books and five children. "I never admit it to those audiences," she told me, "but I've learned far more from my children than I have from my books. By the time a book is published, the author has learned everything she can from it. But you never stop putting all you have into your kids, and you never stop learning from them."

One of the most distressing issues we face in the future is the proliferation of weapons of mass destruction. In 2003 I was privy to an online discussion of this issue among national security experts, and one man declared flatly that it was ultimately futile to try to prevent proliferation, considering how easy it is for independent individuals to produce biological, chemical, nuclear, and other WMDs.

One of those responding to this paralyzing comment was Valerie Hudson, a political scientist who also happens to be the mother of six children, ages one to nineteen.

"I find myself using my experiences as a mother to process some of these timeless questions," she emailed. "With all these kids, entropy threatens my home every minute of the day. Do I try to stem it? You bet. Do I think I am going to win? Nope. Do I think life would be better if I quit trying? Absolutely not.

"The most important things in life are the most futile, like trying to keep our kids safe from the dangers of the world. Our measure is whether we press on in the face of that futility. Our efforts will not alter the big picture, but they can buy time and avert disaster in specific cases. And we will be judged for those efforts . . ."

Thank you, Valerie! This is timeless wisdom, going all the way back to the Greek myth of Sisyphus, the hero condemned for all of eternity to roll a boulder up a hill, only to have it roll back down every time it almost reaches the top. A sober metaphor for life. And a hopeful statement that life is worth the effort.

A mother's work is never done. But that doesn't mean you don't do it.

CHAPTER 14

Where We Stand Now: The Executive Gender Gap

We recognize women's "rights." But we ignore women's *strengths.*

—Management expert Tom Peters

The thesis of this book is that many women—and men—who have been active, conscientious parents are superbly well equipped to deal with the complexities, irrationalities, and sheer maddening *messiness* of human affairs. People who have taken their child-rearing responsibilities seriously are not likely to be fazed by the crises and the capriciousness of public life or life in the corporation. Contrary to myth, the hand that rocks the cradle has never ruled the world, but maybe it's time it did. We could hardly do worse.[1]

This may sound controversial, but there is actually more agreement on this than is apparent on the surface. Numerous surveys have found that both men and women agree that the most effective modern managerial techniques include the very same skills that mothers and fathers say they learn from their children: the ability to manage emotional relationships; to articulate a compelling shared vision; to listen to others; to practice a respectful, nonegotistical leadership style.

What we might call the *enlightened parent* model of leadership has become the most fashionable approach to management. In a 1996 study of male and female executives in Great Britain, for example, both the men and the women reported that they practiced a democratic style of management, emphasizing people skills and developing talent. Only 19 percent said they led from the top or decisively directed subordinates. (The author of this study speculated that a higher percentage of people might in fact be "leading from the top," but didn't want to admit it.)[2] Similarly, Susan Vinnicombe, director of the Center for Developing Women Business Leaders at the Cranfield University School of Management in England, says that managers today tend to "describe themselves in terms that fit with the prevailing rhetoric of good management practice, now strongly associated with a consultative style and a high level of interpersonal skills."[3]

The growing acceptance of leadership that stresses interpersonal skills, empowerment of others, and a cooperative style is based on one simple fact: It works. Study after study has revealed that managers who practice this style are judged more effective. Interestingly, these managers tend to be women.

When executives are rated by their peers, underlings, and bosses, women score higher than men. The gender differences are often small, and men are sometimes rated higher in such crucial areas as technical analysis and strategic thinking. But, for the most part, female executives are judged more effective than their male counterparts.

Some of these findings, summarized in a special report in 2000 by *BusinessWeek*, are particularly powerful because the researchers were not looking for gender differences. They accidentally stumbled on the executive gender gap while compiling and analyzing hundreds of routine performance evaluations. The participants had no idea that their judgments would end up as part of a study on gender, and the researchers themselves were startled by the results.

In one case, when 425 high-level executives were evaluated by about twenty-five colleagues each, women won higher ratings on forty-two of the fifty-two skills measured. "Women are scoring higher on almost everything we look at," commented Shirley Ross, an industrial psychologist who helped oversee this study. In another study, conducted by Janet Irwin, a California management consultant, women ranked higher than men on twenty-eight of thirty-one measures. Defying stereotypes, women outperformed men in many intellectual areas, including recognizing trends and generating new ideas and acting on them. Several other studies showed similar patterns, including one by Personnel Decisions International, a consulting firm in Minneapolis that looked at a huge sample of 58,000 managers and found that women outranked men in twenty of twenty-three areas.[4]

Again and again, the studies refer to women being more focused on results than their male colleagues, and much less interested in protecting their turf. (As an example, one female vice president of engineering at Apple Computer startled her male peers by volunteering to shift dozens of employees out of her division because she felt they would fit better in a different department. She explained "It's not the size of your organization that counts; it's the size of the results.")[5]

These studies obviously have to be taken with a grain of salt. They may inflate minor differences, or simply reflect the fact that a disproportionate number of executive women work in human resources, which requires greater interpersonal skills than other management positions. Robert Kabacoff of Management Research Group in Portland, Maine, says that his firm, after controlling for differences in men's and women's corporate positions, has found no evidence that women are more democratic as leaders and no strong evidence that women executives have greater emotional intelligence.[6]

Kabacoff has found evidence of gender differences in management style, however, with women superior to men on some measures and men superior in others. Crossculturally, women in leadership are more focused on delivering results, and women do bring greater excitement and enthusiasm to their work, giving them an edge in the ability to motivate people. Men, on the other hand, seem to excel at strategic planning and are likely to be more innovative; advantages, Kabacoff speculates, that may stem from the fact that women still feel less secure in organizations and are therefore less likely to take risks.

The Myers Briggs Type Indicator, which defines sixteen different personality types based on Jungian psychology, also reveals gender differences, with male managers consistently coming out as traditionalists and female managers emerging as significantly more initutive, and superior as catalysts and motivators.

Whatever their origins, gender differences and a wide range of strengths are obviously a good thing for organizations. A recent study by Catalyst found that major companies with more women in senior management perform better financially than companies with proportionately fewer women at the top. Clearly, gender diversity and superior financial performance were related (although this link doesn't prove that one *causes* the other). Because men outnumber and outrank women in most workplaces, that would argue for promoting more women or persuading men to vary their style. And sure enough, flourishing consulting businesses have sprung up to advise male executives to be more like women—or, if you prefer, more like good parents.[7]

London-based management consultant James R. Traeger, for example, runs a three-month seminar for men to improve their abilities to communicate, listen to others, build teams, and develop flexibility. "If you were to ask which of these qualities men had an upper hand at," says Traeger, "the answer would be none."[8]

Traeger's program, like Bill Ury's at Harvard, explicitly tries to convince male managers that the aggressive, controlling, and competitive executive is the opposite of a good manager. The tips he offers men will by now sound familiar.

*   Don't overcontrol or micromanage. Rigid, bossy bosses are bad bosses. Let go.

* Empower your employees to design their own jobs. Be open to others' suggestions, and be willing to change when the consensus goes against you.
* Admit you don't know everything.
* Treat each employee as an individual, and build on their particular strengths.
* Learn to listen. You can't solve all of your problems, but your staff probably can.

Tom Peters, the wildly successful management writer and speaker, unabashedly links the most effective leadership styles to women. In 1990, Peters wrote that, "There is little disagreement about what businesses must become: less hierarchical, more flexible and team-oriented, faster and more fluid. In my opinion, one group of people has an enormous advantage in realizing this necessary new vision: women."[9]

I heard Peters speak at a conference of executive women sponsored by Accenture in the late 1990s, and he repeated his view that women have exactly what it takes to be leaders in the twenty-first century, especially in the service and experience sectors of the economy (health, travel, entertainment, etc.) which are increasingly more important than the older, male-dominated extractive and goods-manufacturing sectors. "Women should rule the roost; everything tells me that," he told his female audience. "The enormous social good of women's increased power is clear . . . this is bigger than the Internet."

By 2003, Peters, who gives some eighty speeches a year, was preaching this message at the top of his lungs. In his latest book, *Re-Imagine!* he declared himself a "difference feminist," aligned with those who believe that women are more empathetic, patient, and sensitive than men, less obsessed with rank, better at reading nonverbal cues, doing and thinking several things at once, negotiating, communicating, and cooperating. Calling women "a woefully untapped source of effective leaders," he urged his business readers to turn their "whole-damn-enterprise Upside Down Right Now!—to embrace the Staggeringly High-Potential Women's Thing."[10]

Peters' casting call for female leadership is only one part of a much deeper cultural shift. Creeping into the popular descriptions of the good leader are images that closely resemble the good mother: someone with a calm, wise head, a firm but fair hand, an ear that listens, and a heart that feels your pain. In poll after poll, people repeatedly indicate that what they want is "kinder, gentler" and "compassionate" as well as strong leadership. Management experts extol the efficacy of "benevolent" leaders who manage relationships rather than control from the top down. Almost imperceptibly, the concept of legitimate authority is shifting and broadening to include attributes of the mother as well as the father. Referring to this development, and to the widespread disillusionment with traditional male-dominated institutions, Carol Gilligan, a developmental psychologist now at New York University, argues that "We might be close to a time similar to the Reformation, where the fundamental structure of authority is about to change."[11]

The problem, of course, is that the still overwhelmingly male power structure is largely ignoring the shifting sands. A huge proportion of leaders, particularly in corporations and at the highest levels of government, don't practice what Peters, Ury, and other management experts preach. As the Wellesley report on female leadership delicately put it, "The rise in popularity of a participatory style of leadership does not necessarily mean that actual workplace practices have changed."[12] To a very large degree, they haven't.

On the commanding heights of political and economic power a patriarchal ideal of authority still prevails. In 2000, only two of the 500 largest companies had female CEOs; of the top 1000 companies, only six, or roughly one-half of 1 percent, were headed by a woman. As Margaret Heffernan, a former CEO of CMGI, notes, "Most men and women in business have never *seen* a female CEO—much less worked with one." Only sixty-three, or 2.5 percent, of the top 2,500 earners at the Fortune 500 companies were women. In the immortal words of Heffernan, who has run five businesses, ". . . women still get screwed in the world of business."[13]

In government, from the Pacific to the Potomac, from the Terminator governor to the president in the flight suit, our leaders embody a macho, rather than maternal, image of power, an image given a brand-new lease on life after the frightening attacks on September 11, 2001. The personification of the tough-guy leader is secretary of defense Donald Rumsfeld, who has bullied four-star generals and combat officers as if his main mission were to prove that war begins at home. At one point, the secretary kept a glass bowl in his office. He told visitors that every time he said something nice about someone, a coin was put in the bowl. He then pointed out that the bowl was almost always empty.

Not surprisingly, Rumsfeld was said to be detested by many members of the uniformed military. One senior general, when asked if he liked Rumsfeld, replied, " 'Like' is such a strong word."

Sheer sexism also plays a part in all this. Robert Kabacoff and Helen Peters completed a study in 2002 on how CEOs and corporate boards view upper management and found clear evidence of a bias against women. Male CEOs and senior vice presidents got high marks when they were forceful and assertive, and lower scores when they were empathic and cooperative, indicating that male executives still cling to the command and control model of leadership. But when female CEOs exhibited these so-called masculine traits they were downgraded. Women were looked upon more favorably when they were feminine and cooperative, but those traits were not as highly valued. In other words, the women couldn't win however they behaved. They could be nice and looked down on or strong and disliked. Kabacoff concluded that, at the highest levels, male bosses are still evaluating people in the most stereotypical ways. As the report on this research put it, "Outdated stereotypes about how men and women ought to behave still appear to play a part in today's corporate reality."[14]

The negative cumulative effects of even the smallest biases can be severe. Research shows that a tiny bias in favor of men, accounting for only 1 percent of the variability in promotions, run through a series of promotions in an eight-level hierarchy, can result in a top level that is 65 percent male.[15]

Moreover, the men at the top of organizations are still evaluating leadership itself in the most stereotypical ways. Their ideas of what it takes to be an effective leader have hardly changed since Alexander the Great. There is still a yearning in the corporate world, as in the political realm, for the charismatic savior who can come in, take charge, and whip everything and everybody into shape. This glorification of the charismatic leader persists in the face of ample evidence that the man on the white horse often has feet of clay.

Numerous recent studies, for example, have found little or no correlation between a company's financial performance and its CEO's charisma quotient. Harvard Business School professor Rakesh Khurana, in his book *Searching for a Corporate Savior: The Irrational Quest for Charasmatic CEOs*, argues that 30 to 50 percent of a company's performance depends on the industry it is in, while another 20 percent depends on the state of the economy. Neither factor is under the control of a CEO. After taking into account all other variables—the quality of its product, employee performance and productivity, and so on, Khurana finds that charisma cannot be a large factor in a company's success or failure.[16]

Similarly, Jim Collins, author of the best seller *Good to Great* and one of the most popular management thinkers today, has examined the leadership of the best companies in the United States over the last several decades. He found that those companies that moved from a so-so to an outstanding performance (as measured by the long-term performance of the stock) were not led by charismatic attention-getters but by people he calls "plow horses not show horses." Often they are executives who've been with the company a long time, rather than high-priced superstars brought in from outside to save the day. They succeed because they have a deep understanding of their business and respect for the skills and experience of their employees.[17]

Collins's job description of the kind of CEO who can take an organization from merely good to great (his so-called Level 5 leaders) might read like this:

"Wanted: People who can relate well to others. Who are grown up and won't jump into the shallow end. Who are responsible and committed to the welfare of the company, not simply to their own personal gain. Who want to build, not just get. Who are determined, strong-willed, and won't give up. Who have personal humility and compelling modesty rather than huge egos."

Doesn't this sound like a help-wanted ad for a good parent?

The fact that the enlightened parent model of leadership has not yet percolated to the top of organizations poses a real dilemma for women, particularly those who know that their own maternal management styles are effective. Should they play that card? Or hold it close to their vest until more people in power get it? This is a high-wire moment, filled with tension, swaying backward as well as forward. To paraphrase Rochelle Sharpe of *BusinessWeek*, women are ready and able to help lead us into the future, but how can they if the powers-that-be are still living in the past?

CHAPTER 15

Hide It or Flaunt It? Is the World Ready for Child-Rearing on a Resume?

In 1997, Barbara Mossberg applied for the position of president of Goddard College in Vermont. When she was asked to write about her most important accomplishments, she responded, "I don't know if one's children can be seen as 'accomplishments,' but certainly I view creating a nurturing structure in which to witness and guide the growth of unique human beings my most important goal to achieve. I don't take credit for my children, but to me they feel like fabulous accomplishments of my life."[1]

Mossberg not only got the job, but her response was posted on the college Web site.

How nice for her, you may be thinking. Maybe this argument works in the sheltered environment of a liberal arts college, or in the social services. But what about out there in the cold, capitalist economy, where bragging about your skills as a mother to a job interviewer could be akin to bragging about your skills at group sex in a Kansas City church group?

"Can you really picture going to an interview for a professional position and telling them that you have 'time management and prioritization' skills because you pick your kids up from school on time?" asks Mary Ann Wiley of Houston. "Or that you have 'project planning and organizing' skills because you planned your kid's birthday party? I can just picture the look of disbelief on the interviewer's face."[2]

Wiley admits she may think this way because she's always worked in male-dominated fields. The trouble is, most of them are.

Virtually all the highly successful mothers I interviewed for this book agreed that being a parent made them more proficient in their professions. But did they dare list child-rearing among their credentials? I have their resumes, and not one did.

Patricia M. Wald is an interesting case in point. Wald spent ten years as a stay-at-home mother of five children after graduating with honors from Yale Law School in 1951. She then went back to work in various part-time capacities, and was assistant attorney general during the Carter administration before being named to the twelve-member Court of Appeals for the District of Columbia, widely regarded as the second most important court in the United States.

Wald's resume does not include any mention of that decade at home, nor does it mention her children. But I happened to see a copy of the resume of her husband, a prominent Washington attorney. On it he listed all five children and their numerous advanced degrees. The proud father, who had not been the family's primary caregiver, was not shy about taking credit for their accomplishments, but the mother who raised them did not.

When I queried roughly one hundred members of Mothers and More, a national support organization, on the resume question, the consensus was the same: better not. These well-educated professional women by and large felt that claiming parenting as a credential on a resume would be career hara-kiri. As one said in an email, "Employers are looking for tangible, related, paid-work experience. I would never mention 'soft skills' in an interview, would you?"

When the question was thrown back at me, and I was asked if I would have put parenting experience on my own resume, say, when applying for a job at the *New York Times*, my answer was an unequivocal no. And how right I was. A few weeks later I was on a panel at Columbia University with Lisa Belkin, a work-family columnist for the paper. She told the audience that Howell Raines, the paper's then-managing editor, had sent out a memo stating that he wanted "unencumbered" reporters, free agents who were ready, willing, and able to jump whenever and wherever they were needed—not a description that fits many mothers. (As noted earlier, one of Raines' "unencumbered" reporters was later discovered to be unencumbered by journalistic ethics as well.)

The fundamental issue, of course, is not resumes, but what we value as a society and how we assess a person's worth. The question is whether we have reached the stage in women's equality where the traditional female work of nurturing and producing the next generation is considered highly skilled labor, as worthy of serious respect as other life accomplishments.

The answer is important to literally millions of women. Old-fashioned housewives may be a thing of the past, but stay-at-home moms (SAHMs), whose principle work is child-rearing, are very *now*. Well-educated women ages thirty to thirty-four are increasingly likely to stay home after their first child's birth, according to the Census Bureau.[3] If the United States mandated paid maternity leaves, like almost every other country in the world, even more mothers of young children would be at least temporarily out of the work place.

Among women in their thirties, the most common occupation by far is full-time housekeeping and child-rearing.[4] In 2002, more than ten million American mothers with children under the age of 18 were not in the labor force—twenty-eight percent of all mothers with children under eighteen.[5] Fully two-thirds of all employed mothers between the ages of twenty-five and forty-four work fewer than forty hours per week, which means that they are not in positions that pay well or lead to higher advancement.

Even very highly educated women are spending years working at home. More than one out of four female MBA graduates have spent time out of the labor force, primarily to care for young children. Of the female business-school graduates from the Harvard classes of 1981, 1986, and 1991, only 38 percent are still working full-time today.[6] The business schools of both Stanford and Harvard have studied this phenomenon, which Sharon Hoffman, the MBA program director at Stanford University, calls "stopping out."

How many of those mothers plan to be unemployed or partially employed for the rest of their work lives? How many are indifferent to their job prospects, earning power, and future economic independence? It is probably safe to assume very few. In the uncertain world we live in, it is no longer unusual for mothers, fathers, or anyone else to embark upon entirely new careers. Child-rearing, full- or part-time, is more than ever before just one among many occupations a person may have in a lifetime. It is time to consider it as such, and not look upon it as a separate sphere that involves no transferable skills or is "only" a labor of love. In my experience, just because you love being a parent, that doesn't mean it doesn't take time, talent, and hard work, or is the only work you could ever love doing.

So, how far are employers from seeing child-rearing as a serious occupation, or a credential that is relevant to other occupations? How hard is it for people who've spent a few years raising children to reenter the work force or be welcomed back on a career track? I only have anecdotal information, but based on my interviews with more than one hundred mothers, I would say that change is in the air, and respect for parents' skills is increasing, particularly as more people with child-rearing experience gain power. But it is going to take a more vigorous push from mothers themselves to make things move faster.

Reports from the Field

One of the more encouraging stories I heard involved a friend in Washington, D.C. Kit Lunney was thirty-nine when she had her only child, after having been deputy attorney general of the state of Maine and a practicing attorney in Portland. She was determined to take motherhood as seriously as anything else she had ever done and, in order to "do it right" by her lights, she switched to a job as general counsel of a small company in order to have more flexible hours.

This arrangement ended after only a few years, when her husband accepted a position with the Federal government in Washington. The family relocated and, suddenly, Kit was in a situation in which she knew almost no one, where her only identity was that of an unemployed wife and mother. Her daughter was now in primary school, and she began to look for a job.

Three years went by, and she still had not found anything suitable. She had virtually given up all hope when one night at a dinner party she found herself seated next to the general counsel of the Commerce Department. At forty-three, he was five years younger than Kit, with a full-time employed wife and two children with whom he was deeply involved.

Kit mentioned that she was looking for a full-time job, explaining that she was an attorney who didn't want to practice law but loved management. Her dinner partner, as luck would have it, loved law but hated management, which was a problem, since he had to manage hundreds of attorneys. He suggested they meet for lunch.

She arrived early for the appointment, bringing with her a file describing all of her recent volunteer projects and an expectation of rejection. She was stuffing pictures of her daughter's soccer teammates into envelopes when he walked in.

"I'm always so impressed how you mothers can work on ten different tracks at once," he commented. "You make *great* managers." This insightful and wonderful man then hired her on the spot.

She became deputy general counsel of the Commerce Department with some 300 attorneys reporting to her. She was expected to sort out their disputes, clarify rules, and settle grievances—a job, she said, that was is exactly like managing a school full of bright, rambunctious children.

We had dinner after her first two weeks, and she was still ecstatic. "I feel like this angel came down and tapped me on the shoulder," she sighed. "I still can't get over it." Since she had started to work full time, her husband had cut back on his extensive travel schedule, and was now spending more time with their daughter. "She thinks she has died and gone to heaven," Kit commented.

A few days after she started at the Commerce Department, Kit was asked to make a decision on whether to allow a talented female attorney, a mother, to switch to a thirty-two-hour week. "My first reaction was 'Don't we have a policy permitting this?' " she said. "We didn't, so my second reaction was 'Of course we let her do it!' Can you imagine the trouble and the expense of replacing an experienced attorney like that?"

Her only complaint, she said, was with the forms she had to fill out for the Federal government.

"I really resented having to put 'unemployed' down for all that time I spent at home."[7]

There is an amazing postscript to this story. A few years later, after the Bush administration came into office, a lawyer who had spent fifteen years as a stay-at-home mother was chatting at a field hockey game with a fellow parent. She told him she was about ready to go back to work, and he said, "Well, we have an opening you'd be perfect for . . ." It was the same job Kit Lunney had held during the Clinton administration, and she got it.[8]

These two women admittedly had good connections which eased their re-entry. What about someone who is really out there on her own, with few contacts, trying to resurrect her career after eighteen years out of the job market? That was the situation copy editor Helen Chongris found herself in midlife. Her story is more typical of the many women who have to convince a skeptical stranger that raising children doesn't cause your brain to atrophy.

Chongris, a graduate of Northwestern University, left a copy-editing job at the *Charlotte Observer* in 1985 to marry a man in New England and start a family. She planned to return to editing soon after her first child was born, but she discovered that newspapers in the Boston area were reluctant to hire someone with family responsibilities. By the time her second child was in preschool she was told that she'd been out of the newsroom three times as long as she'd worked in it (six years versus two), and that she could understand why, with rapidly changing technology, she was old news. One recruiter told her she would be put on the bottom of any applicant list, and another informed her that she was wasting his time and that her clips packet was taking up needed space on his desk.

"It was an all-out shut-out," Chongris told me. She gave up, and started a small business selling needlework supplies.[9]

Years went by, the family moved to north Texas, and her oldest daughter started looking at colleges. Her own "twisted postcollege path" started to haunt her, and she decided to do something about it. She got an interview with the *Dallas Morning News* and reminded an editor that one of her job offers right after college—twenty years earlier—had been from their business copy desk. She hadn't taken that job then, but now she was available and more seasoned with real-world experience.

The interviewer—a woman in her early sixties—was sympathetic. She told Chongris she had guts, and agreed to give her the required editing tests. Her score on the first was the highest since the test had been administered, and she had one of the highest scores ever on the other test. This performance earned her another interview, this time with a male editor.

He asked her, "What have you done in the last eighteen years that could lead me to believe that you can do the kind of juggling copy-editing requires?"

She laughed out loud. She ran through a typical mother's juggling act under pressure: the time she had to pick up one child at school while the other was running a fever and racing to the doctor's office before it closed and then running to the pharmacy to pick up the prescription while calling the plumber on her cell phone and trying to persuade him to wait until she got home.

"I've been working with a sense of urgency all along, and believe me, something clicks and you set your priorities and you get everything done," she told him. "If the only thing holding me back from this job is deadline pressure, then let me assure you I can handle it."

"I really don't think you're speaking to the matter at hand, Helen," he replied.

Three months went by. She hit upon the idea of a transferrable skills resume—taking the general skills she had developed as a mother household manager, and small-business owner, and showing how each applied to the business world. This included things like "how to be a critical thinker," and "never point out a problem without having a solution." [See Appendix] The document got their attention again and she went in for another interview with the boss of the previous editor.

He told her that she might be a good copy editor, and her maternal skills might be transferrable, but the technology had changed so much since the mid-eighties that it didn't matter—she probably couldn't handle the new technology.

She reminded him that she had been helping her children do their assignments on a computer for years, and that she could learn whatever needed to be learned in a short training course.

I asked if the technology was really all that more complicated.

"It's easier!" she exclaimed. "To learn to copyedit on the latest computer programs, all you really need is a day and a half of instruction. They just thought I was a technophobe because of my age."

She was forty-two.

Chongris finally talked the *News* into admitting her into a thirteen-week internship program, so they could see how she functioned in the real world under deadlines. Twice as old as many of the others in the program, she did just fine, and when we spoke she was filling in on a 4:00 P.M. to 1:00 A.M. night shift for a few weeks while the *News* pondered whether to offer her a permanent job. "When they're desperate," she remarked wryly, "they don't think of the ususal objections."

> *I thought I had gone through all the tough stuff, the selective university, the children growing up. (Her son is now a freshman in high school.) I thought any idiot could figure out that I was employable. But it wasn't true. You take one step out of the path, and take a road people aren't comfortable with, and you're back to square one. I had too much scary mommy baggage, and they didn't want to take a chance on me.*
>
> *It might not have been that way had I stayed in Charlotte, where people knew me, but I married someone who wasn't from Charlotte. You can't always marry the perfect person or stay in the perfect place. For years I was living with my own private shame . . . I had started to doubt myself, until I realized that I wasn't alone. There are a lot of high potential women out there who've had a hard time getting back in. It's not just me.*
>
> *"We need to make noise."*

I got two things out of Helen Chongris's story. First, if attitudes are ever going to change women have to be determined to convince others that their different experience is valid. Tom Peters warns that women will never be truly powerful as long as they try to play by the men's rules. We must assert our own strengths, stand up for our own priorities, and eventually make our own rules. So hard, but so true!

Women in Power Can Help

The second message of Chongris's story is that it helps immensely to have a sympathetic woman in power. I have heard my share of stories about unhelpful female bosses, and they are definitely all too common. But I've been persuaded that as more women come into positions of real authority, the more they will alter workplace norms to fit women's lives. As Chongris described her encounters with interviewers, the women "saw me as a glass half full, and the men saw a glass half empty." The women got it and could see the courage and tenacity in the years she had spent as a conscientious mother.

A powerful story about a woman in charge giving another woman a break is recounted in Madeleine Kunin's autobiography, *Living a Political Life.* While governor of Vermont, Kunin was asked to make a choice between two strong candidates for the position of legal counsel to the state's Department of Banking and Insurance. She interviewed both. The first candidate was an energetic young man in his mid-thirties, then working in another area of state government.

"Do you think you could transfer your skills from that department to this?" she asked him.

"No problem. The work is very comparable. I have no doubt that I can do it."

"Even though the fields are different?"

"Yes. I'm a quick study."

The second candidate was a pleasant-looking woman in her forties who had recently completed law school with honors. Kunin noticed a fourteen-year gap between her graduation from Radcliffe and her entry into Georgetown Law School. It turned out that she had married, had two children, and spent several years working at home and in unpaid volunteer activities. "I know this woman," thought the governor. "Her life could have been mine."

(When she herself was thirty, Kunin was sitting one day with a friend in a café near Harvard Square, while their one-year-old babies dozed side by side in their strollers. Between sips of espresso, the two friends wondered whether those "child-fragmented years would spell nothing, like the magnetized alphabet letters stuck helter-skelter on the refrigerator door." If only, Kunin thought years later, someone had tapped her on the shoulder and whispered, "Not to worry, someday you will be governor of Vermont.")

The female job seeker explained that she had worked in a field related to banking and insurance in Washington, but she took great care to specify that the work had not been precisely in the same field. She drew a clear line between what she knew and what she did not. As Kunin put it, "honesty did not permit her to cross it even when what she wanted was just on the other side."

Kunin believes that if she had been a male governor, she would have recognized herself in the young man and hired him. She imagines this governor's reasoning process:

"The woman? Qualified, perhaps, but not enough confidence. I need an aggressive person in this job who can take on the big boys in this business. His resume moves up in a straight line . . . and it shows serious intent, commitment, and ambition. She took time off to have a family. Now I fully understand that. My wife did the same thing. But it slowed her down. She's lost ten years. She'd be well qualified to work somewhere in the department, but not at this level."

What was going through Kunin's mind as she pondered her decision?

She read between the lines of the woman's resume and saw the value of those so-called lost years she had spent as a homemaker. She saw a special kind of ambition in the act of going to law school after raising a family.

"It requires tremendous drive to succeed while meeting the demands of both family and school," Kunin thought. "If she gets this job she will see it as a new beginning, a delayed fulfillment, more motivating perhaps than immediate success would have been for the man. Something tells me that she will give this job her all."

The governor hired the former stay-at-home mom. Within four years, she had become Vermont's commissioner of banking and insurance.[10]

Probably no head of any institution in America has done more to advance women than Princeton University president Shirley M. Tilghman, a molecular biologist. By 2003, after two years as head of the university, Tilghman had appointed women as deans of admission, the college, the Woodrow Wilson School of Public and International Affairs, the school of engineering, and provost, and was calling for an increase in the percentage of women on the faculty, then only 21 percent.

More significant than all the high-profile appointments is the fact that under Tilghman the university became a place where women, and specifically mothers, felt accepted. Marilyn Marks, a former reporter for the *Miami Herald* who had been handling media relations for Princeton, told me a story about her own experience. She had taken the job at the university when her daughter was two, thinking it would be less stressful than daily journalism. She soon discovered that her new hours were just as unpredictable and demanding. Reporters would call her at home while she was preparing dinner, getting her daughter ready for bed, and even after the family was asleep. When another position with more regular hours opened up, as editor of the *Princeton Alumni Weekly*, she applied for it.

At the end of the selection process she had to have an interview with Tilghman. The president didn't make the appointment, which was decided by a group of alumni, but she could have vetoed it. She asked Marks why she wanted to change jobs. After listing her professional reasons, she pointed out that Tilghman herself had once said that when she knew that her children were in good hands, she could concentrate fully on her work, and when she was at home, she could concentrate fully on her family. Marks explained that her current job didn't allow her to do the latter.

Tilghman said she understood perfectly, and Marks got the new job. The point, she told me, is that she felt very comfortable telling the president of the university the truth, and the president understood.

"If she had been someone else, I would never have said anything like that. I would have just mentioned the professional part. But she made me feel like my feelings were perfectly legitimate. I'll never forget that."[11]

This ability to change the conversation and the norms in their organization was a point of pride with many of the women I interviewed. Kit Lunney was delighted to be able to change the work rules at the Justice Department to permit a short work week. Ruth Harkin was proud of introducing flexible schedules for mothers and fathers in

United Technologies' Washington office. Under Cheryl Bachelder's leadership, Kentucky Fried Chicken became much more sensitive to work/family conflicts. Bachelder told me this story with approval: When a junior marketing director at KFC discovered that her annual budget presentation was scheduled at the same time as her mother's seventieth birthday party, she told her boss that she couldn't present her budget on that day. The senior executive in charge said, of course, you shouldn't miss your mother's birthday.

Jamie Gorelick made it her business, when she arrived at Fannie Mae, to assure people that there would be no stigma attached to anyone who took advantage of the company's flexible policies. There was quite an array on the books, but almost no takers. When Gorelick left a few years later, about one-third of the people in the company were on some sort of individualized work schedule: a four-day week, flextime, and so on. Fannie Mae's family-friendly policies had become one of the organization's major attractions as an employer.

Does all this mean that the time is ripe for parents to be more candid about their backgrounds? Some prominent women think so. Madeleine Albright, former secretary of state, never put parenting on her resume, but she recently told a reporter that if successful people who had done a stint as a full-time parent did add that to their curriculum vita it could go a long way toward challenging negative stereotypes.[12]

When university president Shirley Strum Kenny half-jokingly declared, in a humorous essay in *The New York Times*, that being a parent was the best career preparation in the world, she was inundated with enthusiastic letters. She told me that nothing she had ever written had received such a response.

"I still meet people, men and women, who have clipped and saved the article," said Kenny. "Just recently I met a young single black man, a professional who is helping young kids, who said, 'Oh, *you're* the one who wrote that article!' "

Kenny admitted she would never have dared to publish such a piece when she was younger—much less put *parenthood* on a resume. "I would have been written off as not serious, and probably would not have gotten tenure," she said flatly. But once she was secure professionally, she was free to say what she thought, and everyone loved it.

The Squeaky Wheel Gets the Grease

I also heard stories about less established women who had the courage to lay their maternal cards on the table, including a mother of ten who walked into a retail store in a newly opened mall, and talked an executive there into hiring her as store manager. She persuaded him that anyone who had successfully raised ten kids could manage anything.

Margaret McLaughlin faced the resume dilemma when she started looking for a full-time job in 2001, after eight years out of the paid labor force. She had a PhD in biochemistry from Columbia University and had worked as a science policy analyst for the Congressional Office of Technology Assessment before she stayed at home with her children. Her professional credentials were excellent, but she couldn't figure out how to deal with those years at home. On the one hand, she could just omit that period entirely. However, that would leave a huge time gap, even considering that for four of the eight years she had been a part-time freelancer. On the other hand, she worried that if she put caregiving on her resume, she would risk turning off some prospective employers.

At the time, her husband, who had been laid off, was also job hunting. He showed Margaret's resume to people at the outplacement office where he was getting help, and they were horrified by her solution: a heading of "Full-time Parent, 1994–98." They insisted that this was a terrible mistake. It looked so unprofessional!

McLaughlin remembered that back in the days when she herself had been hiring people, she was always uncomfortable when there was a gap on the resume. She wondered what they'd been doing during those years, and always imagined the worst. Strung out on drugs? Jail? Involuntary commitment? So she went with her gut. She stuck with "Full-time Parent" and listed it on the second page of her CV, under Other Experience. She decided that any employer that had a problem with that was probably not someone she would want to work for anyway.

Some interviewers noticed the item and commented on it, mostly women who had spent time caring for small children themselves. She'll never know whether anyone disliked it enough to decide not to interview or hire her. But so what? Of the thirty companies that received her resume, seven called her in for an interview, and four offered her a job.[13]

I also heard a fair number of heartening stories from mothers who had negotiated more livable work situations. My favorite, for obvious reasons, was the *BusinessWeek* reporter who called me for comment on an article, and then confided that my book *The Price of Motherhood* had changed her life. She explained that she had a young child, and had always done what her editors had demanded, from traveling at the drop of a hat to working late. She reasoned that no one had forced her to have the baby; it was her choice, and so it was her sole responsibility to handle whatever difficulties or consequences might arise.

After reading the book, she realized that parents have a right to workplace norms that reflect their lives and responsibilities. The next time the magazine asked her to go out of town for a conference, she said, "Okay, I'll be happy to, but I need you to arrange for someone to come in and take care of my child while I'm gone, or I can take her with me and you can pay for a baby-sitter while I'm at meetings and interviews."

Once they had gotten over the shock, the editors said okay, proving once again that if you don't ask, you won't receive.

Hollywood producer Lucy Fisher was able to negotiate an incredible amount of flexibility by being good at what she did and by daring to ask. Fisher, who now runs an independent production company with her husband Douglas Wick, has three daughters: Sarah, sixteen; Julia, thirteen; and Tessa, twelve. When she was expecting Sarah, she was executive vice president in charge of production for Warner Brothers. She had to stay in bed the last three months of her pregnancy, so she started having meetings at her house. This worked so well that after the baby came she asked the company to put in her contract that she could have Fridays off. She got it, thereby becoming a heroine among women in the film business.

Her stories of those years are hilarious. One of the first things she did after the baby arrived was to assign her young male assistant an extra job duty: to signal her when her breast milk was leaking onto her shirt. It was also not uncommon for startled employees to see A-list directors like Steven Spielberg and George Miller walking the halls of Warner's calming her crying infant.

Two more babies followed in fairly quick succession. Fisher says that when she went in to tell her boss that she was pregnant a third time, he just looked at her as if she were crazy, and then slowly put his head down on his desk. After the third arrived, she soldiered on for awhile, but three kids under the age of five were ultimately too much. As she put it succinctly, in terms every mother can understand, "I was having a nervous breakdown." So she went to see Bob Daly, the co-CEO at Warner's, and said "Reduce my salary. I want to go down to three days a week."

Fisher had a lot of movies in the works at the time, and was dealing from strength. (As she put it, when we talked over lunch at the Sony studio in Los Angeles, "I wasn't asking when I was limping.") She had been at the studio for more than a decade, overseeing the production of such films as *The Fugitive*, *The Bridges of Madison County*, and *The Witches of Eastwick*. She was highly regarded for her skills with talent and story. One example of her inventiveness: when the premiere of *The Fugitive*, a film she had been working on for five years, was scheduled on the same night as a kindergarten camping trip, she called the star, Harrison Ford, and asked if he wouldn't mind pretending that *he* couldn't be available that night, and would they please change the date. He made the call, and they did.

Still, she was definitely pushing the envelope in asking for a three-day week. So what happened? Daly told her, "Work your three days. Take full salary and add a year to your contract."

Eventually, the deal was too good to be true. After a few years Daly asked her to go back up to four days a week. She asked him if anyone had been complaining about her performance. "Is Steven Spielberg complaining? Ivan Reitman? Neil Jordan?" she asked, mentioning some of the directors she had worked with. Daly said no. "So, what's the problem?" she wanted to know.

"Well, I have to come to work five days," said her boss.

By this time, Mark Canton, then chairman of Columbia Tristar, was pleading with her to come on over to his group, and she decided to accept the offer. She told Daly that she was leaving because she now had a chance to become co-chair (the boss) of a company and still have a four-day work week. Better yet, she made sure that her new official title was vice chair—not co-chair—of the Columbia TriStar Motion Picture Group (Sony Pictures Entertainment's movie arm). "That way when I had to leave early, I could say 'So what's the big deal? I'm only the vice chairman,' " Fisher explained.

In the next two years, under the co-leadership of this lively, confident, and competent mom, Columbia TriStar broke all industry records for domestic gross revenues and had the highest worldwide gross in history. Among the films she supervised were *Men In Black* and *Jerry Maguire*. Her mommy schedule even helped the studio land Jack Nicholson, the star of *As Good As It Gets*.

The studio was nervous about the film's cost, and was refusing to meet Nicholson's financial demands. So, Fisher, who knew the actor from working with him on previous films, went to his house, and asked what she could do to get him on board. She told him she couldn't get him more money, but she could give him Fridays off. She had Fridays off and so could he. He liked the idea.

She went back to the studio and told them she had gotten him for the money, but they would have to reschedule the shoot. This turned out to be its own nightmare, but they had their star, thanks to a mother's flexible workweek.

Where Parenting Skills Are Most Relevant

Obviously parental skills are more relevant in certain fields than in others. As Fisher's story illustrates, industries that crave creative talent, including film, television, advertising, and many high-tech, high-performance fields, are likely to care less about an employee's gender, family arrangements, or work schedule as long as the job gets done. Shelly Lazarus of Ogilvy & Mather told me that good people can write their own tickets in the advertising business today. "There's a shortage of talent now, and my business is *all* about talent," said Lazarus. "Advertising is an idea-driven business; you can't care who has them. I'll do anything I need to do to get talent! I had a creative director [a man] who lived on a ranch in Penelope, Texas, and worked in New York City. . . . The world works around people who are indispensable. But you do have to know the power you have."

Apparently, talented women in advertising still haven't woken up to the fact that they have that kind of power. According to a 2002 study by *Advertising Age*, men occupied the top five positions, including creative director and associate creative director, by a ratio of 2.77 to 1 in more than two hundred agencies surveyed. The problem is the same old story: the top people on the creative side are required to spend a lot of time traveling on shoots, and mothers can't travel that often. As a result, most commercials are made from a male point of view and inevitably fail to resonate with female customers. For example, one TV ad for an allergy medication portrayed the mother of a twenty-something man as a frumpy old woman. Not surprisingly, women are offended by such ads. An amazing 58 percent of women say they are annoyed by advertising pitches aimed at them.[14] Ultimately advertising agencies have to get the message to get more mothers on the job—which may be one of the reasons Young and Rubicam recently selected Ann Fudge, an experienced executive and a mother, as its new CEO.

Education, where inspiring, guiding, and mentoring *is* the job, and the caring professions, including medicine, the social services, counseling, and the ministry are likely to be more congenial to caregivers than fields in which their skills are beside the point. (Construction work, auto mechanics, pure scientific research, modelling, and movie stardom come to mind).

And what about all the jobs in sales and marketing, which require skills of persistence, persuasion, and negotiation? What about financial advisory services, insurance, travel and hospitality, automobiles, and real estate, where women make up a huge percentage of the customers? The only one of these industries that actively recruits mothers is real estate.

(Several years ago I saw an ad for real estate salespeople showing a woman smiling confidently with her briefcase over her shoulder. "Raising a family isn't just a wonderful accomplishment," the ad declared. "it's perfect training. To raise a family, you must care about people, be organized, and know financial planning. It's perfect training for a successful career in real estate.")

The ministry is slowly being transformed by the mothers in its ranks. Margaret Moers Wenig, now a teacher at Hebrew Union, a Reform Jewish seminary in Manhattan, told me that more than 50 percent of the seminary's applicants are female, and many are applying after years spent raising children. "They will be some of our best rabbis," says Wenig. She added that if a mother tries to get a job in a field she left years earlier, it might be difficult, "but if you change fields, and go back to school, you might be looked on very favorably."

The slight, petite rabbi had a synagogue on the upper West Side of Manhatten for sixteen years, and she believes that having a baby when she took over her rabbinate at age twenty-five made her much more sensitive to the needs of the entire community. She reinstituted a Hebrew school at the synagogue, the first in twenty years, and worked hard to make the synagogue child-friendly. She actually paid out of her own pocket to have child care during services on high holidays, until she persuaded the elderly congregation to support it.

She faced a great deal of opposition to the idea of reopening the Hebrew school from members of the synagogue who wondered why they should have to pay for a program for other people's children. "I was trying to say that this was a community endeavor," Wenig told me. "That these are not just the children of individual families; they are the future of our community."

The rector of an Episcopal parish in Salem, Massachusetts found that a maternal persona was welcomed and needed by many parishioners. Those who were going through childbirth felt especially comforted by the presence of a cleric who had been through the same ordeal. Catherine Powell described one young couple who had been terribly excited about an expected baby, then had a stillborn child. They called her in the middle of the night and asked her to come to the hospital to comfort them in their grief. "To me, it had to do with my experience with children," said Powell, who has two.

Even the media has discovered that mothers can contribute something special. Soledad O'Brien, who had two babies in rapid succession, says that "Having children helps audiencewise. The bulk of our audience, like the majority of Americans, are parents. They've been through the whole thing with me, my pregnancies, watching me get big, then bigger, then showing off the baby pictures . . . People stop me all the time and ask how's Cecilia; how's Sofia? I'd say that 95 percent of the people who sit down with me on the show ask me, 'how are the girls?' "

O'Brien, who is married to an investment banker, went into physical training after giving birth twice in less than three years and got herself back into the best shape she'd ever been in. She even managed to complete a 10K race. She was deluged with emails from other working mothers, cheering her for making the time to do something for herself. Clearly this widespread identification with her "comeback" worked to the advantage of NBC, her then-employer.

It's Still Uphill

Still, the obstacles to mothers attempting to reenter the work force remain formidable. This is especially true in times of high unemployment. In late 2003 there were 9 million unemployed people in the United States, and another half a million or so *discouraged* workers, the official term for people who are not currently looking for work because they have given up hope of finding what they want. (Mothers with children at home are not included in any of these numbers, because they are not officially in the labor force.) The women I spoke with who were trying to get back into the hard-hit IT industry, for instance, were having no luck at all.

When I interviewed New York Congresswoman Louise Slaughter in May of 2003, she startled me by stating flatly that "anyone who's stayed at home for six years, let's say, is not going to get a job, period. You'd be doing people a disservice to suggest otherwise. There are no jobs. She'll have to get in line behind everyone else, and there aren't going to be any left for her. I don't think you realize how bad it is out there." Boom.[15]

Moreover, there is no doubt that the longer a person has been out of the job market the harder it is to get back in. People do lose professional contacts, they may lose technical skills, and they often lose confidence, which is even worse. It takes a pretty thick skin to face down a disbelieving interviewer who asks, how could you have acquired any relevant skills as a parent? It is difficult for an employer to distinguish between someone who spent years barely functioning at home and someone who read all the parenting books, developed a high emotional IQ, and ran a household as smoothly as a Swiss hotel. The outstanding parent earns no diploma, no honorable discharge, no medals, and no letters of recommendation for a job well done.

Cognitive Bias
All these difficulties are magnified by thinking that confuses mothers with maids. Many people associate housewives and mothers at home

with menial labor and the lowly chores of cleaning, laundry, changing diapers, babysitting. They see a full-time parent and envision those routine tasks rather than the complex problem-solving, the subtle relationship work, the multitasking and motivational skills. New research is shedding a fascinating light on such stereotypical thinking, and discovering that it is much more widespread than has been assumed.

Scholars, including Susan Fiske, a professor of psychology at Princeton who works in the field of *cognitive bias*—how people see and think about other people—have found clear evidence of harmful bias against both traditional and nontraditional women.[16]

"Business women," for example, are seen as quite competent, along with Asians, Jews, and rich people, but they are not liked. Think Glenn Close in *Fatal Attraction*. Housewives, on the other hand, are stereotyped as the warmest people you'll ever meet, but they are ranked low in competence, way down there with the elderly, the blind, housecleaners, and Hispanics. Think Lucille Ball in *I Love Lucy*. It makes you wonder how the species ever survived, with all those ditsy, dimwitted mothers raising the young.

The disdain for service on the home front stands in sharp contrast to the vast overrating of military service. I ran into this a few years ago while chatting with one of the top executives of T. Rowe Price, a Baltimore-based investment firm. I commented that raising a child provided a person with invaluable managerial experience. At first he readily agreed, explaining that he had two daughters who were mothers of young children, and he knew how challenging it was. But when I suggested that parenting should be considered as valuable a credential as time spent in the military, he looked shocked. "But military service is *direct* leadership experience!" he exclaimed.

Most researchers describe this kind of kneejerk stereotyping as unconscious and unintentional. Law professor Joan Williams of American University, who is documenting the pervasiveness of bias against mothers, prefers to call it *unexamined*. This shifts the burden of proof. If an employer (or economist) has a bias against a stay-at-home mother who is returning to the job market, for example, or makes an assumption that a parent who prefers a thirty- or forty-hour workweek, instead of a fifty- or sixty-hour week, is not a committed worker, then it's his problem, and his obligation to reexamine his thinking. Williams argues that discrimination based on bias against parents ought to be as illegal as discrimination on the basis of race or gender. As a remedy, she recommends that a ban on discrimination against people with family responsibilities be added to state antidiscrimination statutes.[17]

Such statutes would protect fathers as well as mothers, for negative stereotyping of housewives extends to househusbands as well. In 2002 there were 189,000 children living with stay-at-home dads, (versus 11 million with stay-at-home moms), and these fathers report that they too suffer a stigma when they attempt to reenter the workforce or take advantage of family-friendly policies. Gary Essig, a forty-six-year-old account manager, stayed home for a year with a newborn while his physician wife worked. When he sought to return to paid work, he thought he would impress prospective employers with how challenging child care really is. He talked about the discipline, resourcefulness, and creativity that was required. Headhunters told him, in effect, to shut up and focus on his past job experience if he wanted to avoid skepticism or even hostility.[18]

Steven Greenfield, a forty-year-old software-development administrator in San Jose, California, spent four years at home with three young daughters before looking for another job. He told a *Wall Street Journal* reporter that one interviewer asked him if he was gay or just "weird." Another accused him of failing to keep up with technology, without bothering to ask him about his specific capabilities. And a third seemed at a total loss for words when he learned that Greenfield was at home raising his kids. The interview ended quickly.[19]

At least men may be somewhat better equipped to handle rebuffs. Psychologists have found that men have *positive illusion*, frequently thinking they are better-looking, smarter, more capable than they really are. Women, on the other hand, often have *negative illusion*, the sense that they are not as good as they actually are. Men with little knowledge of a subject, for example, often have no trouble opining at length about it, and guys with no apparent qualifications apply for the most unlikely jobs. Obviously change will come much sooner if women overcome their own cognitive bias. Until mothers themselves put a high value on their work outside the paid labor force, they can't expect others to do so. As one stay-at-home mother commented, "The more we value ourselves and exude the confidence in the skills that make a family successful, the more those same skills will be noticed and sought after . . ."

"If an ever-increasing number of mothers put parenting on their resumes," adds Dagmar Kauffman, a German-born member of Mothers and More in Chicago, "corporate America will get the message sooner or later!" Doing her part, Kauffman, a mother of two grown children, has put different titles on her joint tax return, like "executive director of household affairs." Every year the papers are returned with a line drawn through the fancy title and "homemaker" written in.[20]

Can't fool those bureaucrats!

In *The Price of Motherhood* I told a story about a female German parliamentarian who had a dream in which she interviewed a young man. "Oh, you have such outstanding credentials," she enthused. "But we are looking for well-rounded people. We see you have never spent any time with children. But there's still time. You're still young. Come back when you've had broader life experience."[21]

Joyce Fletcher, a management expert, has the same dream. She imagines that someday, employers will realize that when people have multiple life roles they can understand customers, colleagues, clients, and constituencies better than someone who leads a narrow, all-business life. She even imagines a time when employee development programs would include some form of caretaking work for people who aren't parents, such as coaching or being a team leader in a youth group. Companies might require either parenting or community involvement as a necessary condition of advancement or continued employment.[22]

In the meantime, back in the real world, you may be wondering whether Helen Chongris ever got that copyediting job at the *Dallas Morning News*. When I called her several weeks after she had expected to be hired on a permanent basis, she was still working the graveyard shift and still waiting to hear. Then, a couple of weeks after that, I received an email with this subject: "I Got the Job I Wanted!"

The Mommy Bunny

As far back as the 1930s, mothers were wishing that someone would notice their talents and put them to good use in the world. In *The Country Bunny and the Little Gold Shoes*, a 1939 children's book by Du Bose Heyward and Marjorie Flack, this maternal dream is the theme.

The book is ostensibly about the selection of Easter bunnies. Five are chosen every year, and they must be "the five kindest, and swiftest, and wisest bunnies in the whole wide world." A young country bunny dreamed of becoming an Easter bunny some day, but she was plump and brown, not the sleek, classic white, and when she grew up she had twenty-one babies who kept her busy for years. But she trained them well, with a special blend of organization and caring, and they learned to do all the household tasks. Her home ran very, very smoothly.

One day, a new Easter bunny contest was announced, and the mommy bunny went to watch the competition, a little sadly because she had little hope that she could ever fulfill her lifelong ambition.

A wise grandfather rabbit was to choose the new lead bunny. The first round of competitors leaped and ran, and proved that they were swift and clever. But they showed no signs that they were also kind and wise.

Then the grandfather noticed the brown mother bunny standing on the sidelines with her twenty-one children, all perky and well-mannered and meticulously turned out. He questioned her and was impressed with her tale of how she organized her household and how happy her children seemed to be. He concluded that she must be both clever and kind. She showed how swift she was as she rounded up all her children in a wink. He concluded she must be wise as well. And he chose her.

On Easter night, he challenged her to one more hurdle: to travel far and wide to bring happiness to a sick child. She met the challenge, and was awarded the golden shoes that symbolize her permanent position as the Easter bunny who can serve in the most difficult tasks.

Katherine Marshall of the World Bank, who called my attention to this story, draws two messages from it. First, the maternal experience is relevant in selecting an Easter bunny, or any other kind of leader. Kindness, wisdom, and courage, for example, are as important as cleverness and speed. Second, the extraordinary way this particular mommy bunny performed her tasks, with good humor, organization, and efficiency, revealed her capacity for leadership. Not all mommies have this capacity, but when you see one, you know you've found someone who deserves the golden shoes.

I see one more thing in this sixty-five-year-old story. The mommy bunny has to depend on a wise old male bunny to recognize her talents. I don't think mommies can afford to be that passive anymore and wait to be noticed. We can recognize the Easter bunny in ourselves.

Mothers Are Everywhere and Times Are Changing

In conclusion, I'd like to summarize two of the major impressions that came out of my research. First, mothers are everywhere, in every profession, from the head of the National Science Foundation to the head of missile systems for a major defense contractor. One of the best moms-are-everywhere stories is about the female minister who was offering communion. Two school-age children leaned over the railing as she approached with the host. "Look," one exclaimed, "It's a mommy!"

Second, mothers are slowly changing the work world—its language, its atmosphere, and, more glacially, its norms.

Let's take the first impression first. I am well aware of the daunting obstacles to combining motherhood with a serious career, so daunting that most women, even educated women, don't combine these two things. I am also cognizant of the fact that most working women are still clustered in traditionally female occupations, which helps keep their wages lower than men's.

However, these truths shouldn't blind us to the remarkable economic progress that mothers have made. Women with children are running the most unexpected organizations, and doing the most unexpected things. For example, high-achieving married women (defined as those earning more than $55,000 a year or having a graduate or professional degree) are just as likely to have children as other married women who are working full-time. More than three-quarters (78 percent) of married high achievers and other married full-time working women have at least one child by age forty.[1]

"Everyone is now saying that family life is detrimental to success; that most successful women have no family life," says Irene Natividad, a Philippine-American businesswoman who was on *Working Mother* magazine's list of the twenty-five most influential working mothers in the country in 1997. "But it's not true! The one thing feeds the other; you can be *more* successful at work because of the other experience at home. If we can't show the correlation women will conclude that the only way to succeed is to be alone."[2]

Even at the very pinnacle of female success, among *Fortune* magazine's fifty most powerful women in business, the percentage who are mothers is almost as high as for other working women. By my calculation, in 2002 three-quarters (76 percent) of the fifty superstars had kids. So much for the myth that the women who get ahead have to abandon the dream of children, and the equally insidious myth that a woman who has children has to abandon her dreams of a career. Neither is true.

This hit home for me after two back-to-back interviews in New York City with the dean of the School of International and Public Affairs (SIPA) at Columbia University and the chief executive officer of Time Inc.

I graduated from SIPA in the 1960s. When I was a student the dean was a remote, courtly white-haired gentleman named Andre Cordier, with whom I never exchanged a word. Today, the dean is an accessible, down-to-earth political scientist in her early fifties named Lisa Anderson, a Middle East expert who speaks Arabic and has two school-age children. She represents a sea change for the institution and for female students.

The day after I interviewed Anderson I found myself in the Time-Life Building in midtown Manhattan, where I worked in my first job after graduating from Columbia. In those days the chairman of Time Inc. was a remote, courtly gentleman named Andrew Heiskell, and the women working at the company's magazines were for the most part relegated to low-level jobs. Today the CEO is Ann Moore, a no-nonsense marketing whiz who worked her way up in a company that no longer sets any limit on what a talented woman can achieve.

When I visited Moore on the thirty-fourth floor, the inner sanctum of Time Inc.'s top executives, I noticed that the halls were crowded with brown cardboard boxes, cleanup bins, and piles of discarded papers. Moore, who had just been named the new corporate chairman, was cleaning house. One of her first decisions as head of the company was to ask everyone to clean out their offices and closets. All the accumulated junk was going on sale at the end of the month to benefit a charity.

"I don't think anyone had cleaned out these shelves for forty years," she commented, waving an arm at the walls of bookshelves in the chairman's vast office. All of her predecessors had been men, who no doubt had never noticed the gathering dust.

Many people feel the jury is still out on the question of whether women change institutions when they gain power, or whether power changes women, by enabling them to act more like men. Up until now women holding power outside the family have been so rare that it's been hard to draw any conclusions.

My interviews convinced me that an answer is emerging. People like Lisa Anderson and Ann Moore are not just men in drag. They are changing the workplace, imperceptibly for the most part, and still around the margins. But in a few unmistakable ways, they and other mothers in positions of leadership are making a difference.

Maternal Metaphors

In the first place, the language of power is changing as more mothers make the workplace their space. Maternal metaphors are popping up everywhere, replacing the sports and military metaphors preferred by males. Author Robin Gerber heard the new language while interviewing the female mayor of a French city, who spoke of connecting with voters as if through an umbilical cord.

Norwegians heard the new language when Gro Harlem Brundtland, their first female prime minister, accused her conservative opponent of running "a government that leaves the dirty dishes for others once the meal is over."[3]

And Argentines heard it when Elisa Carrio, a reform politician, described the economic crisis of the summer of 2002 in this way: "We are witnessing the painful birth of a different kind of Argentina. The one thing not to do when a woman is trying to give birth is close her legs. That is what the old political classes are doing by holding on to power. It means the birth is going to be very painful."[4]

Jamie Gorelick unabashedly uses the new language. She tells a story about a popular children's book called *If You Give a Mouse a Cookie* in which a mouse comes up to a little boy and asks for his cookie. The mouse eats the cookie, and then asks for a glass of milk. When he gets the glass, he asks for a straw and then a napkin . . . and so on and on until the two of them have made a tremendous mess that they have to clean up. At the end, as the boy and the mouse lie exhausted, the mouse says he's thirsty, and wants another glass of milk. . . . The point is, if you give a mouse a cookie, his demands will never stop.

There is a scene in the movie *Air Force One* in which the president, played by Harrison Ford, is in the cargo area of the presidential plane dodging terrorists. He is also on the phone with the vice president, Glenn Close, who is back at the White House. The terrorists are executing hostages, and have just finished off the national security advisor, and the president says to the vice president, "We can't give in to their demands. It won't end there."

"And if you die on that plane, will it end there?" asks the vice president.

"Look," replies the president. "We've got a job to do, whatever the cost. If you give a mouse a cookie . . ."

The vice president finishes the sentence, "he's going to want a glass of milk."

Gorelick believes that this story represents a new type of conversation among powerful people. The shorthand is not football or basketball or hockey, sports that are familiar as power symbols in Washington, D.C. The shorthand is a kid's book and the conversation is between two extremely powerful people who identify themselves as parents.

"I submit to you that this little bit of movie dialogue would not have been remotely conceivable twenty-five years ago when I started my professional life," Gorelick told a group of Washington women in 1999.

This particular mother of two isn't the least bit shy about bringing references to her kids into the office. "At the Justice Department we would have these meetings every evening around five in the attorney general's cavernous conference room to plan for the next day," Gorelick told me. "We'd go around the table, and once, when we got to the head of legislative affairs, he started in with all the problems: 'we're under assault about this, we're taking incoming on that,' one thing after another. And I said 'Andy, you're sounding like Eeyore. You need more of a Tigger attitude.' Everyone there who had kids exploded with laughter. The next day I brought in toy figures of Pooh and Eeyore and he carried them around the rest of the time he was at Justice, saying 'Let's get a better attitude around here!' "

It is hard to overstate what a change this represents. Not so long ago, upwardly mobile female executives were afraid to put their children's pictures on their desks for fear that they wouldn't be taken seriously. Distinguished women like biologist Rita Colwell felt that they couldn't even mention the fact that they had children.

"In my age group, you had to mask it," said Colwell, who is in her sixties. "I couldn't let anything 'feminine' or 'maternal' enter into a discussion. I had to be one of the guys as much as possible. I couldn't ever say something like, 'You know, you're acting like a two-year-old.' "

"Did you ever think that of someone?" I inquired.

"Of course!"

Today's female executives, in contrast, say that talking about their kids can be an asset rather than a liability in the office. Pamela Thomas-Graham, the young mother who is CEO of the CNBC cable channel, told me that being able to talk about her kids has deepened her relationships at work. Whereas previously, she was a bit of an anomaly as a black female among predominantly white male colleagues, now she can exchange anecdotes about the kids. "I now have different and more interesting conversations with people," she confessed. "Men love to talk about their kids, and many of them have a lot of them! We can joke about them, the way men joke about sports or whatever."

"Children are a wonderful shared interest between men and women," Cheryl Bachelder confirmed. "I would look totally incompetent if I tried to use sports analogies; it would be 'there's Cheryl, trying to talk about sports.' But there are two things I can talk about with male executives: children and books. I find men like to talk about their families, and it's liberating for them to be able to do that with the boss. I get very positive feedback on this—it makes me seem more human, accessible, personable, and not so intense and cutthroat."

Bachelder added that many men in her former company were relieved to hear her message that she's a better leader *because* she's a parent, not *in spite of it*. "They want a more balanced life too, and by my example I give them the freedom to express that desire," she said. "My leadership team is about 50-50 male–female, and the men are just as likely as the women to say things like, 'I've got to take time off to get to my daughter's graduation.' "

Gorelick has had the same reaction from the men she's worked with. One morning, she arrived at an early morning meeting in the Justice Department completely stressed out after taking her kids to school.

"The kids were such brats in the car this morning," she grumbled, whereupon F.B.I. Director Louis Freeh, the father of six boys, and Drug Enforcement Agency head Tom Constantine, a father of nine, spent the next twenty minutes sharing their techniques on how to get kids to behave in a car. "It was a real bonding experience," said Gorelick.

Mothers Do Make a Difference

Finally, I do have the impression that when a mother is at the very *top* of an organization—the president of a university, the governor of a state, the CEO or the head of a major division of a corporation—two important changes occur. First, the *worker norm* changes, and the *typical* worker begins to be seen as someone with family responsibilities rather than someone with no life outside of work. When that perception shifts, as it has at Fannie Mae, at Princeton, and elsewhere, the organization becomes a much more comfortable place for parents to work. Conscientious parents are no longer in the closet, but free to be honest about their values.

Second, when mothers have real power in an organization, and are able to express themselves freely, the institution begins to benefit from a new form of diversity. Diversity of *experience* is just as important as diversity of race, gender, age, ethnicity, and so on. When people with direct experience of raising children, who have previously been screened from positions of authority, come into their own, the effect is the same in an organization as it is in biology. The result is hybrid vigor, or *heterosis*, the increased energy and capacity for growth that results from cross-breeding and cross-pollinating.

Here's how I see what is happening. During the women's liberation movement of the 1960's and early 1970's, the struggle was for reproductive freedom and educational and economic opportunities, including the right to gain entry to professions that had largely been closed to women. The task was to learn from men, and to accustom men to working with women, who had historically been seen as different. Different was synonymous with inferior. Women had to prove that they were as good as, if not the same as, men.

In this stage, which lasted roughly from the late 1960s to the 1990s, and persists even today in some hold-out areas, women entered the professions in large numbers and were admitted into corporate management. They were expected to accept the rules of the game as it had always been played, and in some cases to even dress like men (still a requirement in some traditionally male jobs like law enforcement and security).

This period is not over until men are comfortable with women in public life, and can see that they are in no way inferior or less competent or even all that different as people. As long as women are still the *other*, they are under pressure to be the same, and their potential value added—the diversity of experience and insights they can offer—is wasted. But once women become part of the in crowd, so to speak, they can finally dare to express their differences without endangering their status. They can raise new issues, broaden the range of ideas that can be taken seriously, and extend the boundaries of accepted discourse. In this stage, the men start learning from the women, and norms start shifting, organizations start doing things differently, and our view of reality itself expands.

Redefining Reality

We are clearly entering this exciting stage of women's advance in public life. Deb Henretta of Proctor & Gamble can testify to what happens when an organization's leadership begins to include people who were previously excluded:

> *The nice thing about having a mother with babies come in [as president of Global Baby Products], is it brought a whole wealth of insights that hadn't been considered, or had been considered and rejected or sidelined. The whole organization is now thinking about the business in an entirely different way. We're bringing together people who*

can solve problems very differently—or solve very different problems. We're bringing together the experts on technology, who can conceive what's possible, and people who can think about how to commercialize the technology so it will connect with the moms who buy the product. And it's not just the women—the men are thinking differently now and are coming up with all sorts of new ideas.

As a company we've learned a lot from this. One type of thinker is not enough. You need diverse points of view. When you bring such diversity together, it creates magic! This is what separates the great business success stories from the rest.

Henretta added that she's "not just trying to get women in, but people who are parents, or not even just parents, but people who've had experience with children. An experienced dad may have as many insights as a mother would. Or a woman who is a deeply involved aunt. I'm trying to get people who have a love of children and experience with children into the mix. . . . I'm also trying to get cultural diversity. I'm in charge of our global baby business, and people in the Philippines, Latin America, central and Eastern Europe all have different cultural attitudes about children and we need all that in the mix."

This expansion of the concept of diversity to include the caregiving experience challenges the reluctant language companies use when they talk about *giving* parents flexibility, or *accommodating* the needs of families, or *adjusting* to nontraditional ways of operating. This is the unenthusiastic language of toleration. The real breakthroughs occur only when employers begin to realize, as Henretta does, that parents can add enormous value to an organization, and to a culture's understanding of itself.

Some of the most exciting changes are occurring in the religious realm. As more and more women become ministers and rabbis, they are bringing a maternal sensibility to bear on our spiritual understanding. This potentially revolutionary development is already affecting the more liberal faiths, in everything from children's religious education to the interpretation of the deity.

Catherine Powell was one of the first women ordained in the Episcopal church, in 1979, four years before her first child was born. At first, she hoped "they wouldn't stick me with the kids" by asking her to teach Sunday school. In those days, Sunday school was relegated to the church basement and the women in the congregation joked, "Go down to the basement, that's where you'll find the women and children."

Once her own two daughters were born, Powell began to pay closer attention to children's religious education, and noticed how "horrible" it really was. "It was, 'read a story, color this picture,' " she explained. "Until recently, there wasn't a sophisticated approach to children's spirituality or any incorporation of developmental issues. It was mothers, listening to our own children, who decided to change that."

Every parent knows that children grapple with the most profound spiritual questions, often prompted by the death of a grandparent or a beloved pet. Where do we come from? Where do we go when we die? Where does the world come from? When Powell's second daughter was about four, for example, she came into the kitchen and asked, "Mommy, what's going to happen at the end of the day?" Powell started to talk about the end of that particular day, and the child interrupted, "No, I mean at the end of *the day*!" She meant, what is at the end of everything?

When her oldest daughter was about five, a child in her nursery school died, and another friend's grandfather died at the same time. Shortly thereafter, her little girl told her that she had a dream, in which she and her friend had visited heaven to see her friend's grandfather and the child who had died. "They wanted us to know that they've been praying for us, and they wanted us to tell other people that everything is okay. They can watch us and we can see them."

Powell decided to teach a Sunday school class that combined Montessori techniques with contemplative spirituality for young children, and now such classes are found in increasing numbers of churches. Children are given the basic parables, and rather than told what the story *means*, they are encouraged to play with figures representing the key figures in the story (such as the good shepherd and his sheep) so that they can work out the meaning for themselves, as they understand it. One day she found a three-and-a-half-year-old boy sitting and staring at a little box containing wooden figures around a table, depicting the Last Supper. She asked what he was thinking.

"You know, if Jesus could give a friend a party, he'd invite the whole world," replied the child.

This is obviously a long way from conventional Bible class. And we wouldn't be in this sensitive and sophisticated place without mothers in the ministry.

Powell says that women in the clergy have made another noticeable difference: They enabled the Episcopal church to deal much more effectively with their sex scandals than the Catholics have.

"We approached the problem much more aggressively," she told me, "because the women clergy were much more willing to talk about it and to report it."

I commented that they must have been successful because I hadn't even heard of any sex scandals in the Episcopal church. "Well, ours tend to be heterosexual," she confided.

"God Is a Woman and She Is Growing Older"

The profound reinterpretation of the deity that women are bringing to organized religion can be glimpsed in a sermon written in 1990 by Margaret Wenig. The sermon, which was reprinted in an anthology of great sermons of the twentieth century, is entitled "God Is a Woman And She Is Growing Older."

In it, Wenig describes God as an elderly woman sitting alone at a kitchen table, thinking back on her grown children's lives and wishing, with bittersweet longing, for them to return to the warmth of her hearth. She remembers their hurts and sorrows, the quarrels and disappointments, but she is steadfast in her unconditional love. The poem-like sermon concludes with a vision of God waiting patiently, with her door open and the candles burning, for her children to return to her on Yom Kippur.[5]

Another sermon, delivered at the National Cathedral in Washington by Catherine Powell, uses the metaphor of birth. Written in the 1980s during a time of upheaval and bloodshed in Central America, it has an eerie timeliness today.

Powell reminded the congregation that all social change is like childbirth. It can be unexpected, as in the case of Abraham's aged wife Sarah; dangerous, as in the case of Moses' mother; and even shocking, as in the case of Mary, who conceived out of wedlock and was perhaps ostracized. Above all, giving birth is painful. This we need to understand, so that we don't recoil from the future.

"We look at the swirling chaos of the world and respond with fear. . . .

"We look at the groaning of the world and we want to protect ourselves. We want to remain calm and quiet, secure in our own place and role in the world. . . .

"We look at the flailing of the world and sometimes we are self-righteous. Well, if they had done things our way; if they wouldn't insist on ruling themselves unprepared; if they had our form of government; if they were more prudent; if they wouldn't be so extreme. . . .

"We face a groaning world, as we stand with unsteady feet in a universe caught up in the convulsions of labor . . . Give us wisdom not to turn away, but to see the struggle as a process of birth, a pushing forward. Give us compassion to see conflict and hostility as symptoms of pain and blocked dreams trying to be born. . . ."

This is a mother's wisdom, using a metaphor that the male priesthood has not had at its disposal. It reminds us that the world is imperfect, bloody, and frightening, but still worthy of embrace. Mothers can offer us hope for new life.

Appendix

How would an individual who has spent some time out of the job market raising children present that experience in the most favorable light? Exactly how could she or he put it on a resume?

One way to begin might be to do a skills inventory on yourself, listing all of the transferrable skills you have picked up informally, including all of the volunteering at schools, churches, and other nonprofit groups. It will obviously help if you have been active in community, school, religious, or civic organizations, and can claim familiarity with fund-raising, recruiting and directing volunteers, publishing newsletters, publicity, Web page creation and maintenance, and the like. But a parent's skills alone could easily include financial management, organizational skills, mediating, negotiating, motivational speaking, tutoring, child psychologist, event planning, catering, household procurement.

The point is, don't be shy. In almost everyone's case the raw material is there. As writer Robin Gerber has pointed out, a resume line that reads "successfully mediated the conflicting demands of household stakeholders" is as legitimate as "led negotiations for product development."

Many women who have been at home for a few years do lose

confidence, and need a reminder of all that they have accomplished. A friend of mine tells the story of her neighbor in the Berkshires, a stay-at-home mother of four, who was applying for a franchise to open a Body Shop. "Do you think I can do it?" she asked, uncertain of her abilities after years of unpaid labor at home.

"Are you kidding?" my friend replied. "You've managed a household of six people on $40,000 a year! You have the skills of a controller with a tight cash flow; the organization of an efficiency expert; the ability to motivate people to do their best; you've managed and defused destructive rivalries; worked twelve to fourteen hours a day at hard physical, emotional, and mental labor; kept on top of a million details at once without even being aware of it—and you don't think that is directly transferrable into the business world?"

One mother who wasn't shy about drawing up a list of her "transferable skills" was Helen Chongris of Plano, Texas. Here is a slightly edited version of a unique separate resume that helped Chongris win a job as a copy editor at *The Dallas Morning News*, after twenty years out of journalism:

TRANSFERABLE SKILLS

In addition to my traditional resume, enclosed, following is a list of functional skills defining my fusion of experience as a [parent and/or other unpaid activity] and as a [specified profession].

*   **Organized negotiator**
    Knowing what to accomplish in an exchange; staying focused on addressing only those issues
*   **Keen listener**
    Grasping what is said and immediately processing that thought to the next level of complexity
*   **Critical thinker**
    Skeptical of any information presented as fact; passionate about determining its accuracy

* **Savvy researcher**
  Can wade through repetitive misinformation to pinpoint best sources to check facts
* **Persuasive pitcher**
  Seasoned in opening and luring with nouns and verbs and in closing and sealing with adjectives
* **Absorbent sponge**
  Eager to learn, can be taught, and can continue learning when applying lessons
* **J-dotter and X-crosser**
  Attentive to detail beyond I-dotting and T-crossing
* **Student of the competition**
  Constantly observing how producers and marketers of similar products do business
* **Motivated contributor**
  Caring to improve climate of the workplace by developing rapport with coworkers and initiating discussion among them about constructive approaches to chronic concerns
* **An adult, but not a parent**
  Inviting cooperation by suggesting, "Yes *we* can," rather than risking shutdown by declaring, "No, *you* can't!"
* **Inspiring teacher**
  Enjoying the sharing of knowledge so much that, bit by bit, others not only learn mechanics of getting a job done but also, by following example set, model their excitement about doing it well
* **Resourceful problem-solver**
  Independently suggesting how to cut costs, streamline processes, and bring about better outcomes, never pointing out a problem without providing a solution
* **Lifelong learner**
  Willing to invest time and money into professional and personal growth

* **Confident survivor**
  Bouncing back promptly from adversity or rejection with a positive attitude and a new direction
* **Adrenaline junkie**
  Accustomed to working with strong sense of urgency; can meet a deadline and keep going
* **Professional worrywart**
  Always infusing an overdeveloped sense of responsibility into every project

Other ideas on transferable skills can be gleaned by looking at the qualifications demanded by various paid positions. For example, Jen Grey, a former nurse, was filling out an online job application from Blue Cross/Blue Shield in North Carolina when she came across the following major responsibilities:

* Consistent demonstration of leadership behaviors (training, mentoring, assisting peers with issue resolution)
* Demonstrated success in coaching, giving constructive feedback and developing employees
* Demonstrated ability to promote and support teamwork and team decision-making
* Excellent negotiation, decision-making, and relationship-building skills
* Demonstrated analytical thinking skills. Ability to identify issues and recommend and implement solutions
* Ability to make sound and independent business decisions in often high-pressure situations.
* Excellent interpersonal and organizational skills.

Which of these, Grey wondered, is *not* part of being a parent? All of these skills could legitimately be listed on a full- or part-time parent's resume.

• • •

The Department of Labor's Occupational Information Network (O*NET) contains a list of skills used to analyze the demands of specific jobs in the paid labor force. Here's the list, in ascending order after the most basic skills (reading, writing, basic math, etc.):

SOCIAL SKILLS (Many parents have clearly mastered these.)
* Social perceptiveness (being aware of others' reactions and understanding why they react the way they do)
* Coordination (adjusting actions in relation to others' actions)
* Persuasion (persuading others to approach things differently)
* Negotiation (bringing others together and trying to reconcile differences)
* Instructing
* Service orientation (actively looking for ways to help people)
* Complex problem solving (in real world setting)
* Problem identification (identifying the nature of problems)
* Information gathering (knowing how to find information and identifying essential information)
* Information organization (finding ways to structure or classify multiple pieces of information)
* Synthesis/reorganization (reorganizing information to get a better approach to problems or tasks)
* Idea generation
* Idea evaluation (evaluating the likely success of an idea in relation to the demands of the situation)
* Implementation planning (developing approaches for implementing an idea)
* Solution appraisal (observing and evaluating the outcomes of a solution to identify lessons learned)

Next in the O*NET skills list come TECHNICAL SKILLS, those skills used to design, set up, operate, and correct problems with machines and technological systems. Here, being a parent is irrelevant. It's hard to see how child-rearing does anything to enhance your ability to write computer programs, conduct software tests, install or maintain technical equipment, and so on.

The next item is SYSTEMS SKILLS, defined as the skills used to understand, monitor, and improve organizations and systems. These include *visioning*, or imagining how a system should work; *systems perception*, or determining when important changes have occurred or are likely to occur in a system; identifying *downstream consequences*, or the long-term outcome of a change in operations; and *systems evaluation*, or looking at indicators of system performance, taking into account their accuracy.

Sounds pretty technical, but is there any doubt that a competent mother or father envisions their child's future; monitors the important changes taking place as the child develops; identifies the long-term consequences of developments; and monitors performance with long-term goals in mind? If anyone fits the definition of a *systems thinker*, it is a mother. Just ask any nursery-school head or college admissions officer.

Lastly, the RESOURCE MANAGEMENT SKILLS, used to allocate resources efficiently. Here's where moms and dads really come into their own. These skills include:

* Time management (of one's own time and the time of others)
* Management of financial resources (determining how money will be spent to get the work done, and accounting for these expenditures)
* Management of material resources (obtaining and seeing to the appropriate use of equipment, facilities, and materials needed to do certain work)
* Management of personnel resources (motivating, developing, and directing people as they work, identifying the best people for the job)

Looking at this official list of the skills needed in the paid labor force, it seems pretty clear that the work of raising a child provides direct experience in many, if not most, of them—with the important exception of specific technical skills. I would note that the top management in many organizations also lack these specialized skills. How many high-ranking executives do you know who can barely use a computer? At senior levels, what counts most is judgment, maturity, efficiency, honesty, dedication, and emotional intelligence. Those qualities, with the important addition of love of the job, virtually define a good parent.

On a lighter note, Holly Butkovich of Ypsilanti, Michigan, a former preschool teacher who is now a SAHM (stay-at-home mom) says she could draw up a resume containing these skills (among others):

Multitasking—Being able to do two additional things while breast feeding.

Self-starter—Being the only one in the house who seems to know how to operate the dishwasher, laundry appliances, and vacuum.

People person—The ability to BS my way through a check-out line where an elderly woman seems to think that I want to hear all about her grandchildren while my kid screams in my ear and the cashier talks on the phone.

Restaurant critic—Knowing the best places to dine where you can diaper a kid.

Crisis prevention—always bring a diaper.

As for that all-important answer to the awful question posed by strangers at parties, "What do *you* do?" here are a few of the totally legitimate answers a stay-at-home parent could choose:

Manager of a small business (for example, Butkovich & Sons)
Estate manager
Private investor

Investor in human capital
Owner of a cleaning/catering business
Executive director of an early education project
Coach
Guidance counselor
Research associate in child development
Human development consultant
Human potential trainer

The list is limited only by your own imagination.

Then there's this story, which has been circulating on the Internet: A few months ago I ran into my friend Emily, who was fuming with indignation. It seemed she had just returned from renewing her drivers' license at the County Clerk's office. Asked by the female recorder to state her occupation, Emily had hesitated, uncertain how to identify herself.

"What I mean is," explained the clerk, "do you have a job, or are you just a . . ."

"Of course I have a job," Emily snapped. "I'm a mother."

"We don't list 'mother' as an occupation . . . 'housewife' covers it," said the recorder emphatically.

I forgot all about this story until I found myself in the same situation, this time at my own town hall. The clerk was obviously a career civil servant, poised, efficient, and possessed of a title like town registrar. "What is your occupation?" she inquired.

What made me say it, I do not know. The words simply popped out: "I am a research associate in child development and human relations."

The clerk paused, ballpoint pen frozen in midair. She looked up, and I repeated the title slowly, emphasizing every word. Then I stared in wonder as she wrote my impressive occupation down in bold black ink on the official questionnaire.

"Might I ask," said the clerk with new interest, "just what you do in your field?"

Coolly, without any trace of fluster in my voice, I heard myself reply, "I have a continuing program of research (what mother doesn't) in the laboratory and in the field (normally I would have said indoors and out). I'm working for my masters (the whole darned family) and already have four credits (all daughters). Of course, the job is one of the most demanding in the humanities. (Anyone care to disagree?) And I often work fourteen hours a day (twenty-four is more like it)."

There was a new note of respect in the clerk's voice as she completed the form, stood up, and personally ushered me to the door. As I drove into our driveway, buoyed up by my glamorous new career, I was greeted by my lab assistants—ages thirteen, seven, and three. Upstairs I could hear our new experimental model (six months) in the child-development program, testing out a new vocal pattern. I felt triumphant.

Biographies
of Interviewees

LISA ANDERSON is dean of the School of International and Public Affairs (SIPA) at Columbia University in New York City. Prior to becoming dean, Anderson served as chair of the department of political science. Professor Anderson is an expert on the Middle East and North Africa, and a human rights advocate. She is married and has two sons, born in 1985 and 1990.

CHERYL BACHELDER, forty-eight, was president and CEO of Kentucky Fried Chicken from early 2002 until September 2003. She is married and has two daughters, who were seventeen and eleven in 2003. Even while president of the world's second largest food chain, she was personally responsible for her daughters' calendars. "All of the logistics of their lives are in my Palm Pilot," she says. Bachelder honed her skills as a marketing manager at Gillette, Proctor & Gamble, RJR Nabisco, and Domino's Pizza, where as executive vice president she was responsible for planning, marketing, research, and product and concept development.

JUDITH A. BLADES, senior executive vice president of property–casualty operations at The Hartford Financial Services Group Inc., is one of the highest ranking women in the insurance industry. She is responsible for approximately $7 billion in annual written premiums, and more than five thousand employees, or nearly one-fifth of The Hartford's 27,000 workers, report to her. Blades, fifty-seven, worked her way up through the ranks at the company, and married a fellow Hartford employee. In 2002, Blades was named Insurance Woman of the Year at a ceremony at the Russian Tea Room in Manhattan. In her off-the-cuff remarks, she told the assembled executives that her family, including her parents and four children, had taught her all of her leadership skills. She never graduated from college, but all her children have.

CAROLE BROWNER, an attorney, was the head of the Environmental Protection Agency in the Clinton Administration. She is married, and her only child, a son, was three years old in 1993 when she went to the EPA. She had previously run the environmental regulation department of the state of Florida. She is now a consultant in Washington, D.C.

LINDA CHAVEZ-THOMPSON is the executive vice president of the AFL-CIO and the highest ranking woman in the labor movement. A second-generation American of Mexican descent, she was also the first person of color to become an executive officer of the AFL-CIO. She rose through the organizing ranks of her union, the American Federation of State, County, and Municipal Employees (AFSCME) in Texas and in the Southwest. Among other things, she also serves as vice chair of the Democratic National Committee. She has two children and two grandchildren.

DR. RITA COLWELL, a microbiologist, was the first woman to become director of the National Science Foundation, in 1998. Under her leadership the agency has established major initiatives in nano-technology, biocomplexity, information technology, and the twenty-first century workforce, among others. Dr. Colwell was previously president of the University of Maryland Biotechnology Institute, 1991–1998, and a professor of microbiology and biotechnology at the university. She has authored or coauthored sixteen books and more than six hundred scientific papers, produced an award-winning film, *Invisible Seas*, and served as president of the American Association for the Advancement of Science. She and her husband, a physicist, raised two daughters; one is now a professor of medicine and the other is an expert on women's health in developing countries.

LINDSAY CROUSE is a veteran actress of stage, screen, and television. For seven years, she was a member of the Circle Repertory Company in New York, and she has performed in regional theaters all over the country. Some of her best known films include *All the President's Men*, *The Verdict*, *House of Games*, *Places in the Heart*, for which she was nominated for an Academy Award, and *The Insider*, with Al Pacino. In television, she has guest-starred on numerous series, including *Hill St. Blues*, *L.A. Law*, *Law and Order*, *E.R.*, *NYPD Blue*, and *Dragnet*. She starred in the CBS Movie of the Week, *Laura Ingalls Wilder: Beyond the Prairie*. She is married and has two daughters and a stepson.

NANCY DROZDOW is a principal and cofounder of the Center for Applied Research in Philadelphia. She provides executive coaching and consulting to the heads of closely held, family-owned businesses. Her advice enables managers to analyze and act on issues of risk, delegation, competition, growth, and exit strategies, and what they often see as messy emotional issues. She has an MBA in strategy from the Wharton School.

LUCY FISHER has had one of the most successful careers in Hollywood, all while raising three children. She began as a story editor at

United Artists, was vice president of production at 20th Century Fox during the 1970s and, from 1981 to 1995 was at Warner Bros. She produced such successful films as *Gremlins*, *The Color Purple*, *The Witches of Eastwick*, and *The Bridges of Madison County*, and she persuaded Warner to open the movie industry's first daycare facility. In 1996, she became vice chairman of Columbia TriStar pictures, where her team, including her husband, producer Douglas Wick, turned out one profitable hit after another: *Jerry Maguire*, *My Best Friend's Wedding*, *Men In Black*, *Air Force One*, *The Mask of Zorro*, and *As Good As It Gets*. Since 2000, when she left Columbia, the Fisher and Wick partnership has produced several more films, including *Peter Pan*.

One of their children has diabetes, and Fisher has been an active fund raiser in the battle against that disease.

Naomi Foner is a screenwriter and producer in Los Angeles and the mother of two successful young actors, Jake and Maggie Gyllenhaal. Foner, a native New Yorker, began her career as a producer in public television. She was at the Children's Television Workshop for ten years, where she developed *The Electric Company* and worked on the popular show *3-2-1 Contact*. After her children were born she and her husband, a director, moved to Los Angeles and she began writing independently.

Foner's original screenplay, *Running on Empty*, was nominated for an Academy Award for Best Original Screenplay. She also wrote and produced *A Dangerous Woman*, *Losing Isaiah*, starring Jessica Lange and Halle Berry and *Bee Season*, starring Richard Gere. Her family was recently given the Torch of Liberty Award by the ACLU for their body of work on First Amendment issues.

Mike Fossaceca, thirty-eight, is a senior vice president for global cash management at JPMorganChase in New York City. He heads a large sales group whose task is helping Fortune 1000 companies find short-term solutions for managing their liquidity, from investing in treasuries to better handling of payables and receivables. He and his wife have two girls, who were four-and-a-half years and seventeen months old when we talked in December 2002.

LOUISE FRANCESCONI is president of Raytheon's $3 billion missile systems division, based in Phoenix, Arizona. She oversees more than forty production and development programs and a workforce of approximately 11,000 employees. (Her division produced weapons used in the hunt for Osama bin Laden in Afganistan and in the Iraq War.) Before joining Raytheon following the merger of Raytheon and Hughes Aircraft Company, she was a twenty-four-year veteran of Hughes and president of Hughes Missile Systems Company. She has one grown son and a stepson.

LESLIE GAINES-ROSS, author of CEO *Capital: A Guide to Building CEO Reputation and Company Success* (2003), is one of the country's foremost experts on CEO and corporate reputation. She is currently chief knowledge and research officer at Burston-Marsteller, a global communications consultant. Before joining Burston-Marsteller, Dr. Gaines-Ross was communcations and marketing director for *Fortune* magazine from 1988 to 1997. She has two grown daughters and a teenaged son.

JAMIE S. GORELICK, a graduate of Harvard and Harvard Law School, was Pentagon general counsel and deputy attorney general in the Clinton administration. From 2001 to 2003 she was vice chair of Fannie Mae, the nation's largest buyer of home mortgages, where she was in charge of government policy and minority lending. She also served on the National Commission on Terrorist Attacks Upon the United States. Gorelick, an attorney, is married and has two school-age children.

RUTH R. HARKIN is a senior vice president at United Technologies Corporation, in charge of international affairs and government relations. An attorney, Harkin was one of the first women in the U.S. to become a prosecutor, in Iowa in the early 1970s. She later became deputy general counsel in the Agriculture Department, and from 1993 to 1997, was president and CEO of the Overseas Private Investment Corporation (OPIC). She is married to Iowa senator Tom Harkin and has two grown daughters.

DEB HENRETTA, forty-three, is president of the Global Baby Care division at Proctor & Gamble in Cincinnati, Ohio. Henretta has spent her entire career at Proctor & Gamble, where she established her reputation by successfully managing the company's popular Tide brand, among others. But she didn't get out of "laundry," as she calls it, until 1999, when she was appointed general manager of P & G's North American baby-care business. She was the first woman to run the company's diaper business and her assignment was simple: rescue the ailing Pampers brand. Pampers, once the bestselling diaper in the world, had been losing market share for several years. Henretta, thirty-eight at the time, brought a mom's eye to the problems, and turned the situation around. She is married with three children ages nine, seven, and two.

MADELEINE KUNIN served three terms as governor of Vermont, and was subsequently appointed deputy secretary of education by President Bill Clinton. She later served as U.S. ambassador to Switzerland, where she was born. Her family, who were Jewish, left the country in the 1930s and emigrated to the United States, where she was educated, married, and raised four children.

SHIRLEY STRUM KENNY raised five children with a "very supportive" husband while both were struggling professors. After earning her doctorate at the University of Texas, she taught English at Catholic University before being appointed president of Queens College in New York City. She is now president of the State University of New York at Stony Brook. When we met in the mid-1990s her children included a rabbi, two PhDs, one MBA, and one undergraduate.

GERALDINE LAYBOURNE is chairman and chief executive of Oxygen Media, a multimedia company in New York with a cable network for women. Laybourne got her start in television at Nickelodeon, where her first hit show, *Double Dare*, more than doubled ratings in less than six months. As president, she turned the once money-losing children's channel into a hugely profitable business. She also served as president of Disney/ABC Cable networks before founding Oxygen Media with Oprah Winfrey, among others. She and her husband raised two children.

SHELLY LAZARUS is chairman and CEO of Ogilvy & Mather Worldwide, one of the world's largest advertising agencies. A 1970 graduate of Columbia Business School, where she was one of four women in her class, Lazarus has spent nearly her entire career at Ogilvy. Under her leadership, the company has won several massive global accounts, including IBM, Kodak, Motorola, and Oracle. She and her husband, a pediatrician, have three children.

VERONICA LOPEZ is a parent educator and counselor based in Staten Island. She is married and has one teenaged son and twin teenaged daughters.

ANN S. MOORE is the chairman and chief executive of Time Inc., the world's leading magazine publisher and a direct marketer of music and videos. Moore began her career at Time in 1978 and in the early 1990s became publisher and then president of People magazine, which became even more profitable under her leadership. Moore launched several other successful publications, including *InStyle, Teen People,* and *Real Simple.* She is married and has one son.

IRENE NATIVIDAD is a longtime leader of the women's movement in the United States. A native of the Philippines, in the 1980s she was president of the National Women's Political Caucus, a bipartisan organization dedicated to electing and appointing more women in public office. She has served as executive director of the Philippine American Foundation, and was Director of the 1992 and 1994 Global Summit of Women. She is married and has one son.

SOLEDAD O'BRIEN has been co-anchor of CNN's *American Morning* since 2003. Before joining CNN, she hosted NBC's *Weekend Today*, MSNBC's *Morning Blend*, and was a reporter for NBC *Nightly News*. A Harvard graduate, she and her husband, an investment banker, have two children. She is proud of her unusual Latino, Irish, and African-American heritage.

SARAH PILLSBURY is a film producer and philanthropist based in Los Angeles. At the age of 25, in 1976, she co-founded the Liberty Hill Foundation, whose mission is "Change, not Charity," in support of local community activism and environmental efforts. She has produced such well-regarded independent films as *Desperately Seeking Susan* and *How to Make an American Quilt*, and the Emmy Award–winning HBO film *And the Band Played On*. She has one daughter, an undergraduate at Yale, and a son in high school.

CATHERINE R. POWELL is Chaplain to the Lower and Middle Schools at National Cathedral School in Washington, D.C. Her Sunday title is Preschool Catechist at St. David's Episcopal Church in Washington. She previously served in churches in D.C., North Carolina, and Massachusetts. She has two daughters, ages 20 and 16.

JUDITH RAPOPORT, chief of child psychiatry at the National Institutes of Mental Health and a former psychoanalyst, is the author of the bestselling book, *The Boy Who Couldn't Stop Washing*. She is married and has two grown sons.

ANN RICHARDS was a volunteer in local and statewide political campaigns for twenty years while raising four children in Austin,

Texas. In 1976, she ran for her first political office, as county commissioner, and won. Six years later, she won a race for state treasurer, becoming the first woman elected to statewide office in Texas in 50 years. In 1990, she was elected governor of Texas, serving one term before being defeated by George W. Bush. She is currently a senior adviser to a Washington, D.C.–based law firm, and has six "nearly perfect" grandchildren.

MARIAN N. RUDERMAN is a group director of Research at the Center for Creative Leadership in Greensboro, North Carolina. Her research focuses on leadership development processes with special attention to the development of women leaders. She is co-author of the book *Standing at the Crossroads: Next Steps for High-Achieving Women* and co-editor of *Diversity in Work Teams: Research Paradigms for a Changing Workplace*. She holds a PhD in organizational psychology from the University of Michigan.

HAROLD SAUNDERS is director of international affairs for the Kettering Foundation and a former secretary of state for Near Eastern and South Asian Affairs under President Carter (1978–81). He was a key member of the team that mediated five Arab–Israeli agreements between 1974 to 1979, including the Camp David Accords and the Egyptian–Israeli peace treaty. He has since developed a framework he calls "sustained dialogue" for improving strained ethnic and racial relationships. He has two grown children.

PAULINE A. SCHNEIDER is a partner in the Washington, D.C. office of the law firm of Hunton & Williams, where she specializes in public finance transactions. She has been bond counsel for billions of dollars of financings for airports and state and municipal governments. A graduate of Yale Law School, she is on numerous boards and has served as president of the D.C. Bar. She has two grown children, a son and a daughter.

SHAUNNA SOWELL has spent her entire career at Texas Instruments, starting as a mechanical engineer almost twenty years ago. She served as vice president of Worldwide Environmental Safety and Health Programs, vice president and manager of Worldwide Facilities and, in 2001, became the first woman vice president and manager of a semiconductor plant, a manufacturing operation whose 800 employees produce $1 billion worth of product annually. In 2002, she was runner-up as *Working Mother* magazine's Mother of the Year.

PAMELA THOMAS-GRAHAM became the president and CEO of CNBC in July 2001. She previously spent ten years at McKinsey & Co., becoming the management consulting firm's first black woman partner. She is a graduate of Harvard and has written three novels. Thomas-Graham and her husband have a six-year-old toddlers.

PATRICIA WALD, a graduate of Yale Law School, worked briefly as an attorney before spending ten years raising five children. She was an assistant attorney general in the Justice Department from 1977–1979, and was then appointed to the U.S. Court of Appeals, D.C. Circuit, the second highest Federal court in the United States. She served twenty years, including a five year stint as chief judge from 1986 to 1991. After retiring in 1999, she served as a judge on the International Criminal Tribunal for the Former Yugoslavia, and in 2004 she was named to the Federal Commission investigating the failure of intelligence on Iraqi weapons of mass destruction.

RABBI MARGARET MOERS WENIG served as rabbi of Beth Am, The People's Temple, in New York City for sixteen years. The once-dwindling congregation flourished under her spiritual leadership. Rabbi Wenig is an expert preacher and serves as instructor in Homiletics at the Hebrew Union College-Jewish Institute of Religion. She is a frequent guest preacher and lecturer and her writings have been anthologized in *Best Jewish Writing 2003*, edited by Arthur Kunzweil.

Notes

Introduction

1. Marian N. Ruderman et al., "Benefits of Multiple Roles for Managerial Women," *Academy of Management Journal*, 45 No. 2 (2002), pp. 369–386. A number of other studies have also found that people with multiple roles have higher levels of well-being, and that learning from one life role can be incorporated in another, in a process called *role accumulation*. *See* Marian N. Ruderman and Patricia J. Ohlott, *Standing at the Crossroads: Next Steps for High-Achieving Women* (San Francisco: Jossey-Bass, 2002), pp. 113–115. A few studies of male executives have also confirmed this process. One found that such experiences as coaching children's sports taught fathers lessons of leadership: McCall, M.W., Jr., Lombardo, M.M., & Morrison, A.M., *The Lessons of Experience: How Successful Executives Develop on the Job* (Lexington, MA: Lexington Books, 1988).

2. Erkut, S., and Winds of Change Foundation (2001). *Inside women's power: Learning from leaders* (CRW Special Report No. 28), Wellesley, MA: Wellesley Centers for Women, Wellesley College, p. 79.

3. Quoted by Mary Meier, "U.S. Leaders Say Managing Kids Prepared Them to Be Boss," WOMENSENEWS, October 16, 2001.

4. Telephone interview with author, 2003 (Drozdow).

5. *pregnancytoday.com,* "Pregnancy May Make You Smarter." Also *see* Fox News Online, "Study: Pregnancy, Nursing May Make Women Smarter," November 11, 1998.

6. Census Bureau, "Children's Living Arrangements and Characteristics" (March 2002).

7. Annual Demographic Supplement to the March 2002 Current Population Survey. Also see Ann Crittenden, *The Price of Motherhood* (New York: Metropolitan Books, 2001), pp. 24–26.

8. Families and Work Institute, "2002 National Study of the Changing Workforce" (New York, 2002).

9. Telephone interview with author, 2002 (Brest).

10. Stephen R. Covey, *The 7 Habits of Highly Effective Families* (New York: Golden Books, 1997), p. 2.

11. "Personal Business Diary: What Would Happen If Mom Ran the Show?" *New York Times,* May 11, 2003.

12. Personal interview with author, New York City, March, 2003. (Margaret Moers Wenig) There is even some evidence that caring for adults, as in nursing, develops a superior ability to integrate emotional, cognitive, and behavioral data and enhances skills of complex problem-solving. *See* Joyce K. Fletcher, *Disappearing Acts: Gender, Power, and Relational Practice at Work* (Cambridge, Massachusetts: The MIT Press, 2001), p. 114.

13. Erkut, *op. cit.,* p. 81.

14. Lisa Belkin, "The Opt-Out Revolution," *New York Times Magazine* (October 26, 2003), p. 58.

15. Personal Communication, 2003. (Segal)

Chapter 1: Multitasking

1. Quoted in Kristin Rowe-Finkbeiner, "Juggling Career and Home," *Mothering* (March–April 2003).

2. Shirley Strum Kenny, "From Parenting, a Presidency," *New York Times*, Education Section (November 3, 1991).

3. Interview with author, Washington, D.C. 1995 (Kenny).

4. Jeanne Boydston, *Home and Work: Housework, Wages, and the Ideology of Labor in the Early Republic* (New York: Oxford University Press, 1990), p. 114.

5. Quoted by Robin Gerber, author of *Leadership the Eleanor Roosevelt Way* (New York: Portfolio, 2002).

6. Sally Helgesen, *The Female Advantage: Women's Ways of Leadership* (Doubleday: New York, 1990), pp. 8–10. For a brief discussion of Henry Mintzberg's ideas, see Michael Skapinker, "In Search of a Balanced Society," *Financial Times*, September 16, 2003.

7. Ruderman, *et al.*, *op. cit.*, pp. 369–386. Also *see* Nancy P. Rothbard, "Enriching or Depleting? The Dynamics of Engagement in Work and Family Roles," *Administrative Science Quarterly*, 46 (2001), pp. 655–684.

8. Helen Fisher, *The First Sex* (New York: Random House, 1999), p. 5.

9. Kinsley, C. H., *et al.*, "Motherhood Improves Learning and Memory: Neural Activity in Rats Is Enhanced by Pregnancy and the Demands of Rearing Offspring," *Nature*, 402 (1999), pp. 137–138; Tomizawa, K., *et al.*, "Oxytocin Improves Long-lasting Spatial Memory during Motherhood through MAP Kinase Cascade," *Nature Neuroscience*, 6 (2003), pp. 384–390; Wartella, J., *et al.*, "Single or Multiple Reproductive Experiences Attentuate Neurobehaviorial Stress and Fear Responses in the Female Rat," *Physiology and Behavior*, 79 (2003), pp. 373–381.

10. Telephone interview with author, December, 2003 (Lambert).

11. Quoted in Katherine Ellison, "The Mind of the Married Mom," *Working Mother* (February 2003).

12. Interview with author, Los Angeles, February 2003 (Pillsbury).

13. Telephone interview with author, 2003 (Ruderman).

14. Ruderman, *et al.*, *op. cit.*, p. 374.

15. Interview with author, Washington, D.C., 2002 (Rapoport).

16. Telephone interview with author, 2002 (Bachelder).

17. Conversation with author, Dordogue, France, July 2003 (Mander).

18. Conversation with author, Los Angeles, February 2003 (Edwards).

19. Mary Catherine Bateson, "Holding Up the Sky Together," *Civilization* magazine, May–June 1995, pp. 29–31.

20. Helgesen, *op. cit.*, p. 34.

21. Interview with author, New York City, December 2002 (Lazarus).

22. Conversation with author, Los Angeles, February 2003 (Crouse).

23. Conversation with author, New York City, March 2003 (O'Brien).

24. Madeleine Kunin, *Living a Political Life* (New York: Alfred A. Knopf, 1994), p.78.

25. Interview with author, Los Angeles, February 2003 (Foner).

26. Interview with author, Bethesda, Maryland, May 2003 (Morella).

27. Abigail Trafford, "Mommy Track—Right to the Top," *Washington Post* (May 19, 1989).

28. Email to author from Sara Eversden, 2002.

29. Email to author from Miriam Sapiro, 2003.

Chapter 2: How to Spot a Baby When You See One

1. Telephone interview with author (2003, Ruderman)

2. *New York Times* (November 17, 1995), p. B12.

3. Alice McDermott, "What (and Why) Mothers Always Know," *Washington Post* (May 10, 1998).

4. Interview with author, New York City, November 2002 (Moore).

5. Interview with author, Washington, D.C. 2001 (Colwell).

6. Allison Pearson, *I Don't Know How She Does It* (New York: Alfred A. Knopf, 2002). pp. 39–40

7. Haim G. Ginott, *Between Parent and Child.* (New York: Avon Books, 1969), p. 88.

8. Interview with author, Washington, D.C., September 2002 (Browner).

9. Interview with author, Washington, D.C., September, 2002 (Schneider).

10. Interview with author, Washington, D.C., 1996 (Wald).

11. Interview with author, New York City, December 2002 (Fossaceca).

12. Interview with author, Los Angeles, February, 2002 (Fisher).

13. Interview with author, Los Angeles, February 2002 (Cook).

14. "An Infantile Perspective on Bureaucracy," unpublished essay by Katherine Marshall.

15. Telephone Interview with author, November 2002 (Francesconi).

16. Telephone interview with author, New York City, November 2002 (Anderson).

17. Interview with author, Washington, D.C. 1996 (Kenny).

18. Interview with author, Washington, D.C., September 2002 (Gorelick).

Chapter 3: Win–Win Negotiating and the Irrational No!

1. Email to author from Kate Lauderbaugh, 2002.

2. Interview with author, New York City, October 2002 (Okun).

3. Richard E. Neustadt, *Presidential Power* (New York: John Wiley & Sons, Inc., 1960), pp. 9–10.

4. William Ury, *Getting to Peace* (New York: Viking, 1999), p. 104.

5. Others have noted that this process of giving and getting is the essence of leadership. As Garry Wills writes, "Great leadership is not a zero-sum game. What is given to the leader is not taken from the follower. Both get by giving. That is the mystery of great popular leaders like Washington, Lincoln, and Roosevelt." Garry Wills, *Certain Trumpets* (New York, Simon & Schuster, 1994) p. 34.

6. William Ury, *Getting Past No* (New York: Bantam Books, 1991) pp. 39–40.

7. Jane E. Brody, "Well-Chosen Words Point Children to Right Track," *New York Times* (December 16, 2003).

8. *Getting Past No*, p. 53.

9. Thomas Gordon. *P.E.T. Parent Effectiveness Training: The Tested New Way to Raise Responsible Children.* (New York: New American Library, 1970) p. xiv.

10. Thomas Gordon. *L.E.T. Leader Effectiveness Training: The No-Lose Way to Release the Productive Potential of People.* (New York: Bantam Books, 1977) pp. 8–15.

11. *Getting Past No*, p. 111.

12. Numerous management coaches have reported that their business clients use their teachings at home, and parent educators say that people who complete their classes often win promotions after applying parenting techniques in the office. *See* Linda Culp Dowling and Cecile Culp Mielenz, *Mentor Manager Mentor Parent* (Burneyville, OK: ComCon Books, 2002).

13. Abby Ellin, "When It Comes to Salaries, Many Women Don't Push," *New York Times*, February 29, 2004, citing "Women Don't Ask: Negotiation and the Gender Divide," by Sara Laschever and Linda Babcock (Princeton University Press, 2003). The *Times* article also cited a 2003 study by Lisa A. Barron, an assistant professor of organizational behavior at the Graduate School of Management at the University of California at Irvine.

14. Sally Helgesen, *op. cit.*, pp. 247–8.

15. Leonard Greenhulgh, *Managing Strategic Relationships: The Key to Business Success* (New York: The Free Press, 2001).

16. Telephone interview with author, 2002 (Mills).

Chapter 4: The Importance of Listening

1. Interview with author, Washington, D.C. 1998 (Richards).

2. Jane Mansbridge, "Feminism and Democracy," *The American Prospect*, November, 1991, p. 134.

3. Interview with author, Des Moines, Iowa, 2003 (Miller).

4. Telephone interview with author, 1996 (Laybourne).

5. Tom Peters. *Re-imagine!* (New York, Dorling Kindersley, 2003), p. 172, 175, and Margaret Heffernan, "The Female CEO ca. 2002," *Fast Company* (August 2002).

6. Marian N. Ruderman and Patricia J. Ohlott. *Standing at the Crossroads* p. 118.

7. Telephone interview with author, 2002 (Henretta).

8. Helgesen, *op. cit.*, pp. 21–2.

9. *Ibid.*, p. 243.

10. *Ibid.*, 243.

11. Fletcher, *op. cit.*, pp. 74–5.

12. Interview with author, Washington, D.C. 2002 (Chavez-Thompson).

Chapter 5: Practicing Patience

1. Interview with author, Washington, D.C. March 2003 (Powell).

2. Interview with author, Los Angeles, February 2003 (Crouse).

3. Ernst & Young is one of the most family-friendly accounting firms in the country. In 1996, the firm initiated steps to retain women, primarily by allowing the parents of young children to work fewer hours while remaining on a career track. It is not uncommon now for a mother to be promoted to partner while working a four-day week. The percentage of women at the partner, principal, and director level is 15 percent—still low, but up from only 7 percent in 1996.

Chapter 6: Empathy: The E.Q. Factor

1. Telephone interview with author, May 2003 (Moorhead).

2. Harold S. Kushner, *When Bad Things Happen to Good People* (New York: Schocken Books, 1981), p. 133.

3. Telephone interview with author, 2002 (Dietch).

4. Simon Baron-Cohen, *The Essential Difference* (New York: Basic Books, 2003), p. 2.

5. *Ibid.*, pp. 32–3.

6. *Ibid.*, pp. 55–6.

7. *Ibid.*, p. 54.

8. *Ibid.*, pp. 127–8.

9. Telephone interview with author, 2003 (Gaines-Ross).

10. Telephone interview with author, 2003 (Fletcher).

11. Interview with author, Los Angeles, CA, February 2003 (Romano).

12. Wills, *op. cit.*, pp. 32–3.

13. George Packer, "War after the War," *The New Yorker* (November 24, 2003).

14. Irene Tinker, "Quotas for Women in Elected Legislatures: Do They Really Empower Women?" (unpublished paper, 2003), p. 17.

15. Kunin, *op. cit.*, p. 85, 363.

16. Personal communication, San Francisco, 2001 (Treat).

Chapter 7: Appreciating Difference

1. Telephone conversation with author, October, 2002 (Patricia J. Ohlott), citing one of the participants in her study of female leadership for the Center for Creative Leadership, Greensboro, North Carolina.

2. Telephone interview with author, January 2002 (Juergens).

3. Ann Crittenden, "Babies Are Born Different," *McCall's*, September, 1984; citing Stella Chess's 1965 book, *Your Child Is a Person*. The final conclusions of the Chess-Thomas study were published in the *American Journal of Psychiatry* in 1984.

4. Richard Smith and James M. Citrin, *The 5 Patterns of Extraordinary Careers* (New York: Crown Business, 2003), p. 64.

5. Polly LaBarre, "Marcus Buckingham Thinks Your Boss Has an Attitude Problem," *Fast Company*, Issue 49 (August 2001), p. 88.

6. Telephone interview with author, October 2002 (Sowell).

Chapter 8: Growing Human Capabilities

1. James MacGregor Burns, *Leadership* (New York: Harper Torchbooks, 1979), p.462.

2. Burns, *op. cit.*, p. 50.

3. Sharon Begley, "Expectations May Alter Outcomes Far More Than We Realize," *Wall Street Journal* (November 7, 2003).

4. William J. Holstein, "The Case for a Benevolent Chief Executive," *New York Times* (August 24, 2003).

5. Fletcher, *op. cit.*, p. 122.

Chapter 9: Letting Go

1. Mrs. Franklin D. Roosevelt, "Building Character," *The Parent's Magazine* 6 (June 1931), p. 17.

2. Conversation with author, Matawan, New Jersey, November 2002 (Graver).

3. Interview with author, San Francisco, California, April 1993 (Hancock).

Chapter 10: Habits of Integrity

1. Interview with author, Salt Lake City, Utah, June 2003 (Hudson).

2. Interview with author, New York City, November 1996 (Cutler).

3. This is not to imply that male heads of state haven't demonstrated the same kind of bravery. When Teddy Roosevelt was wounded by an assailant in the 1912 presidential campaign he went on to deliver his scheduled speech with blood oozing from his shirt. Twenty-one years later, his cousin Franklin Roosevelt sat unflinchingly in an open car as a gunman fired five bullets at him, missing the president but mortally wounding the mayor of Chicago, who was standing next to him in the car.

4. Interview with author, Fort Meade, Maryland, October, 1997; quoted in Ann Crittenden, "Fighting for Kids," *Government Executive*, December 1997.

5. Interview with author, New York City, October 2002 (Osomobor).

6. Interview with author, New York City, October 2002 (Boccio).

7. By 2002, more than 20 percent of Reform rabbis and more than 50 percent of Reform seminary students were women. And, in 2003, North America's Reform rabbis elected a woman as their president, the first female head of a major rabbinical association. The Conservative branch of Judaism began ordaining women in 1985 and, by 2002, 11 percent of its rabbis were women. The Orthodox seminaries still exclude women, and in most Orthodox synagogues women are not even allowed to read publicly from the Torah.

8. Lydia Polgreen, "A Fire Kills Two Children Found Alone," *New York Times* (October 13, 2003); Nina Bernstein, "Daily Choice Turns Deadly," *New York Times*, October 19, 2003. Four months after Ms.

Brathwaite's arrest the Brooklyn district attorney dropped the charges against her, according to her attorney, Douglas G. Rankin. In a telephone conversation Mr. Rankin told me that the prosecutor agreed that this was a tragedy that should not result in prosecution—I would add persecution—of the grieving mother. Ms. Brathwaite was on a leave of absence from McDonald's and in therapy, with the assistance of a fund that had been raised on her behalf. Sadly, the person most responsible for charges being brought against Braithwaite was another woman, the head of the Crimes against Children Bureau in the district attorney's office. "She was not willing to recognize that this was Hobson's choice," said Mr. Rankin.

9. Fletcher, *op. cit.*, pp. 33–4.

Chapter 11: A Sense of Perspective

1. Kunin, *op. cit.*, pp. 102–3.

2. Interview with author, Stockholm, Sweden, 1997 (Hatt).

3. Ruderman and Ohlott, *op. cit.*, p. 127.

Chapter 12: Playing Fair

1. Telephone interview with author, October 2003 (Mossberg).

2. Nicholas Wade. "Genetic Basis to Fairness, Study Hints," *New York Times* (September 18, 2003).

Chapter 13: The Future Matters

1. Clyde Farnsworth, "Planet Earth's Preacher, with Canada His Pulpit," *New York Times*, December 28, 1994. Polls in the U.S. consistently show that women are more concerned about the environment than men, and leaving a healthy environmental legacy for their children is a major reason. Eight national environmental organizations are headed by women, including American Rivers, the League of Conservation Voters, and World Wildlife Fund.

2. Email from Valerie Hudson on post nonproliferation failure, September 2003.

Chapter 14: Where We Stand Now: The Executive Gender Gap

1. Ann Crittenden, "Nations Are Like Children," *The Nation* (February 4, 1991), pp. 119–23.

2. *See* Judy Wajcman "Desperately Seeking Differences: Is Management Style Gendered?" *British Journal of Industrial Relations* 34, 3 (1996), pp. 333–48.

3. "The Debate: Do Men and Women Have Different Leadership Styles?" by Susan Vinnicombe. *www.som.cranfield.ac.uk/som/news/manfocus/downloads/p12_13*

4. Rochelle Sharpe, "As Leaders, Women Rule," *www.business week.com*, November 20, 2000.

5. *Ibid.*

6. Telephone interview with author, December 2003 (Kabacoff).

7. Catalyst, "The Bottom Line: Connecting Corporate Performance and Gender Diversity," 2004. This study, sponsored by BMO Financial Group, looked at the 353 companies that remained on the Fortune 500 list for four out of the five years between 1996 and 2000. Those with the highest representation of women in their senior management had a 35 percent higher return on equity and a 34 percent higher total return to shareholders than companies with the lowest proportion of women at the top. The result was the same after controlling for industry and company differences. The link between female leadership and financial performance was particularly strong in consumer discretionary, consumer staples, and financial services companies.

8. Sharpe, *op. cit.*

9. Tom Peters, "The Best New Managers Will Listen, Motivate, Support. Isn't That Just Like a Woman?" *Working Woman* (September 1990).

10. Tom Peters, *Re-Imagine!* (New York: Dorling Kindersley, 2003), p. 272.

11. Quoted in Michael Norman, "From Carol Gilligan's Chair," *New York Times Magazine*, November 9, 1997, p. 50.

12. Sumru Erkut, *op. cit.*, p. 39.

13. Margaret Heffernan, "The Female CEO ca. 2002," *Fast Company*, August 2002.

14. Helen Peters and Rob Kabacoff, "A New Look at the Glass Ceiling," *MRGI Research Report: Leadership and Gender* (Portland, Maine: Management Research Group, 2002), p. 5.

15. V. Valian, *Why So Slow? The Advancement of Women* (Cambridge, Mass.: MIT Press, 1998), p. 3; describing a computer simulation carried out by Martell, Lane, and Emrich in 1996.

16. *See* Rakesh Khurana, *Searching for a Corporate Savior* (Princeton: N.J., Princeton University Press, 2002).

17. Jim Collins, *Good to Great* (New York: Harper Business, 2001), pp. 24–36.

Chapter 15: Hide It or Flaunt It? Is the World Ready for Child-rearing on a Resume?

1. "Considerations of Leadership" for Goddard College, 1997 by Dr. Barbara Mossberg.

2. Email from Mary Ann Wiley, 2002.

3. Barbara Downs and Kristin Smith, U.S. Census Bureau, "Maternity Leave Among First-Time Mothers," paper for the annual meetings of the Population Association of America, Washington, D.C., March 29–31, 2001.

4. Occupational data for women of working age was supplied by Steve Hipple of the Division of Labor Force Statistics, Bureau of Labor Statistics, March 6, 2000.

5. Bureau of Labor Statistics, "Employment Characteristics of Families in 2002," USDL 03-369, Table 5 (July 9, 2003).

6. Catalyst, "Women and the MBA: Gateway to Opportunity," May 2000. Findings of the report based on research by Catalyst, the University of Michigan Business School, and the Center for the Education of Women at the University of Michigan, are summarized on *www.womeninbusiness.bus.umich.edu/research/womenandtheMBA*.

6. Belkin, *op. cit.*, p. 44.

7. Conversation with author, 2000 (Lunney).

8. Telephone conversation with author, May 2004.

9. Telephone interview with author, November 2003 (Chongris).

10. Kunin, *op. cit.*, pp. 358–61.

11. Conversation with author, 2002 (Marks).

12. Kristin Rowe-Finkbeiner, "Juggling Career and Home," *Mothering* (March–April, 2003), p. 32.

13. Email from Margaret McLaughlin, 2001.

14. Peters, *Re-Imagine!*, p. 171.

15. Interview with author, Washington, D.C., May 2003 (Slaughter).

16. Fiske has produced several papers on stereotypical thinking with Thomas Eckes of the University of Hagen in Germany, Amy J.C. Cuddy of Princeton, Peter Glick of Lawrence University, and Jun Xu of UCLA.

17. Conversations with author, Washington, D.C. 2001–2003 (Williams).

18. Kemba J. Duncan, "Stay-at-Home Dads Fight Stigma," *Wall Street Journal* (August 26, 2003).

19. *Ibid.*

20. Email from Dagmar Kauffmann, 2002.

21. Ann Crittenden, *The Price of Motherhood* (New York: Metropolitan Books, 2001), p. 274.

22. Fletcher, *op.cit.*, pp. 135–36.

23. Katherine Marshall, "Choosing Leaders: Lessons from an Easter Tale," unpublished, 1997.

Postscript: Mothers Are Everywhere and Times Are Changing

1. This data comes from the Current Population Survey (CPS), representing more than 30 million women working full-time. Also see "Creating a Lie: Sylvia Ann Hewlett and the Myth of the Baby Bust," by Garance Franke-Ruta, in *The American Prospect*, July 2, 2002.

2. Interview with author, Washington, D.C., 2002 (Natividad).

3. Gro Harlem Brundtland, *Madam Prime Minister* (New York: Farrar, Straus and Giroux, 2002), pp. 236–7.

4. Sophie Arie, "Elisa Carrio in Lead to be Argentina's President," *www.womensenews.org*, July 18, 2002.

5. "God Is a Woman and She Is Growing Older," by M. M. Wenig, p. 116ff in *Best Sermons* 5, ed. James W. Cox (San Francisco: Harper San Francisco, Harper Collins, 1992).

Acknowledgments

My first and most profound thanks go to all the mothers—I stopped counting when their number went over one hundred—who generously shared their insights and the details of their lives. It wasn't always easy for them to do. One night I attended a potluck supper with a group of mothers in Maryland and, a few hours before the dinner, I got this email, sent to me mistakenly by a member of another mother's group:

"There is a working mothers group at my church and one of the women is having a dinner at her house tonight. Ann Crittenden is coming to this dinner. She is researching her new book and wants to hear funny stories from us mothers and how we use parenting skills in the workplace. What pressure! I'm going to this dinner and my mind is totally blank! I can't even remember a funny story about my kids. Can someone give me a good story I can pass off as my own?"

I sort of took that night off, and didn't come home with any stories. The last thing I wanted to do was add to the already horrendous pressures on working mothers. On the contrary, my goal in writing this book was to add to the feelings of competence and self-confidence that all mothers should have. That so many took the time to help me on this project confirms my conviction that if you've raised kids, you truly can do anything.

In addition to the many who are already mentioned in the book, I owe a special debt of gratitude to the following friends and acquaintances, who contributed contacts, research, ideas, feedback, and ever-sustaining enthusiasm.

Jessica Brando at Princeton and Alicia Maxey at Catalyst, a nonprofit organization advocating the advancement of women in business, provided valuable research assistance. A number of people helped me with ideas and contacts for interviews, including Linda Juergens, Rhonda Kave, and Lori Slepian of the National Association of Mothers Centers; Joanne Brundage and Debra Levy of Mothers and More; Karin Lissakers, Martin Mayer, Kathleen Patterson, Rosemary Ripley, Margo Roosevelt, and Janice Thomas. I also especially want to thank Irene Addlestone, Abigail Taylor and Valerie Young of MOTHERS D.C., Eleanor LeCain, Abigail Trafford, Valerie Hudson, and Veronica Lopez for their support.

I owe a very special thanks to Mary Edsall, whose insights, intellect, and wisdom have sharpened my thoughts for years, and who gave the first rough draft a perceptive read; and to Katherine Marshall, who also vetted the manuscript and shared her own profound thoughts on the topic of maternal leadership.

I want to acknowledge the much-appreciated support of my very talented agent, Katinka Matson of Brockman Inc., and my capable publishers at Gotham Books, Lauren Marino and her assistant Hilary Terrell. A very special thanks to my husband, John Henry, a man who not only loves strong women, but thinks it's time they ruled the world. And finally, my deepest appreciation to my son, James Crittenden Henry, without whom I never would have gained the insights that inspired this book, and who has made me wiser than I ever dreamed I could be.

A Note from the Author

I would love to hear from readers who have been affected by this book, and who would be willing to share their own stories about how being a mother or father enriched and enhanced their professional lives. I can be reached at *story@anncrittenden.com* To find out more about my writings, please visit my Web site at *www.anncrittenden.com*. For information on issues affecting mothers, particularly mothers' economic situation, visit the Web site of the advocacy group MOTHERS, at *www.mothersoughttohaveequalrights.org*.